PEUGEOT 205
THE COMPLETE STORY

OTHER TITLES IN THE CROWOOD AUTOCLASSICS SERIES

AC COBRA Brian Laban

ALFA ROMEO 916 GTV AND SPIDER Robert Foskett

ALFA ROMEO SPIDER John Tipler

ASTON MARTIN DB4, DB5 & DB6 Jonathan Wood

ASTON MARTIN DB7 Andrew Noakes

ASTON MARTIN V8 William Presland

AUDI QUATTRO Laurence Meredith

AUSTIN HEALEY Graham Robson

BMW M3 James Taylor

BMW 5 SERIES James Taylor

BMW CLASSIC COUPÉS James Taylor

CITROËN DS SERIES John Pressnell

FERRARI 308, 328 AND 348 Robert Foskett

FORD ESCORT RS Graham Robson

FROGEYE SPRITE John Baggott

JAGUAR E-TYPE Jonathan Wood

JAGUAR XK8 Graham Robson

JENSEN INTERCEPTOR John Tipler

JOWETT JAVELIN AND JUPITER Geoff McAuley & Edmund Nankivell

LAMBORGHINI COUNTACH Peter Dron

LAND ROVER DEFENDER, 90 AND 110 RANGE James Taylor

LOTUS ELAN Matthew Vale

MGA David G. Styles

MGB Brian Laban

MGF AND TF David Knowles

MG T-SERIES Graham Robson

MAZDA MX-5 Antony Ingram

MERCEDES-BENZ CARS OF THE 1990s James Taylor

MERCEDES-BENZ 'FINTAIL' MODELS Brian Long

MERCEDES-BENZ S-CLASS James Taylor

MERCEDES-BENZ W124 James Taylor

MERCEDES SL SERIES Andrew Noakes

MERCEDES W113 Myles Kornblatt

MORGAN 4/4 Michael Palmer

MORGAN THREE-WHEELER Peter Miller

PORSCHE CARRERA – THE AIR-COOLED ERA Johnny Tipler

RELIANT THREE-WHEELERS John Wilson-Hall

RILEY RM John Price-Williams

ROVER 75 AND MG ZT James Taylor

ROVER P5 & P5B James Taylor

SAAB 99 & 900 Lance Cole

SUBARU IMPREZA WRX AND WRX STI James Taylor

SUNBEAM ALPINE AND TIGER Graham Robson

TRIUMPH SPITFIRE & GT6 Richard Dredge

TRIUMPH TR7 David Knowles

VOLKSWAGEN GOLF GTI James Richardson

VOLVO P1800 David G. Styles

PEUGEOT 205
THE COMPLETE STORY

ADAM SLOMAN
FOREWORD BY ARI VATANEN

THE CROWOOD PRESS

First published in 2015 by
The Crowood Press Ltd
Ramsbury, Marlborough
Wiltshire SN8 2HR

www.crowood.com

© Adam Sloman 2015

All rights reserved. No part of this publication may be reproduced or transmitted in any form or by any means, electronic or mechanical, including photocopy, recording, or any information storage and retrieval system, without permission in writing from the publishers.

British Library Cataloguing-in-Publication Data
A catalogue record for this book is available from the British Library.

ISBN 978 1 84797 867 7

Dedication
For Sarah, Lily and James. None of this would have happened without the wonderful and never-faltering support of my family.

Acknowledgements
The process of writing a book is a daunting one and I would like to thank the following for their support during the project: Andrew Didlick, Ari Vatanen, Max Vatanen, Barrie Farrington, Ben Foulds, Coventry Museum of Transport, Gerard Hughes, Ian Robertson, Jonny Smith, Vicki Butler-Henderson, James Baggot, Craig Alexander, Craig Cheetham, Richard Gunn, Ian Hartnell, The Society of Motor Manufacturers and Traders (SMMT), Sue Baker, Damien Kimberley, Louise Aitken-Walker, Kevin Jones, John Evans, Herve Charpentier, all at Peugeot UK, Rebecca Mansfield, Vauxhall Motors UK, Kate Thompson, Volkswagen Group UK, David Hill, Ford Motor Company, British Motor Heritage Trust, Alex Vieira, Renault UK, Rebecca Ruff, Artcurial Motorcars, Eugenio Franzetti, Peugeot Italia, Puneet Joshi, FIAT Group Automobiles UK, Simon Rose, Dimma UK, Terry Pankhurst.

Unless otherwise stated images are from the Peugeot Press Office.

Typeset by Jean Cussons Typesetting, Diss, Norfolk

Printed and bound in India by Replika Press Pvt Ltd

CONTENTS

Foreword by Ari Vatanen		6
Introduction		7
Timeline		8

CHAPTER 1	PEUGEOT BEFORE THE 205		13
CHAPTER 2	THE ARRIVAL OF THE SUPERMINI AND THE REORGANIZATION OF PSA PEUGEOT		24
CHAPTER 3	M24: DESIGN AND DEVELOPMENT OF THE 205		34
CHAPTER 4	TURNING POINT: THE LAUNCH OF THE PEUGEOT 205		47
CHAPTER 5	ARRIVAL OF THE GTI: THE BIRTH OF A LEGEND		64
CHAPTER 6	GROUP B, RALLYING AND THE 205 T16		81
CHAPTER 7	SPECIALS AND VARIANTS: FROM COMMERCIALS TO THE CTI		126
CHAPTER 8	BUYING, MAINTAINING AND MODIFYING THE PEUGEOT 205		144
CHAPTER 9	PEUGEOT AFTER THE 205		164

Appendix: The 205 in Numbers		187
Index		190

FOREWORD

My earliest memories of Peugeot come from Eastern Finland, my home, from Tuupovaara – it's the centre of this planet!

In a country village you have a few notable people, teachers, police chief, and the guy who runs the forests, and a doctor and a pharmacist. I remember we had the same family run the pharmacy for decades. He had a Peugeot and so did our long-standing priest. He had a Peugeot 403. Peugeot was considered to be a little bit old fashioned – for middle-aged, old-fashioned people.

That was the image of Peugeot for me. That was still in the back of my mind when the 205 and the rally project came along (in September 1983).

I always remember one English mechanic who had been something to do with Talbot saying to me, 'Oh Ari, you mustn't go to Peugeot! You know those French people!' It was very typical of that Anglo-French rivalry! When I saw Jean Todt regarding the project, I asked 'Is it true you will only use French components and French people at any cost?' He replied, 'No Ari, we use whatever it takes to win!' This was his first answer to me and it reassured me.

Despite not having a common language with the team, we had such a strong bond. On the second stage of the Corsica Rally, I set the fastest time. There was something about this whole outfit that I liked. It was not just a technical approach, it was all about people.

From my subjective point of view, very few, if any drivers have enjoyed such a special period in their lives. Not just as a driver but also as a human being. I am very privileged. I'm privileged because I am here to tell the tale. It formed me as a human being, it opened my eyes. You don't come out of an accident as the same person. Rita always says that before the accident I was like a racehorse with blinkers on. At least now they are a little bit more open.

I only had two cars that fitted me like a glove in my hand: Escort RS1800 and Peugeot 205 T16. With the Peugeot a little turn got it as sideways as it could be, but the front wheels were straight all the time. You can floor it all the time. Just a fantastic car.

I remain very fond of the 205. That was my car and my team. Anything else would have been unnatural. I was at home with that team in that car. Had I been with any other team or in any other car I would have been a mercenary. You see the difference? It's a big difference.

My heart was there. It still is.

Author Adam Sloman with Ari Vatanen, Paris, 2013. AUTHOR

Ari Vatanen,
Paris,
12 April 2013

INTRODUCTION

The 1980s were a boom time for hatchbacks yet few cars have had the impact of the 205. It changed Peugeot's fortunes, saved the company and became an automotive icon in the process.

While the regular 205 proved itself as an adept city car, the GTI became the must-have hot hatch of the 1980s, while the sharply styled CTI convertible added even more appeal.

From simple French hatchback to turbocharged World Rally winner, the Peugeot 205 found favour like no Peugeot before during its thirteen-year production run.

It was great looking, even better to drive and its story featured as many twists and turns as the B-roads it loved so much.

This is the story of the Peugeot 205.

The 205 GTI would become a 1980s icon, but it was only part of the 205's incredible story. PEUGEOT

TIMELINE

1942
The 205's designer, Gerald Welter, is born.

1960
Welter joins Peugeot's styling team, working initially on the Peugeot 204.

1977
Development of the 205, codenamed M24, begins.

September
First exterior styling model completed by Peugeot's design team. Design studies for the interior begin.

1978
February First full-size model presented to Peugeot's management.

November
Styling model revised and presented once again to management.

1979
In December, management select the Peugeot design proposal ahead of the rival scheme from Pininfarina.

1980
Audi's Quattro makes its rallying debut.

1981
Dashboard and other interior element designs are signed off for production.
   Prototype 205 is produced and begins development testing.

October
Jean Todt is asked to head up a new motorsport department within Peugeot. He accepts and Peugeot Talbot Sport is born.

November
Future Peugeot driver Ari Vatanen is crowned World Rally Champion in a Ford Escort RS1800. The constructor's title is taken by Peugeot subsidiary Talbot, whose Lotus Sunbeam was driven by Guy Frequelin and Jean Todt.

1982
The initial batch of 360 205s is built at Mulhouse.

1983
January–February
European launch of the 205 takes place in Morocco, North Africa.

February
205 Turbo 16 is tested for the first time.

October
205 UK launch takes place in the Republic of Ireland
   Five-door 205 diesel launches in France.

1984
April
205 Turbo 16 is shown to the motoring press for the first time, in Paris.

Pininfarina showcase their idea for a 205 estate, the 205 Verve at the Turin motor show. It does not go into production.
   1.6 GTI goes on sale in Britain priced at £6,245.

May
205 T16 is driven on a rally stage for the first time on 3 May. Ari Vatanen is at the wheel.

August
The 205 diesel is launched in Great Britain. The launch programme sees the cars given limited fuel and challenged to drive from London to Scotland.
205 T16 records its first World Rally Championship win in Finland on the 1,000 Lakes

October
Peugeot and Vatanen win again, taking first place on the Italian San Remo Rally, completing it in eight hours, thirty-four minutes. Jean-Pierre Nicolas' last WRC event. He retired at the end of the 1984 season.
1.6 GTI price increases to £6,645 for the UK market.

November
Peugeot Talbot Sport complete a hat-trick of wins as Vatanen and co-driver Terry Harryman win the RAC Rally of Great Britain. The 1984 season ends, with Peugeot recording three wins from six rallies entered.

December
Three-door is launched in the United Kingdom.

Also in 1984
The 205 is crowned *What Car?* 'Car of the Year'.

1985
January
First 205 limited edition is made available, the 205 Lacoste.

February
Ari Vatanen continues his fine form with the T16 as he and co-driver Terry Harryman win the Monte Carlo Rally. The Finn underlines his championship credentials by winning the Swedish Rally a few weeks later.

March
Vatanen wins again, this time in Portugal. Peugeot lead the World Rally Championship with 54 points, ahead of Audi on 44. Timo Salonen leads the Driver's championship on 44 points, ahead of Vatanen on 40.

At the end of the month, Timo Salonen wins the Acropolis Rally. He leads the championship with 68 points, Peugeot lead the manufacturers table on 92 points, thirty ahead of Audi.

July
Salonen stretches his title lead to twenty-eight points with victory in the New Zealand Rally.
Ari Vatanen suffers a near-fatal accident during the Rally Argentina. It would rob him of the chance to win a second world title.

August
Timo Salonen and Seppo Harjanne win the 1,000 Lakes in Finland. It would be Peugeot's final win of the 1985 season. Salonen leads the championship with 124 points, Stig Blomqvist is a distant second, on 75.

October
The first British-built Peugeot, a 309, leaves the firm's Coventry factory at Ryton-on-Dunsmore.

November
Peugeot Talbot Sport win the World Rally Championship, while Finnish driver Timo Salonen takes the driver's title. Louise Aitken-Walker and Ellen Morgan finish 16th overall on the Lombard RAC Rally in a 205 GTI.

December
1,000,000th Peugeot 205 is built.

Also in 1985
- The first CTIs are completed by Pininfarina
- Peugeot UK form the 'Peugeot 205 GTI Club'
- German magazine *Auto Motor Und Sport* vote the 205 'Best Small Car in the World'

1986
January
Defending Champion Timo Salonen finishes second on the Monte Carlo Rally.

February
Juha Kankkunen wins the 36th Swedish Rally.

TIMELINE

April
Peugeot UK get their own 205 T16 for use in British rallies.

May
CTI launches in France.

Henri Toivonen and co-driver Sergio Cresto are killed on the Corsica Rally, an event from which Group B will never truly recover. Many teams pull out following Toivonen's death. The rally is won Bruno Saby in a Peugeot 205 T16 E2.

205 Automatic launches in France.

Lacoste 'All White' limited edition launches.

1.6 GTI is revised with power increased to 115bhp.

June
Juha Kankkunen wins the Acropolis Rally in Greece.

CTI 1.6 launches in the United Kingdom priced at £10,680. 205 Junior arrives in three-door form.

July
Another Kankkunen victory, this time in New Zealand. He beats Markku Alen and Miki Biasion to win the rally.

September
Peugeot complete a 1-2 finish on the Finnish 1,000 Lakes Rally. Salonen wins, followed by Kankkunen. The difference is a little over one second. Ari Vatanen makes a public appearance at the rally as a spectator and is warmly greeted by fans.

October
Peugeot unveil the 1.9-litre version of the GTI in France.

November
Timo Salonen wins the British round of the World Rally Championship, with Markku Alen's Delta second and teammate Kankkunen in third.

December
The final Group B World Rally event is held in the United States. Juha Kankkunen finishes second on the Olympus Rally. Peugeot Talbot Sport wins the double again. This time Juha Kankkunen is crowned World Champion, with Timo Salonen finishing third. FISA rule that the Group B cars be banned and the 205 would not contest a World Rally Championship again.

Peugeot completes all of its 205-related launch activities in Great Britain. The 205 is a top-ten best-seller in the UK.

Also in 1986
- The 205 enters the UK's Top 10 best-seller list, with 39,188 sold. 7,000 GTIs are sold and Britain accounts for 20 per cent of the 205's global sales
- 205 XA van launches in France
- The Peugeot GTI Club holds its first national gathering
- GTI-like 'XS' added to the 205 range, replacing the XT

1987

January
Ari Vatanen makes his return to competition in the Paris Dakar Rally. He wins the event.

The GTI 1.9 arrives in Great Britain to a warm response from the motoring press.

July
Five-door 205 Junior launched.

September
Peugeot build the two millionth 205.

Also in 1987
Seppo Niittymaki wins the Division 2 European Rallycross Championship in 205 T16 Evo 2.

1988

January
Juha Kankkunen wins the 1988 Paris Dakar Rally in the 205 T16.

205 range is revised. Dashboard is updated. 205 'Rallye' is launched in Europe.

March
Peugeot launch the GTI Rally Club, one of the first to compete in a Group A GTI was Colin McRae.

June
CJ 1.4 Cabriolet launched.

July
'Junior Special' launched in three and five-door forms.

'Open' limited edition launches, a three-door hatchback with 1.4 petrol engine.

Also in 1988
- The Peugeot 205 Nepala Estate conversion is shown in Brussels. It works by adding a new fibreglass rear section to the 205 hatchback. It does not see production
- Former Talbot rally driver Guy Frequelin wins the French Rallycross Championship in a T16 Evo2
- Matti Alamaki wins Division 2 European Rallycross Championship in 205 T16 Evo 2

1989
GTI Rally Challenge launched.

May
Roland Garros convertible launched.

June
Roland Garros three-door limited edition launched.
Look special edition launched in the UK. 1.1-litre three-door only.
Three millionth 205 built.

October
Limited edition Miami Blue and Sorrento green 205s launch. 1,200 examples are built: 300 blue 1.6s, 300 green; 300 blue 1.9, 300 green.

December
- Matti Alamaki wins Division 2 European Rallycross Championship in 205 T16 Evo 2
- Phillipe Wambergue wins the French Rallycross Championship in a 205 T16 Evo 2

1990
June
Cabriolet version of the Roland Garros limited edition launches.

August
CTI 1.6 gains an electrically powered hood.

September
D turbo model launched with 78bhp 1.8-litre turbo diesel unit and five-door bodystyle.
Anti-lock braking available as an option on GTI. Light units revised with clear indicators at the front and redesigned rear light cluster. Reversing lights are relocated to the rear bumper. CTI gains electric hood.

October
'Trio' and 'Trio Plus' three-door limited edition launches in the UK, with 1.0-litre engine.
'Griffe' GTI limited edition launched in Europe.

Also in 1990
- Richard Burns wins the GTI Rally Challenge in his first season
- Fourgonette or 205F van launches in France
- *Car* magazine votes the Peugeot 205 its 'Car of the Decade'
- Matti Alamaki wins Division 2 European Rallycross Championship in 205 T16 Evo 2
- Jean-Manuel Beuzelin wins the French Rallycross Championship in a 205 T16 Evo 2

1991
February
Style 1.1 and 1.8 Diesel models launched in the UK.
Gentry shown at Geneva Motorshow with 105bhp, 1.9 litre engine.

May
Catalytic converter becomes standard on the majority of the 205 range in Europe.

June
'Trio' 1.0-litre and 1.1-litre 'Trio S' and 'Trio SX' three-door models go on sale.

July
The 4,000,000th 205 is built.

October
1.6 CTI discontinued.
D Turbo launched with three-door bodystyle.
Style models gain a glass sunroof and new interior trim.
Catalytic converters now available on 1.1 and 1.4-litre models and becomes standard on the CTI.
Air conditioning option added to GTI and CTI.
Central locking and headlight warning buzzer becomes standard equipment on the GTI.

Also in 1991
XA Van is face lifted, becoming the XA Multi.
Laser Green metallic paint offered on GTI.

TIMELINE

1992

January
Diesel version of the 'Trio' L.E. launches

March
'Gentry' 1.9 four-speed automatic goes on sale. Features include power steering and a catalytic convertor. Its 1.9-litre engine develops 105bhp. Offered in Aztec Gold and Sorrento Green it costs £12,836.

June
Special Edition Junior model launched in the UK. Joined by three and five-door 'Zest' models (offered with petrol and diesel) and UK 'Rallye' model launched with 1.4-litre petrol engine. Turbo diesel editions of the XR and GR launched.

July
1.1 'Style' launched in three and five-door bodystyle.

September
GTI 1.6 is discontinued, the final list price is £11,375.

October
Catalytic converter becomes standard on the GTI 1.9, which now develops 122bhp.
  IFM Special Edition launched – just twenty-five examples to be made. It makes its debut at the British International Motor Show.

December
1.8 Diesel three and five-door 'Junior' launched alongside 1.1 petrols and 1.6 automatic versions.

1993

February
1.4 'GTX' three and five-door special editions launch.

March
'Style' three and five-door diesel limited editions go on sale.

September
'Sceptre' three and five-door specials launch in the UK with 1.4-litre or 1.8-litre turbo diesel engines.
  1.6-litre Junior automatic launched in the UK in three-door guise.

October
Diesel STDT launched. Stylistically similar to the GTI, but with wheels from the 405 GTX.

1994

February
1.8 diesel 'Trio' launches, in three-door form.

April
Keypad immobilisers are fitted to the GTI and CTI.
  GTI and CTI are discontinued. They are priced at £12,265 for the GTI and £14,195 for the convertible.

July
'Mardi Gras' arrives in three and five-door models. It's offered with 1.1 and 1.6 petrol automatic as well as 1.8 diesel and turbo diesel models.

September
Range reduced to Mardi Gras and D turbo.

1995

February
Mardi Gras limited edition discontinued. Five millionth 205 is produced.

June
1.8 'Aztec' three and five-door diesel launches. It's joined by the 'Inca', a three-door diesel.

1997

January
205 Fourgonette is discontinued and replaced by the Peugeot Partner van.

1999

The final nine 205s leave the production line in Spain.

CHAPTER ONE

PEUGEOT BEFORE THE 205

ABOVE: **The lion was a key factor in Peugeot's branding from early in its history.**

The Peugeot family can trace its businesses back as far as the nineteenth century, but it was the arrival of the industrial revolution in France that set the family on its path to automotive manufacture. Two brothers, Jean-Pierre and Jean-Frédérick, set up a steel mill near Montbéliard in eastern France. At just nineteen, Jean-Frédérick developed a technique that saw the company mass-produce tools such as saws that were both high in quality and low in price. By the 1850s the company was producing everything from animal hair clippers to women's underwear. It was the production of lingerie that ultimately led to the company's move into vehicle production.

Traditionally whalebone had been used in the production of corsets, making them the preserve of only the wealthiest people in the country. Peugeot changed all that by using steel

Tool manufacturing formed the basis of Peugeot's early business. The tools were highly regarded for their quality and affordability.

PEUGEOT BEFORE THE 205

instead of bone, allowing corsets to be made much cheaper. As bicycles became more popular, Peugeot repurposed their machinery to produce spokes for bicycle wheels. Within five years the company was selling its own bicycles and became one of the country's top manufacturers.

FROM TWO WHEELS TO FOUR

With bicycle production now in full swing, the great-grandson of Peugeot's founder, Armand Peugeot, felt the company's future lay in more than just bicycles. He had spent some time in Britain studying production methods. At his behest, the company built its first vehicle, the Type 1, a steam-driven, three-wheeled car.

Armand drove the car from Paris to Lyon, and though it was plagued with reliability issues, it was well received by the visitors to the 1889 Paris Exposition, where Emile Levassor was impressed with the car – though not the engine that powered it. Levassor had just acquired production rights for Daimler's petrol engine. Soon enough Levassor and Peugeot joined forces. In 1890 the company produced its first four-wheeled petrol-driven vehicle and by 1896 Peugeot was producing its own petrol engines. After four years the company had produced seventy-five cars and Peugeot had begun to export the car.

The other members of the Peugeot family did not share Armand's confidence in the motor car and insisted he set up his own plant. He did, and saw the new company's fortunes grow and grow. By the dawn of the twentieth century the company offered fifteen different models.

The rest of the Peugeot family saw the error of their ways and produced their first car in 1905, in direct competition with Armand. In 1911 the two companies joined forces and built a new factory in Sochaux, close to the border with Switzerland, where its operational headquarters remain to this day. Before the outbreak of the First World War Peugeot was producing almost 10,000 cars annually across four factories with a range of eighteen models. During the war the company became involved in the war effort, producing trucks, armaments and aeroplane engines.

While still in its formative years the company enjoyed motor-sport success, winning the French Grand Prix in 1912 and 1913 as well as the Indianapolis 500 in 1913, 1916 and 1919.

Peugeot's move into transportation began with bicycles.

Armand Peugeot – the father of Peugeot's motor cars.

PEUGEOT BEFORE THE 205

The Type 5 (1893–96) was one of Peugeot's early 'horseless carriages' – it was also the first Peugeot to enter competition.

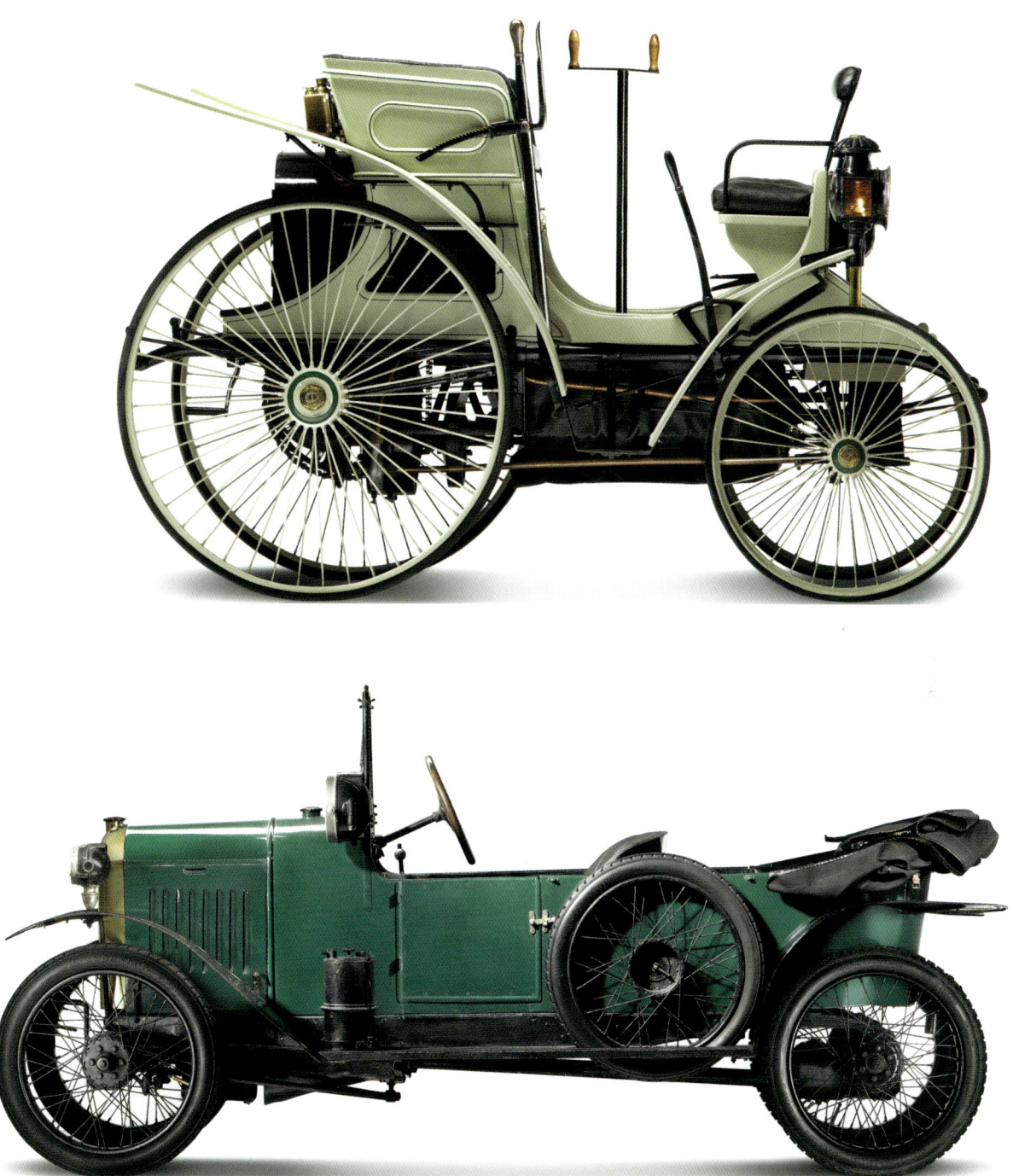

The Quadrilette arrived after the First World War and proved popular thanks to its low cost and impressive reliability.

15

■ PEUGEOT BEFORE THE 205

After the war Peugeot began production of a small car, the Quadrilette. The little 667cc car gained a strong reputation for its impressive fuel economy, and before long it was offered with a larger 720cc engine. Almost 100,000 Quadrilettes were sold between 1920 and 1929.

As the company grew in size, so did the number of employees. The Peugeot family was keen to provide its staff with an activity for their leisure time. Football was becoming increasingly popular across Europe and Jean-Pierre Peugeot, head of the company, set about creating a team for his staff to support. Thanks to the company's success, he had the funding to do it and in 1928 FC Sochaux-Montbéliard was formed.

The club began playing in the lowest tier of the league but quickly gained notoriety when Jean-Pierre admitted to paying his players, something that was strictly forbidden at the time. FC Sochaux became strong advocates for professionalism within the game and were the first club to become professional in 1929, in the process becoming founder members of the French football league. The club went further, too, organizing a competition, La Coupe Peugeot, featuring the best clubs in France. Close links have been maintained with the football club to this day, with Peugeot being principal shirt sponsors of the team and retaining ownership of the club itself.

TWO IS THE MAGIC NUMBER

In 1929 Peugeot introduced the 201, the cheapest four-seater in France, which in 1931 became the world's first mass-produced car with independent front suspension. The

The 201 was launched in 1929 and began the legendary 2 series.

16

PEUGEOT BEFORE THE 205

WHAT'S IN A NAME?

Until the late 1920s each distinct model was given a 'Type' designation by Peugeot, even if it was known to the public by another name. This changed in 1929 when the 201 replaced the Type 190 and a new three-digit naming convention was established. It is simple to decipher: the first digit represents the model size, the middle is always a zero and the final figure(s) represents that particular generation of model. So although the 201 was the 201st Peugeot design, it was also the first generation of the 2 series, hence 201. During the 1930s, some Peugeots were named according to the amount of power they produced, hence the 5CV and 10CV. Peugeot acted to secure every variant of their new naming system, to prevent other manufacturers from interrupting the sequence. This most noticeably forced Porsche to rename its 901 concept the 911, though Peugeot chose not to take action against Ferrari when the Ferrari 308 was unveiled. The naming system was modified in 2012, with the brand-identifying '0' (or '00') remaining in the middle and the end digit becoming '1' or '8' to determine whether the car was intended for established markets, '8' for markets such as Western Europe and '1' for emerging markets.

Peugeot's numbering system survived until the launch of the 208 in 2012.

car's name came from the fact that it was Peugeot's 201st design. (Thereafter all Peugeot models would feature a zero in the middle of the name – *see* box.) Unlike any other car in Peugeot's history, the 2-series range is the only one to have a continuous sequence of models, right up to today's 208.

Improvements in production techniques lifted Peugeot's annual production capacity to 43,000 units and over 140,000 vehicles were built during the 201's lifetime. The more aerodynamic 301 appeared in 1933, followed in 1934 by a convertible model sporting a revolutionary folding roof operated by compressed air, which also opened the boot in order to stow the hood away.

The 202 succeeded the 201 in 1938. Featuring an 1133cc, water-cooled engine it demonstrated once again Peugeot's ability to develop a wide range of vehicles from a single model. It was offered as a four-door saloon, a two-door convertible, a pick-up truck and an estate.

The Sochaux plant fell into Axis hands during the Second World War, though the company managed to continue car production for civilian use, albeit in limited numbers. This came to an abrupt end in July 1943 when an Allied bombing raid destroyed much of the factory.

POST-WAR RESURGENCE

In 1946, with the war over, the 202 was back in production. In response to the shortage of steel, a timber-framed estate was produced. The extra work involved, combined with the cost of the timber, made it an expensive proposition and fewer than 3,000 were made. In 1947 the 202 was joined by the new 203. Like the 202 it was also offered as a convertible, boasted overdrive on its top gear and almost 700,000 units were sold during its twelve-year production run.

Production of the 202 was interrupted by the outbreak of the Second World War.

■ PEUGEOT BEFORE THE 205

The post-war years saw the French manufacturing industry rebuild, with Peugeot playing a key role. The 203 was the firm's first new car following the conflict.

Peugeot's first diesel-powered car – the 403 estate – was launched in 1958. The company had been producing diesels since the late 1920s but this was the first unit refined enough for automotive use.

The 403 was built at the Lille factory in France, and also in Australia, and for a brief time was exported to the United States. The company was quick to offer a full range of 403 models that incorporated saloon, estate, coupé, pick-up and convertible, the latter finding fame on US television in the detective series Columbo, in which the car took on the role of the dishevelled detective's somewhat dilapidated car. Actor Peter Falk, who portrayed the detective, chose the car after he found it sitting in the back lot of Universal Studios.

The 404, another example of a Peugeot with a long lifespan, was launched in 1960. It was offered with a range of engines, including a 2-litre diesel, and boasted modern features such as fuel injection and fully automatic transmission. In excess of two million 404s were built between 1960 and 1972, with the car finding a strong market in Africa, where it won the Safari Rally in 1963, then in three consecutive years from 1966 to 1968. The 404 was still being built under licence in Kenya in 1991.

The 204 followed in 1965 and, much like the Mini, featured a transverse engine with its gearbox in its sump. It was the first Peugeot with all-independent suspension and three years after its debut it became the best-selling car in France.

Arguably the best-known classic Peugeot, the 504, arrived in 1968 and became popular worldwide, with production right across the globe, as it was manufactured in China and Argentina, among other countries. A true testament to its success though was its ability, like the 404 before it,

PEUGEOT BEFORE THE 205

PEUGEOT 204

Production: 1965–76
Body style: Saloon, estate, coupé, convertible and van
1.6 million built

The 204 arrived in the mid-1960s and become Peugeot's best-selling car of the day.

to remain in production. Production continued in South America until 1999, and it was on sale in Kenya and Nigeria until as recently as 2005.

One of the keys to its longevity was Peugeot's development of the 504 platform, with it being offered in a full range of variants: a saloon, estate, coupé and pick-up truck. Its worldwide success was in no small part down to its tough, rugged nature, which made it particularly suited to heavy use and high mileage. Its ruggedness was complemented by a frugal diesel engine, making the saloon version popular with Parisian taxi drivers and the pick-up an obvious choice across Africa, where roads were harsh and fuel quality variable.

GROWTH, COLLABORATIONS AND EXPANSION

By the dawn of the 1970s, the 204 was revised and improved, becoming the 304. At the same time, a new factory opened in Mulhouse, near Sochaux, initially producing components for the group.

The 504 enjoyed a long production life and become one of the best-loved classic Peugeots.

■ PEUGEOT BEFORE THE 205

The 504 also enjoyed considerable success as a rally car, here seen in competition spec.

The company began looking to its French counterparts for research and development of new powertrains, and it was Peugeot's initial collaboration with Renault – to be joined by Volvo in 1971 – that led to the development of the 'Douvrin' family of engines. Spanning sizes from 1-litre through to 3-litre V6 units used in motor sport, these all-aluminium engines saw use in a huge range of cars, and even the infamous gull-winged DeLorean.

An engine from this partnership powered the next car in the Peugeot story, the 104. Launched in 1972 as a four-door saloon, the 104 was Peugeot's first foray into the expanding supermini sector and at the time it was the smallest four-door offered in Europe. It was designed by Paolo Martin, who had worked for Italian styling giants Pininfarina and Bertone, penning such cars as the Fiat 130 Coupé and Lancia Montecarlo prior to creating the 104 for Peugeot. A hatchback followed in 1976, the year in which Ford's Fiesta made its debut. The 104 was later offered as a three-door, in three variants, the ZA, ZL and ZS. The car was popular throughout Europe and remained on sale in its native France until as late as 1988. It also proved to be a widespread choice in Clubman-level rallying throughout Europe.

Peugeot's collaboration with fellow manufacturers led to one of the key moments in the company's history, one that would change it forever. The 1970s were a challenging period for many car manufacturers, with the oil crisis of 1973 hitting makers of larger, thirstier vehicles particularly

PEUGEOT BEFORE THE 205

The 104 took Peugeot into the supermini sector for the first time.

hard. Citroën was one such manufacturer. Having invested heavily in its new CX saloon, the company found the market for big saloons had all but evaporated as smaller, more frugal cars began to dominate the marketplace. In December 1974, facing severe financial hardship, Citroën agreed to sell 38 per cent of the company to Peugeot.

A little under two years later, Peugeot increased that stake to almost 90 per cent, saving Citroën from bankruptcy and creating the PSA Peugeot Citroën group. The Citroën takeover brought the Italian car manufacturer Maserati with it, though the supercar maker was sold on to DeTomaso in 1975.

Peugeot quickly began to address the issues that had led to Citroën's struggles, and new models swiftly followed, based on existing Peugeot platforms. The first of these was the LN, based on the 104, but with a small 600cc 2-stroke engine. These small, frugal cars, combined with an economy still recovering from the oil crisis, meant that Peugeot's takeover of Citroën was a financial success for the company.

PEUGEOT 104

Production: 1972–88
Body style: Three- and five-door hatchback, four-door saloon

Available in three- and five-door versions, the 104 survived until the late 1980s.

21

■ PEUGEOT BEFORE THE 205

SYMBOL OF PRIDE – THE EVOLUTION OF THE LION LOGO

The lion first appeared on Peugeot products in the nineteenth century, specifically on the company's tools. The first lion logo was created by Justin Blazer in 1847 and featured a lion walking on an arrow. When the two Peugeot companies merged, the lion remained, with a full lion used on bicycles and motor cycles, and a lion's head used on motor cars. The lion made its first appearance on a motor car in 1933. In 1948 the company began using the familiar lion in profile, standing on its hind legs, as seen on the Franche-Comté coat of arms. The logo was reworked in 1976 and again in 1998 before a more simple, fluid lion design was unveiled in 2010.

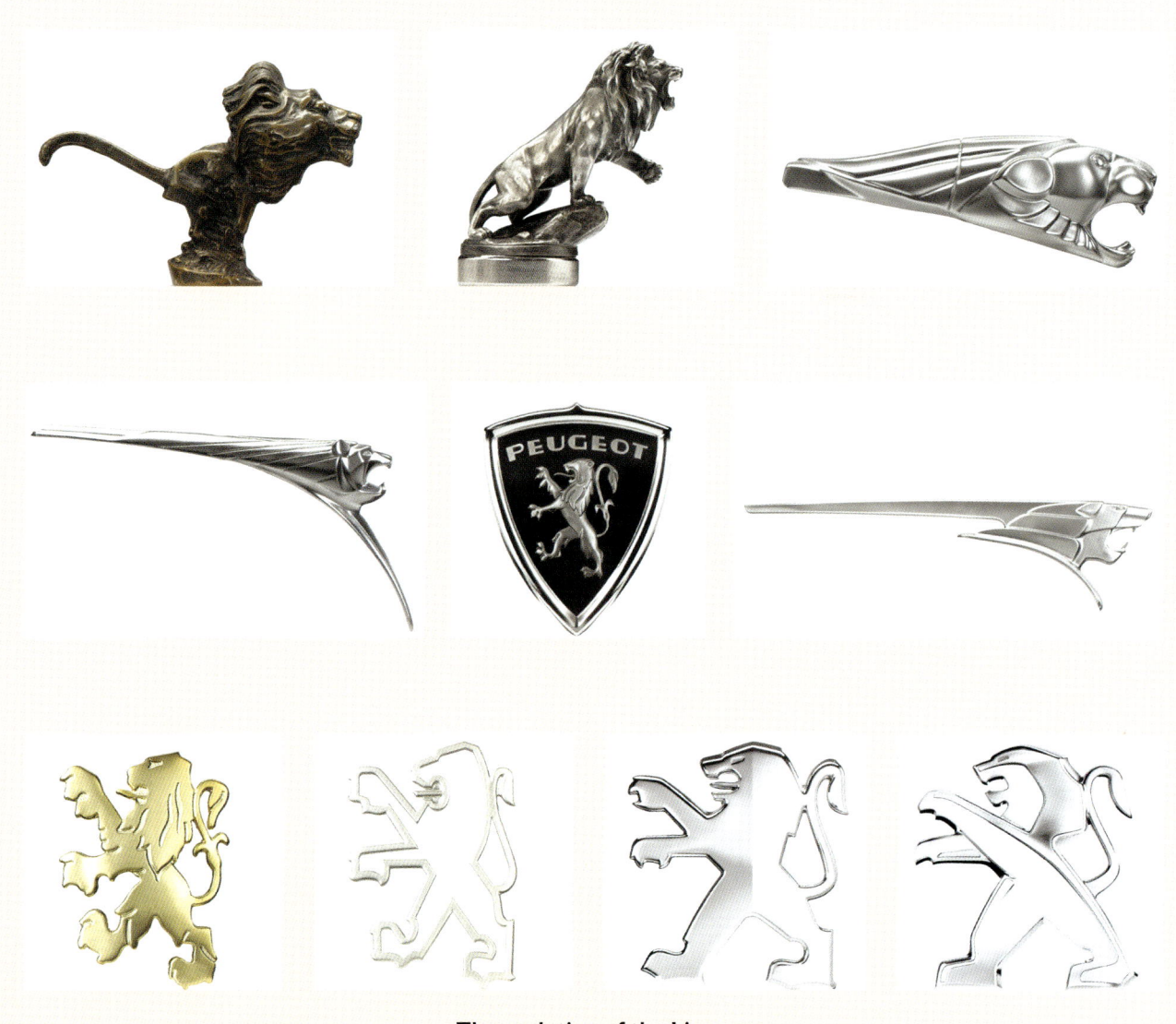

The evolution of the Lion.

PEUGEOT BEFORE THE 205

GLOBAL PLAYER

Peugeot Citroën grew further still in August 1978 when the company announced it had completed the purchase of the struggling Chrysler Europe. The American manufacturer had itself purchased the Rootes Group (comprising such British marques as Hillman and Humber) and French manufacturer Simca in the late 1960s, seeking to replicate the success of General Motors with its Vauxhall and Opel subsidiaries, but failed to understand the European market. In the face of mounting losses and poor sales, Chrysler Europe opted to sell out to Peugeot Citroën, ultimately selling its European operations for just $1.

Peugeot's purchase gave it control of Chrysler's operations in the UK, most notably at Ryton-on-Dunsmore in Coventry, the Simca factories in France, and a smattering of production facilities in Spain. The newly christened Peugeot S.A. group (PSA) became the fifth largest manufacturer in the world, and the largest in Europe.

Coventry was very much at the heart of UK motor manufacturing and Peugeot quickly found the location and its facilities ideally suited to its needs. The first car to emerge from Ryton under PSA ownership was the Talbot Horizon in 1980. Peugeot officially moved into Coventry and the Ryton plant in 1979 and by October 1985 the first Peugeot, the 309, was rolling off the Ryton line.

The company also sought to integrate itself with the local community. In a situation remarkably similar to that of FC Sochaux in France, the company developed a relationship with local team Coventry City FC, using its Talbot brand to sponsor the club for the 1981–82 season. The club's shirt was redesigned to look like the Talbot logo, with prominent branding across the strip. Plans went further, with the football club applying to the Football Association to be renamed 'Coventry Talbot', on the promise of increased investment into the club by the car maker. The FA was outraged, the players were banned from wearing the Talbot kit during televised matches, and the request to rename the club was turned down. Peugeot later became principal sponsor of the club with its name appearing on the team's shirts between 1989 and 1997.

By the mid-1980s the 205 was ready for launch and the 104 was withdrawn from many markets, including the UK, to make way for the new model. Peugeot had now established itself as a truly global brand, with exports to almost 200 countries and factories in Britain and Ireland, Canada, Australia and Argentina.

The Rootes Group plant at Ryton-on-Dunsmore, near Coventry, would become the centre of Peugeot's UK manufacturing.
COVENTRY MUSEUM OF TRANSPORT

23

CHAPTER TWO

THE ARRIVAL OF THE SUPERMINI AND THE REORGANIZATION OF PSA PEUGEOT

It could be argued that all modern superminis owe their existence to one car, the original Mini, as devised by Sir Alec Issigonis of the British Motor Corporation in 1957. When Issigonis's baby hit the market two years later, in 1959, the way small cars were designed would change forever.

Prior to the Mini, almost every car on the planet had mounted their engine longitudinally, with the engine being used to propel the rear wheels. The Mini was not the first vehicle to feature front-wheel drive – the system had existed for almost fifty years and following the Second World War, German company DKW and SAAB both offered vehicles that were driven from the front – but it was the Mini that took the formula, improved it, and applied it to the small-car segment.

The result of mounting the engine transversely meant that 80 per cent of the Mini's available space was freed up for the vehicle's passengers and their luggage. The layout made

BMC's Mini of 1959 revitalized the way small cars were thought about. AUTHOR

THE ARRIVAL OF THE SUPERMINI AND THE REORGANIZATION OF PSA PEUGEOT

perfect sense and it is a format that the majority of vehicles on our roads follow today.

The other dominant vehicle design aspect is the hatchback, but that dominance would take a little longer to come to the fore.

Saloons, in a variety of sizes, had for most of automotive history been the default design layout for a car. This 'three-box' principle (a box for the engine, a box for the passengers and a box for luggage) had been used in everything from the diminutive Mini to large Gallic saloons like the Peugeot 505. This began to change during the 1960s and 1970s with the launch of cars such as the Renault 16 and the Autobianchi Primula. The market for small hatchbacks began to properly emerge during the late 1970s as manufacturers realized that customers liked the practicality that a hatchback afforded.

Initially, saloons were face-lifted to become hatches, so cars such as the Peugeot 104 and the Alfa Romeo Alfasud began to sprout hatches. For small cars, three-box was out, two-box was in.

GAME CHANGER

Things really changed at the dawn of the 1970s. While British manufacturers doggedly stuck to the saloon layout, European car makers were beginning to realize that the future for small cars lay not in the shape of the saloon but in the hatchback.

The start of this revolution began in France and Italy, with Fiat and the 127 and Renault and the 5. The 127 had launched

The Renault 5 showed how well a small hatchback supermini could work and Peugeot realized they needed to rival it. RENAULT PRESS OFFICE

a year earlier as a saloon and was revised in 1972 to feature a hatch; the diminutive Renault had always been intended as a hatch. Up until the 5's arrival, the small-car world had been largely dominated by the Mini, but now a new breed of small car would take on the Mini's revolutionary engineering concepts and build upon them. With its greater refinement, a more comfortable cabin and increased practicality the Renault 5 heralded the dawn of a new market segment – the supermini. The Renault 5 was clever. Thanks to the packaging of the engine and gearbox there was room under the bonnet for the spare wheel, allowing additional space for passengers and luggage.

Ford's new Fiesta would further evolve the supermini concept and arguably bring it into the modern era. Though

The Fiesta arrived in 1976 and quickly became a best-seller in many European markets, including the UK. FORD HERITAGE

25

■ THE ARRIVAL OF THE SUPERMINI AND THE REORGANIZATION OF PSA PEUGEOT

beaten into production by the slightly larger and more traditional Vauxhall Chevette, the Fiesta became a huge success, which underlined how popular the hatchback had become throughout Europe.

The genesis of Ford's supermini began in 1972, when the company felt there was room in its range for a car to sit beneath the Escort in the Ford family. Though Ford was beaten to the punch by its long-standing rival General Motors with the launch of the Vauxhall Chevette hatch in 1975, Ford would respond with a more modern, more compact hatchback supermini that would eventually force General Motors to replace the Chevette in 1982.

Designed by Ford of Europe, but intended for markets across the globe, the Fiesta eventually broke cover in 1975 before being shown officially to the public in 1976. It was launched in mainland Europe in September of that year before arrival in the UK in 1977.

British models were built at Ford's iconic Dagenham plant. The Fiesta very much ushered in an age of modernity for Ford, with its sharp styling, impressive ergonomics package and front-wheel drive. It quickly proved popular and the Fiesta soon began to dominate sales in this sector, becoming Britain's best-selling supermini for five years from 1978 to 1982.

This new breed of car combined city-friendly dimensions with an increased level of comfort and practicality not seen in the previous generation of small cars such as the Mini and Hillman Imp. Every manufacturer wanted a piece of this exciting new market. Slowly but surely, each manufacturer brought its own Fiesta challenger to the market.

Enter the Austin
The Fiesta's fiercest foe, in Britain at least, would at first come in the form of the Austin Mini Metro. The Metro had endured a troubled conception. British Leyland had wrestled since the late 1960s and early 1970s with how to replace the iconic Mini. Sir Alec Issigonis's small car had become a superstar, a mascot for the company known all around the

The Metro took the Mini and made it modern – it arrived in 1980 after a troubled gestation. BMH

26

THE ARRIVAL OF THE SUPERMINI AND THE REORGANIZATION OF PSA PEUGEOT

The 205's rival from General Motors would come in the form of the Vauxhall Nova/Opel Corsa, arriving in the UK in 1983. VAUXHALL MOTORS

Fiat's Uno would arrive almost alongside the 205 and would prove to be one of its strongest competitors early on. FIAT MOTORS UK

had not been a source of profit for the company. Quite the opposite in fact. It is well known that in 1960 Ford bought a Mini and stripped it to bits in an effort to find out how their rival was able to produce and sell the Mini so cheaply. Ford's engineers realized that they could not – each Mini ended up costing the British Motor Corporation (the forerunner to British Leyland) £30.

Whatever car was to succeed the Mini would have to be produced in a more sensible fashion and be able to take on the Fiesta and any other European and Japanese rivals head-on. The first step on the road to Metro arguably came in 1973 when British Leyland began development of the car codenamed 'ADO74'. Intended as a more spacious Mini, ADO74 suffered at the hands of Leyland's infamous mismanagement, and the project dragged on. The company quickly realized it would struggle to find the £130 million necessary to bring the car to production and it was quietly shelved.

Another potential replacement came from Italy, in the form of the Bertone-designed Innocenti Mini of 1974. The Innocenti added more contemporary styling and a hatchback, but retained the Mini's running gear. The Bertone car failed in one all-important area, however: cost. It was more expensive to produce than the original Mini so any chance it had of succeeding its originator ended there and then.

The Metro would finally begin its development in 1974 when British Leyland's management chose to simplify their plans by using the Mini's engine and gearbox in its successor. This car, now named 'ADO88', would continue its development until 1977, evolving into a very Metro-like shape.

British Leyland had determined to build an ultra-low-cost car but, in the wake of the Fiesta, chose at the last minute to revise its forthcoming car, fearing its 'cheap' alternative might be little more than an also-ran when compared with the Ford. The car gained yet another development code, becoming 'LC8', and by 1980 the car was ready for launch.

The Metro arrived to a sea of Union flags and the strains of 'Rule, Britannia!' Leyland deliberately played the patriotic angle with the Metro – it needed its new small car to see off a host of foreign competitors and much of the company's future depended on the little car. Thankfully for Leyland, it worked. Metro proved hugely popular on its arrival and was soon outselling the Mini (which, owing to public affection and continued sales, would remain in production), before eclipsing the Fiesta as Britain's best-selling supermini in 1982.

The next big arrival in this burgeoning sector would be the Opel Corsa, known in the UK as the Vauxhall Nova. The Nova arrived in Europe two years after the Metro, offered as a three-door hatch or two-door saloon. Britain would have to wait until 1983 for the Vauxhall-badged version to arrive, where it replaced the – by now – rather aged Chevette.

By the dawn of 1983 most of Peugeot's rivals were offering a supermini in their range, with Fiat's Uno coming along at almost the same time as the 205. The Uno would become a key rival for the 205, particularly in Europe. It showed once again the trend for front-wheel drive – compact hatchbacks were not a flash in the pan. The Uno was a replacement for Fiat's 127, which had been the Italian company's first front-wheel-drive supermini.

27

■ THE ARRIVAL OF THE SUPERMINI AND THE REORGANIZATION OF PSA PEUGEOT

Peugeot's newest acquisition, Chrysler-Talbot Europe, sold almost 70,000 vehicles in 1981, with production spread between Ryton and Linwood, in Scotland. COVENTRY TRANSPORT MUSEUM

Linwood had been home to the Hillman Imp and later the Avenger. The plant's construction had been a purely political decision and it struggled throughout its brief life. Peugeot closed it in 1981. COVENTRY TRANSPORT MUSEUM

So while development was well advanced on the 205, Peugeot found itself being one of the last manufacturers to join the then-new generation of supermini. As history records, the wait would be worthwhile.

MAKING THE MOST OF IT – PEUGEOT'S CHALLENGE FOR THE 1980s

Peugeot was a company that found itself rather in the doldrums as the 1980s dawned. Having expanded greatly in the 1970s, absorbing Citroën, Simca and Talbot into its ranks, its increased size had put the company under considerable financial strain with a range of vehicles in need of updating. A period of rationalization followed for the newly enlarged PSA Peugeot group. Peugeot had discontinued the Hillman Hunter saloon in 1979 but further pruning was needed.

Figures from the Society of Motor Manufacturers and Traders show that in 1981 Peugeot sold 17,805 vehicles in the UK, representing 1.20 per cent of the market. Chrysler Talbot on the other hand had notched up 68,048 sales, with a 4.58 per cent share of the market. The buyout gave Peugeot a considerable increase in total market share as well as access to a well-established dealer network. As with any takeover, though, there would be changes and Peu-geot wasted no time in making them.

In 1981 Peugeot closed its Lin-

THE ARRIVAL OF THE SUPERMINI AND THE REORGANIZATION OF PSA PEUGEOT

wood factory in Scotland, a plant that had been part of the Rootes Group and had been responsible for building the Hillman Imp. The plant had struggled since its opening in the 1960s. Geographically it was isolated from the heartland of British manufacturing in the English Midlands. This isolation led to some bizarre production practices – engine components, such as cylinder heads, were cast at Linwood before being transported, via train, to Stoke-on-Trent and then Coventry, where engines were completed before being returned to Scotland.

The local workforce lacked experience in the business of car building, which led to ongoing quality issues and, as with many manufacturers during the 1970s, relations between the factory's workforce and management remained under near-constant strain. The last car to be built at Linwood was the Avenger, which had started life as a Hillman, then became a Chrysler and finished as a Talbot when production was relocated from Linwood to Coventry.

ACROSS THE CHANNEL

At home in France, Peugeot had a strong manufacturing, distribution and dealership base behind it. The factory at Aulnay-sous-Bois had opened in 1973 as a Citroën plant a year after Peugeot had opened their Mulhouse operation. It became part of the PSA group following the merger in 1976. Alongside Aulnay there was also the Citroën plant at Rennes. Rennes had opened in 1960, becoming the first Citroën factory outside Paris. Initially it was responsible for producing the Citroën Ami 6. Citroën also had a car production plant at Caen, which opened in 1963, as well as plants in Spain, at Vigo, and Portugal, at Mangualde.

Citroën's Charleville plant handled items such as cylinder heads, engine subframes and crankshafts, while the company's gearboxes were produced in Metz. After the Peugeot-Citroën tie-up the company added an engine plant close to the Metz gearbox site, at Trémery. Construction of the factory began in December 1977. It opened in 1979, having cost 1.8 billion francs, and by 1980 was producing 60,000 engines annually – a figure that would increase exponentially during that decade.

Prior to the mergers and acquisitions, Peugeot had formed a joint venture with Renault and Volvo to open a foundry and engine plant in Douvrin, near Calais. The Française de Mécanique facility opened in 1971, producing crankshafts. By the mid-1970s it was producing the Douvrin V6 and by 1979 it built its first diesel engine and employed 4,000 people.

Compared with the British operation, Peugeot's French acquisition, Simca, was in much better shape, holding around 10 per cent of the French market in 1979. Peugeot's first step was to rebrand the cars as Talbot-Simcas.

Simca's cars remained popular in Europe, notably France and Spain – they joined the PSA family as part of the Chrysler Europe buyout.

■ THE ARRIVAL OF THE SUPERMINI AND THE REORGANIZATION OF PSA PEUGEOT

With Simca came the car plant in Poissy. Alongside Aulnay-sous-Bois, it became the second of Peugeot's Parisian factories. Unlike Linwood, Poissy enjoyed a much stronger position within the French motor industry. The factory was opened in 1940 by Ford just weeks before Germany's invasion of France. Ownership passed to Simca in 1954 before Chrysler took control of that business in 1963.

Poissy was the crown jewels of Chrysler Europe, occupying a huge site and employing 22,000 people to produce some 2,000 cars a day. Under PSA control Poissy continued to build Simcas and Talbots, producing the likes of the Samba, Solara and Tagora. By 1980 the Simca name was phased out, but production at Poissy continued, albeit with the cars now wearing Talbot badges.

Simca also brought with it the Villaverde factory near Madrid, Spain. This factory produced Simca cars and Dodge commercial vehicles. Under Peugeot the truck and bus business was sold to Renault while the factory would continue to build cars such as the Talbot Samba and Solara.

PEUGEOT'S DISPARATE PRODUCT MIX

Small hatchbacks were becoming massively popular yet Peugeot's only offering in this burgeoning sector was the 104. The 104 had launched a decade earlier in 1972 and was starting to look somewhat dated. According to Peugeot's April 1981 price list the 104 was Peugeot's cheapest car – at £3,119.57 for a three-door hatch – but still found itself undercut by the newer, and arguably more fashionable, Austin Mini Metro, which had launched to much fanfare from press and public alike.

The five-door version of the 104 added almost £400 to the price and alongside the three-door remained the only hatchback in Peugeot's range. Contrast this with the likes of Ford, who offered the Fiesta in the 'B' segment, or supermini class, and the Escort in the 'C' segment, or small family car. Ford's faith in the hatchback was underlined by the launch of the Sierra, which replaced the legendary Cortina and

The Peugeot 305 was offered as a saloon and estate. It was smart and spacious, but hardly exciting and unlikely to draw customers to showrooms.

THE ARRIVAL OF THE SUPERMINI AND THE REORGANIZATION OF PSA PEUGEOT

The Pininfarina-designed 604 was what many expected from Peugeot – a big, comfortable Gallic cruiser.

signalled a move away from saloons that all manufacturers would follow. Vauxhall, likewise, had offered the Astra as a hatchback since 1980 and the Cavalier gained a hatchback variant in 1982.

Peugeot, meanwhile, continued with a range of cars that had a small but loyal following – one that would have looked somewhat dated to the new-car buyer in the early 1980s. The 305 had arrived in 1977, styled by long-time collaborator Pininfarina. It was a strong seller in Europe and won the *What Car?* Car of the Year in 1979 but it failed to capture the British public imagination in the same manner.

Further up the range sat the 504 saloon and estate, which had won European Car of the Year in 1969 but was decidedly long in the tooth at the start of the 1980s. It was eventually replaced by the 505, though for a while Peugeot offered both the 504 and 505 alongside each other. Again, the 505 would be a saloon, though it was later joined by the eternally practical 505 Estate with its massive load bay.

Peugeot's flagship at the time was the 604. Another Pininfarina-designed car, it stayed faithful to Peugeot's traditional brand values of building big, laid-back saloons. Power came from either a V6 ohc petrol engine or a 2498cc diesel engine. The 604 was Peugeot's first attempt to compete against established executive marques such as BMW, Jaguar and Rover. It launched in 1975 and received praise from the press for its spacious interior, ride comfort and handling, but commercially the 604 was a failure, with fewer than 200,000 examples sold.

The Talbot Range

Peugeot's range was by no means bad, but it wasn't exactly inspiring. Talbot, on the other hand, had a selection of cars that were arguably more modern and forward-thinking than Peugeot's, boasting hatchback, saloons and even a 'lifestyle vehicle'. Despite this, Talbot remained something of a bit player in Britain, where customer loyalty was split between the likes of British Leyland and Ford, with Japanese manufacturers gaining an increasing market share.

Talbot's line-up included the Samba, the Horizon, the Solara, the Alpine, the Tagora and the Rancho. It was an odd mix of products and components borrowed from PSA Peugeot, Chrysler and Simca – a result of Talbot's merger with Simca before Chrysler sold off its European business to PSA Peugeot.

The Samba was essentially the same car as the 104 and therefore suffered the same drawbacks as the Peugeot. It was joined, further up the range, by the Horizon – a car

31

■ THE ARRIVAL OF THE SUPERMINI AND THE REORGANIZATION OF PSA PEUGEOT

The British-designed Talbot Tagora largely sank without a trace upon its launch.

that had been developed in France and sold initially as a Simca in France and a Chrysler in Great Britain. It underlined the increasing popularity of the hatchback in continental Europe, beating the Astra to the market by two years, the hatchback Escort by three and Austin's Maestro by five. Talbot offered it with a 1.1-, 1.3- or 1.5-litre petrol engine or a 1.9-litre diesel and by 1980 it was being built in the UK, at Ryton, Coventry.

Further up the range sat the family hatchback/saloon duo of Alpine and Solara. Built at Poissy, and later at Ryton, and designed by Roy Axe who had styled many previous Rootes Group cars including the Sunbeam Rapier and the Hillman Avenger, the front-wheel-drive hatchback won European Car of the Year in 1976. Both cars, especially the hatchback, enjoyed considerable success in Europe, particularly in France where the Alpine began life as the Simca 1307.

The duo failed to repeat that success in the UK, where buyers remained faithful to the likes of Ford, who had built a loyal customer base with its Escort and Cortina. Towards the end of the Solara and Alpine's life, Talbot renamed them once again, dusting off the 'Minx' and 'Rapier' nameplates that had once been used on Hillmans during the 1960s and 1970s. Talbot's use of the names was somewhat confusing to buyers. Rather than separate the names so that one covered the hatch and one the saloon, Rapier and Minx were used on both cars, referring not to body style but to trim level.

Talbot's range also included the slightly oddball Rancho. The Rancho was the result of a collaboration between Simca and French engineering company Matra. It was based on the Simca 1100 and, prior to PSA's takeover, was sold as the Matra-Simca Rancho. With its increased ride height, plastic-clad wheel arches, bull bars and driving lamps it looked every

THE ARRIVAL OF THE SUPERMINI AND THE REORGANIZATION OF PSA PEUGEOT

bit the tough off-roader, but nothing could be further from the truth, since it was powered by a 1.4-litre, ohv petrol engine with front-wheel drive and developed 80bhp. With its shrunken Range Rover styling the Rancho was one of the more popular vehicles in the Talbot range but it was arguably out of place in the overall Peugeot Talbot range, which included the 305 Estate, which in some ways could have been perceived as a rival to the Talbot.

Through its $1 purchase of Chrysler Europe, Peugeot found itself with a large manufacturing base behind it. Combined with the manufacturing capacity acquired through the purchase of Citroën, Peugeot had become one of the key players in European motor manufacture. However, it now needed to capitalize on that growth. PSA had taken on significant debts through the buyouts of Citroën and Chrysler Europe. The newly enlarged group found itself under considerable financial strain and a return to profitability was required.

What Peugeot needed now was a new generation of products that met with the demands of a new generation of car buyer. It needed a product to change its image, to awaken interest in the brand and to draw customers into its dealerships.

What Peugeot needed was the 205.

The Rancho was quirky and unique – predating today's modern 'softroaders' by over thirty years.

33

CHAPTER THREE

M24: DESIGN AND DEVELOPMENT OF THE 205

It was clear from the success of some of Peugeot's key rivals that the hatchback had become the de facto architecture for any small car wishing to win over customers in this fiercely fought segment. The war for supermini customers was already raging and Peugeot was one of the last to arrive. However, by studying the alternatives in the market, PSA was able to better its rivals in more than one area.

Codenamed 'Project M24', the 205's development took five years and cost Peugeot in the region of £110 million. Rather than replacing the 104, Peugeot's original intention was that the M24 would sit above the older model and below the larger 305 saloon. The 104 was beginning to become outclassed by alternatives from Ford and Volkswagen, to name just two.

Despite its age, Peugeot felt there was still a place for the 104, particularly in Europe. However, as history shows, the company would quickly withdraw the 104 from the UK market, and the 205 would easily fill the gap left by the older model.

Peugeot's research showed that the market for the small hatchback was growing (in 1982, the year before the 205 arrived, 25 per cent of new vehicle registrations fell into this sector) and it was the tastes of car buyers at the time that quickly helped shape the 205.

The external design for the new car set Peugeot's own styling studio against that of Italian carrozzeria, Pininfarina. The two studios were given a 1:10 scale layout of the new car's key dimensions and datum points and set to work.

The in-house team at Peugeot, based at the Peugeot design studio at La Garenne-Colombes, near Paris, was led by Gérard Welter. Welter had joined Peugeot in 1960 at the age of eighteen and had worked on cars such as the 204 convertible, the 304, the 305 and the 604. By 1975 he had become Peugeot's director of exterior design and, two years into that role, he would lead the design team on the M24.

PSA was determined to make the M24 a success – between Peugeot, Citroën and Talbot the company was struggling with an outdated and often conflicting range. While PSA's management set about reorganizing and restructuring the company, the M24 would be the first of a new generation of Peugeot products and there was no margin for failure. Simply put, the M24 had to succeed.

And so, with the car's importance reiterated, Peugeot began an intensive period of market research, questioning potential customers on the merits of rival vehicles and what they expected from a Peugeot supermini. Some of the 205's key attributes were determined by its rivals. All of its rivals were under 4m (13ft) in length – the shortest was the Metro at 3,406mm (134.1in), the longest Nissan's Micra at 3,746mm (147.5in). It should also be available in both three- and five-door body styles, with a design that lent itself to

Development of the M24 began in earnest. The team was led by Gérard Welter.

34

M24: DESIGN AND DEVELOPMENT OF THE 205

> ### GÉRARD WELTER – FATHER OF THE 205
>
> Gérard Welter enjoyed a long and fruitful career with Peugeot. He joined the firm in 1960, working under designer Paul Bouvot. Welter was part of a small team, made up of fewer than a dozen people. He would stay with Peugeot for almost fifty years and after the 205 would design the 405. He was the first Peugeot employee to build a racing car for Prototype racing. In 1988 the duo built 'Project 400', intended to be the first car capable of reaching 400km/h (248.54mph) during a Le Mans race. They succeeded, hitting 405km/h (251.66mph) at Le Mans in 1990. Later that year Meunier departed and Welter's wife Rachel joined her husband. Between 1993 and 2010 Welter Racing competed in the Le Mans 24 Hours, taking the pole and fastest lap for the 1995 race with the Peugeot 905 Spider. The team maintained a strong relationship with Peugeot, using the manufacturer's engines up until 2008. Today Welter is retired, and survived an attempt on his life in 2011. Welter Racing continues to operate from its base in Seine-et-Marne, in the north of France.

both layouts. Peugeot's management was also keen that the car should appeal to younger buyers – the firm's traditional customer base had been towards the mature end of the scale and the company needed to entice younger buyers in order to expand its market share.

The Renault 5 was France's best-selling car at the time and Peugeot's management was determined to overhaul its rivals from Boulogne. If the 205 were a success it would earn Peugeot some national pride by taking sales from Renault and its 5 as well as spearheading a new range of Peugeot cars, a range designed and built for the 1980s.

The consultation process concluded in 1977 and Welter's team set to work. The M24 was intended to replace the range-topping 305 and the lower-specification 104, with a planned launch in 1982 or 1983. It would have to be a front-wheel-drive 'two-box' (hatchback) measuring no more than 3,800mm (150in). It also had to boast all-round, independent suspension. Furthermore, there was a keen sense within the company that the M24 should be capable of utilizing the diverse range of engines the PSA group had at its disposal (the company had recently acquired Citroën, which gave PSA access to a broader range of front-wheel-drive engines).

PSA's management rightly believed that the M24 needed a broad range of engine options to appeal to the widest possible spectrum of customers. For the designers this meant that the M24's engine bay had to be able to accept either an 'end-on' or an 'in-sump' gearbox arrangement. This would enable the 205 to accept engines ranging from 954cc through to 1500cc – in the case of the old Douvrin or 'X' engine – as well as the larger, newer XU engines that would go on to power the performance-led variants of the M24.

Equal consideration was given to the diesel options for the M24, as Peugeot had a strong reputation for their robust and extremely fuel-efficient oil burners. These engines, together with the XUD-series diesels, would give the 205 anything from 45bhp to 120bhp and ensure there was a 205 suited to as wide a customer base as possible. Peugeot's management had noted the success of the Volkswagen Golf GTi and believed that the new small Peugeot should have its own sporting variant.

The 205's development benefitted from Peugeot's continuing research and development programme, known as VERA (*Véhicule Econome de Recherche Appliquée* or 'economic vehicle applied research'). Much of the VERA work had been based around the 305 and investigated ways of improving aerodynamics and reducing the weight of production cars. Peugeot used this research not only to improve the way their cars were designed and built, but also as a promotional tool.

The design of M24 evolved quickly – there are strong hints of the 205 evident in this model.

M24: DESIGN AND DEVELOPMENT OF THE 205

While the battle for the 205's exterior was fought between France and Italy, the 205's interior was an entirely Gallic affair. Peugeot's styling centre, led by designer Paul Bracq, began interior design studies for the car in September 1977, working in conjunction with the VERA project teams to develop the car's interior. The team also took advantage of new technology, utilizing computer-aided design (CAD) for many of the 205's interior components. The team was keen to create a design that would age well, provide maximum passenger protection and offer ease of maintenance.

By 1981 the first mock-ups of the M24's interior had been completed. These mock-ups were used as the basis for ergonomic tests as well as customer and styling clinics.

Developments in CAD began in the 1960s and came to fruition in the automotive industry in the 1970s. One of the first programs used for vehicle development was UNISURF, the pioneering CAD/CAM (computer-aided manufacturing) system devised by Frenchman Pierre Bézier, an engineer at Renault. The program was first developed in 1968 and by 1975 it was fully operational and one of the key tools used by Renault for new car development.

CAD allowed engineers to develop various components and simulate how those components would behave. CAM could then take those components and refine the manufacturing process, meaning the development of new components could be greatly speeded up. CAM gave the 205's development team the equivalent of production-ready componentry to work with, rather than the rough-and-ready test pieces previous 2-series cars would have been developed with.

The CAD/CAM system gave engineers real-world data on vital areas such as structural rigidity and fatigue, information that could only have been gained previously from hundreds of hours of testing. The 205 was the first Peugeot to truly benefit from this advancement. CAD was also used to underpin what was known as the 'comfort study' for the M24's interior. The computer software determined the ideal driving position in the car, saving hours of experimentation and the need for engineers of various sizes to test the settings.

One of the key areas within the interior brief was the provision of 'extensive storage space'. The M24 delivered this by including a large glovebox, a centre console with additional space for radio and oddments, as well as open areas above and below the dashboard. The addition of door bins (which on some models house the switches for the electric windows) completed the selection of storage options.

THE INTERIOR BRIEF

After the M24's key dimensions had been laid down the styling team developed a brief for the new car's cabin:

- The design should use clean, flowing lines that would not date.
- The mouldings should be rounded to offer improved passenger protection in the event of an accident.
- Should provide extensive storage space.
- Provide ease of maintenance with access to the instruments, which should be perfectly integrated into the dashboard.
- Should contain a degree of 'future proofing' – meaning that the interior could be upgraded or additional instrumentation added without the need for significant redesign or the investment demanded by such work.

Once the brief was agreed development could begin.

While Welter's team worked in Paris, Pininfarina worked on their own take on the M24, presenting Peugeot's management with clay models in early 1977. Peugeot saw sufficient promise in the proposal to request revisions, which the Italian studio duly made, presenting revised models in October 1977.

AND THE WINNER IS...

The competition for the M24's exterior design drew to a close in 1979. Despite Pininfarina's revisions, Peugeot's management opted to go with Welter's in-house design proposal, the Farina study being rejected on the grounds of it being 'too traditional and conventional'. The importance of the M24 could not be overplayed: it was a make or break car for PSA Peugeot. The company needed new customers and the best way to attract them was to offer something genuinely new, necessitating a break with the firm's traditions.

Following some minor refinements, the exterior design was finalized by the start of 1980 and the M24 was at last on its way from drawing board to showroom. It retained the same wheelbase as the 104 – 2,418mm (95.2in) – but

M24: DESIGN AND DEVELOPMENT OF THE 205

Peugeot's design team beat their Italian rivals to it – the 205 would be entirely French in design.

But not before some final revisions to the front – the face of the 205 as we know it today.

the body itself grew by around 80mm (3in). The track was also increased by 70mm (2.75in) and 25mm (1in) at the rear. The increase in overhang and track allowed the 205 to have a large enough engine bay to accommodate the range of engines PSA Peugeot intended to offer with the new car. The increase in track also meant the 205 would hold the road better than the 104 and allow for softer springs, meaning improved passenger comfort.

With the full-size clay model signed off by management, it was then scanned in by computer, mapping out 10,000 points on the M24's body. This meant that software was

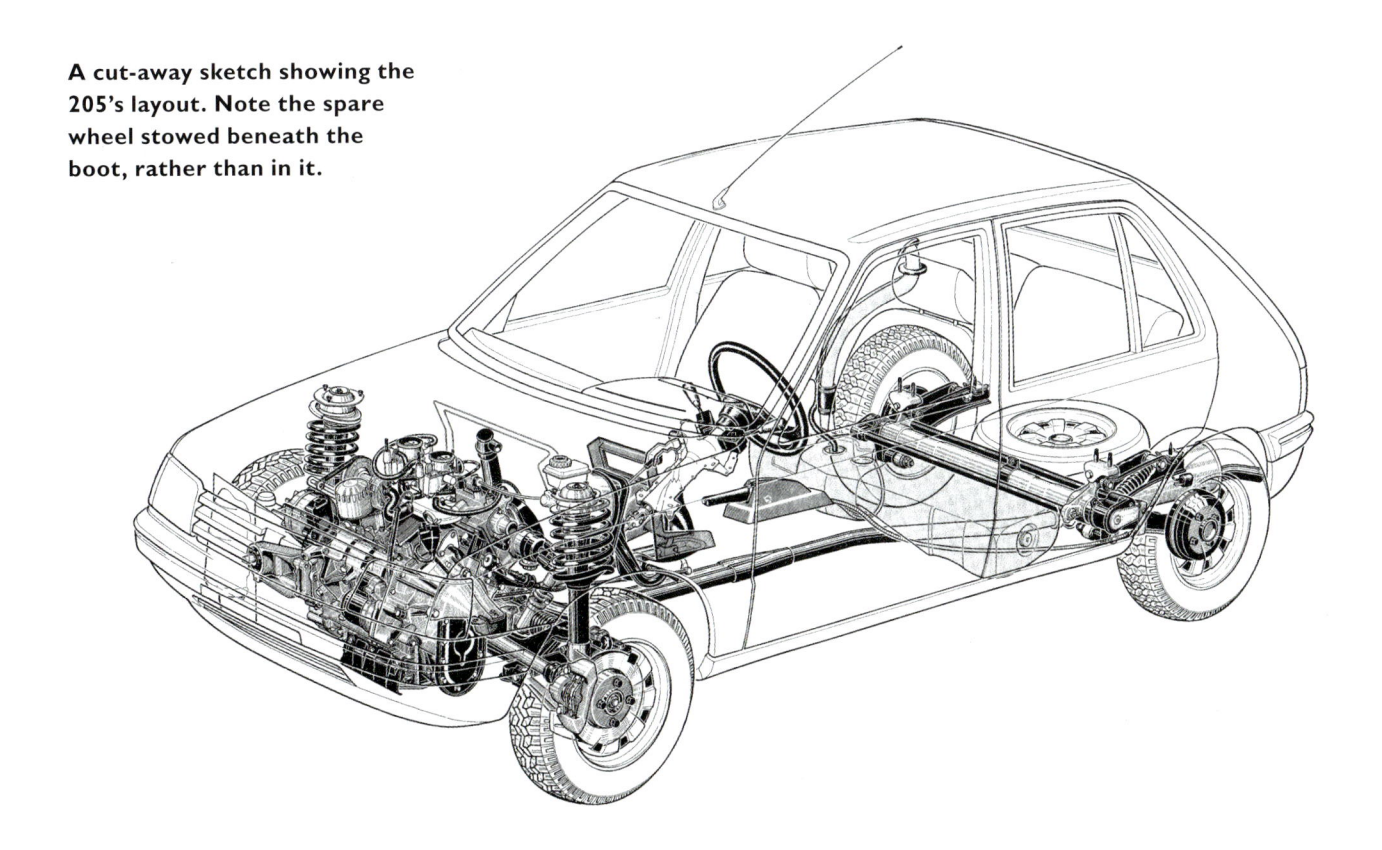

A cut-away sketch showing the 205's layout. Note the spare wheel stowed beneath the boot, rather than in it.

37

■ M24: DESIGN AND DEVELOPMENT OF THE 205

then able to determine the location for the car's mechanical pick-ups as well as the most logical routes for fuel and brake lines. Another benefit of the CAD-scanned body was the way in which it was possible to determine where key structural areas were and were not necessary, meaning that significant weight could be saved from the car's bodyshell. The computer was also able to create a front end capable of accepting the range of engines demanded at the 205's inception.

Safety was becoming an increasingly important focal point for many manufacturers, including Peugeot. The doors were designed to include a brace to add protection from side impact, while the M24's front end was designed so that in the event of an impact the shock would be transferred upwards, away from the passenger compartment. The seat belts were mounted to the seat runners so that the belts remained at maximum efficiency, regardless of the seat's position.

Another area of Peugeot's focus was refinement. The company had a reputation for well refined cars and despite its diminutive dimensions, the 205 was to be no different. The cabin was designed with a rubber-lined bulkhead, while the floors were covered with a thick, polyurethane matting, which was fitted to the floor before the heat-formed carpets were installed.

Passenger comfort was also considered when it came to the M24's heating and ventilation. The heater, for example, was capable of renewing the air inside the cabin every twenty seconds. A complete M24 was also placed in a semi-anechoic chamber, an 'echoless' room, to test the noise levels produced by the car.

These concepts and more were a result of Peugeot's vigorous VERA programme. During 1981, a VERA 305 was put to the test in a series of economy runs to evaluate the success of Peugeot's revisions to the car. It weighed 188kg (414lb) less than a standard 305 sedan, and consequently enjoyed a reduced drag coefficient. The changes made it 33 per cent lighter and the car's fuel economy increased to 91.2mpg (3.1ltr/100km) from its turbo diesel engine – incredible figures for 1981.

The car's compact set-up meant that the spare wheel could be stowed beneath its rear end to maximize load space. To aid the battle against corrosion, 42 per cent of the components were either zinc electroplated or galvanized. The wheel wells and underbody were designed to minimize mud accumulation and the sills were shaped to reduce potential damage from gravel impact.

With the design laid down, a full-scale master model was created using a computer-controlled milling machine. The master was then used to create two prototype bodies. Over 300 components in the model were created by Peugeot's craftsmen, each item requiring the fashioning of a wooden mould from which the components could be cast. One of

The Project VERA 305 taught Peugeot's engineers plenty about aerodynamics and fuel economy.

M24: DESIGN AND DEVELOPMENT OF THE 205

the bodies was for testing purposes, to study the bodyshell's reaction to fatigue, its torsional rigidity and vibration response. The other formed the basis of the first running M24 prototype. Each of the shells took up to 18,000 hours to produce while some of the individual components were the result of almost 70,000 hours of work. Craftsmen were also used to create items such as seats, interior trim and carpets.

Aerodynamic testing was conducted on a full-size shell, allowing the engineering team to determine the location of cooling air intakes, flow lines across windows, whether or not the body should feature rain gutters, and the design of the wing mirrors. Elsewhere, results from VERA testing led to changes in the M24, determining the shape of the front cross section, the use of a flat windscreen seal, a small lip at the rear of the roof panel, and the final decision to go without roof gutters.

Once complete, each component was then tested before full development testing could begin. Many of the new components were put to the test on a newly developed triaxial machine. Peugeot was the first manufacturer to use such a machine, which when linked to a computer was able to record how each part of the system behaved. This system also allowed Peugeot to put the 205's suspension through continuous testing – the rig was run for twenty-four hours a day for seven days, simulating thousands of miles and the harshest of environments.

Every component used, or considered for use, in the 205 was bench-tested, with door locks, window winders and bonnet locks completing over 100,000 opening and closing cycles. The M24's engines were then bench-tested in a chamber, with the exhaust gases collected and analysed by computer before the car could be subjected to the final rolling road and test-track sessions.

By 1981 the first prototype car was ready to begin testing. It was still known as the M24. Although the 104 would initially be sold alongside it the team was expecting to market the new car as the 105. However, Jean Boillot, Peugeot's commercial director at the time, vetoed the use of the 105 name. He saw the M24 as a much more upmarket product than the 104 and wanted to communicate that message clearly to potential buyers. And so the M24 was christened 205.

The 205 now embarked on 600,000 miles (over 950,000km) of testing at Peugeot's Belchamp test facility, near Sochaux, with its road section, cobbles, mud, a water hazard and a high-speed ring, allowing the company to test the car at maximum speed and gauge fuel consumption.

BODYSHELL CONSTRUCTION

The shell's floor was made up of front and rear sections, while the sides contained the door frames, the body's sills and pillars, the rear wings and the seat belt mounting points. The roof was welded on as a separate panel, while the front wings were bolted to the shell. A reinforced panel at the bottom of the bulkhead provided extra bracing in the event of an accident and directed shock away from the cabin in the event of an impact. The 205's shell combined strength with lightness, tipping the scales at 194kg (428lb) without the front wings. The doors also benefitted from computer-aided design, with single-piece pressed frames.

The 205's front subframe was constructed from two side members, connected by a cross member. This was fixed at the front bulkhead and extended under the floor. The side members carried the engine mounts, with rubber mounts to help reduce the noise, vibration and harshness of the 205's engine. To further improve the 205's refinement, the engine was mounted at an angle of 72 degrees, moving it further away from the driver, and the exhaust and inlet manifolds were designed to be harmonically in tune with one another, thus cancelling each other out. Thick, fibre matting was applied to the bulkhead, the dashboard and the area surrounding the 205's pedals. Instead of traditional roof lining, which was prone to echoes, Peugeot fitted the 205 with a piece of fabric-lined, bonded polyurethane foam, greatly reducing the amount of noise and vibration inside the car.

The M24 development car meets an early pre-production 205.

■ M24: DESIGN AND DEVELOPMENT OF THE 205

Construction diagrams show how the 205 remained strong, yet lightweight.

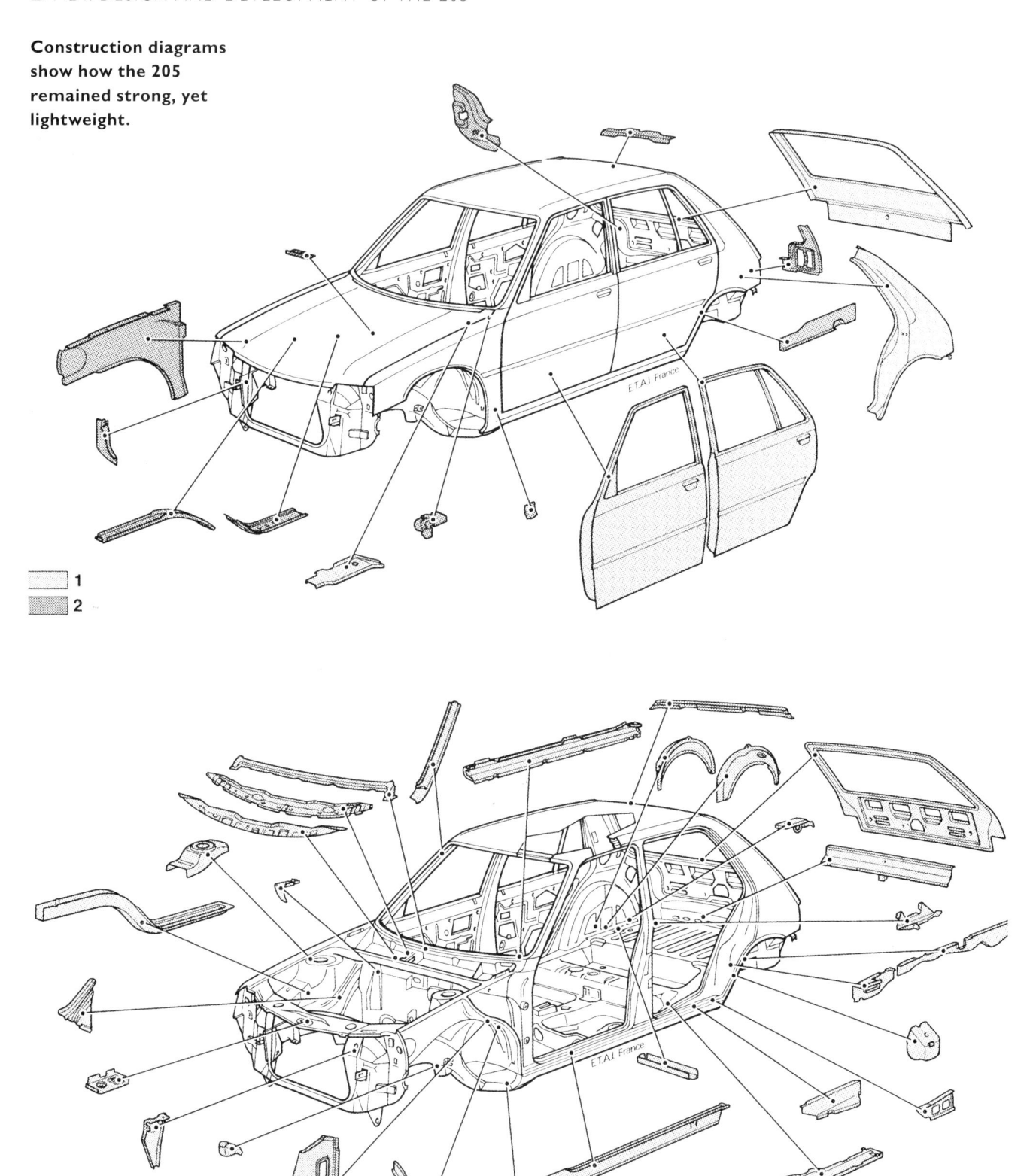

1
2

M24: DESIGN AND DEVELOPMENT OF THE 205

SUSPENSION

VERA also impacted on the M24's suspension, which Peugeot was keen to ensure offered the highest levels of comfort.

The 205's design brief demanded that the new car's suspension be light, simple to service, quiet, resistant to corrosion and still provide a ride befitting of a Peugeot. The engineers opted to use inverted MacPherson struts – similar to what had been used on the 104, albeit with an anti-roll bar behind the front wheel's centre line. Coil springs and shock absorbers completed the set-up.

At the rear, the car used trailing arms with a torsion bar. For the M24s with engines developing in excess of 59bhp, the engineers specified a rear anti-roll bar. The M24's ride height was lower than that of the 104.

Road noise was minimized by the used of rubber mounts for the 205's suspension, six at the front and four at the rear. The front suspension was supported by a cross member beneath the main structure. At either end of that cross member, and in front it, was a lower link with a rubber mounting, helping to reduce the amount of noise from the system. At the outer end of this was the lower ball joint, fixed by a clamp and bolt.

These links were joined by an anti-roll bar, pointing rearwards, on flexible mountings to allow progressive rigidity and maintain refinement. At the top was the suspension strut, featuring a shock absorber and spring, connecting the stub axle to the main structure again via a rubber mounting. The strut was fixed to the stub axle with a clamp. The system was simple, with each component designed to be easily removable and replaceable, making maintenance and servicing on the 205 as easy as possible.

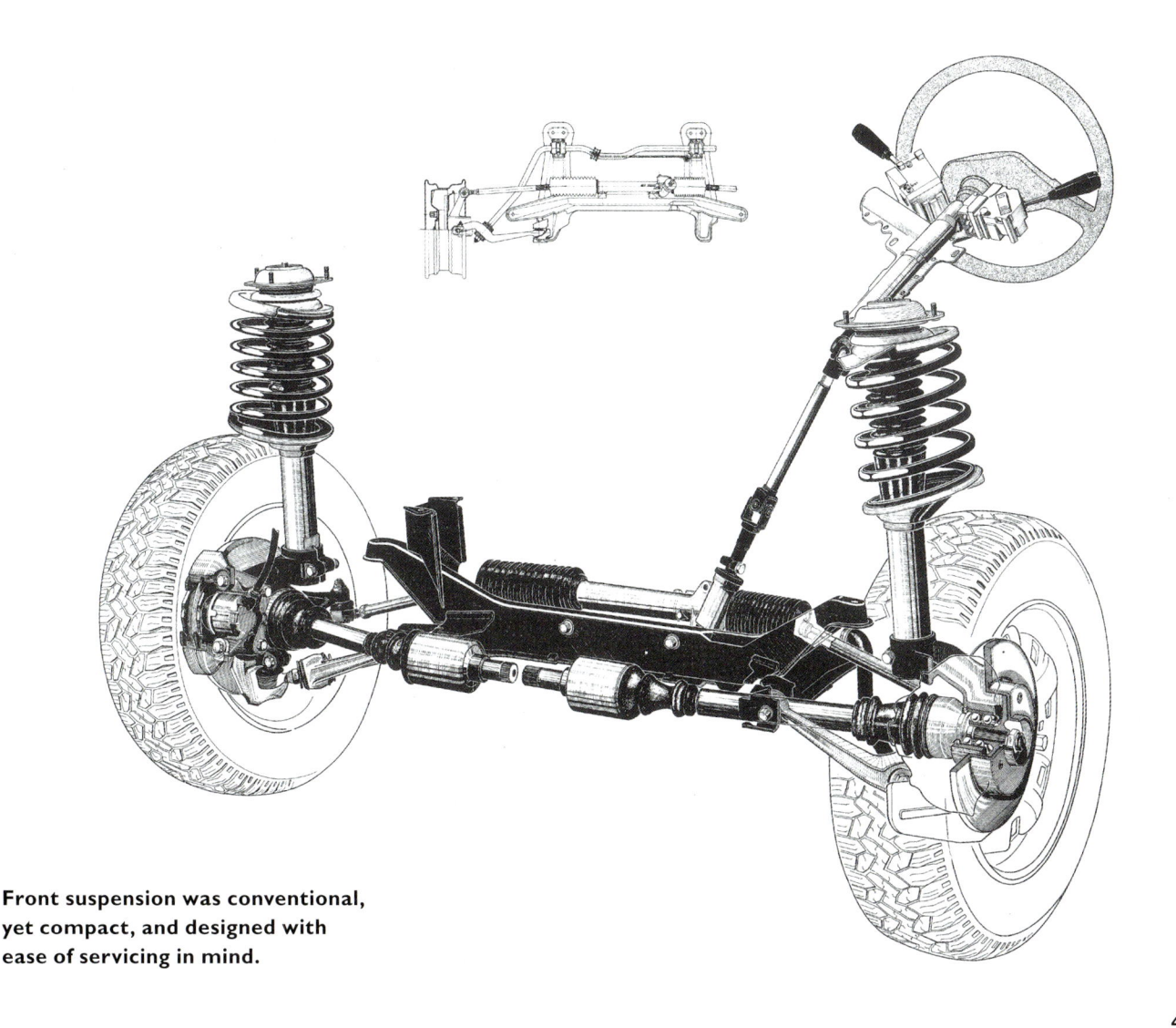

Front suspension was conventional, yet compact, and designed with ease of servicing in mind.

■ M24: DESIGN AND DEVELOPMENT OF THE 205

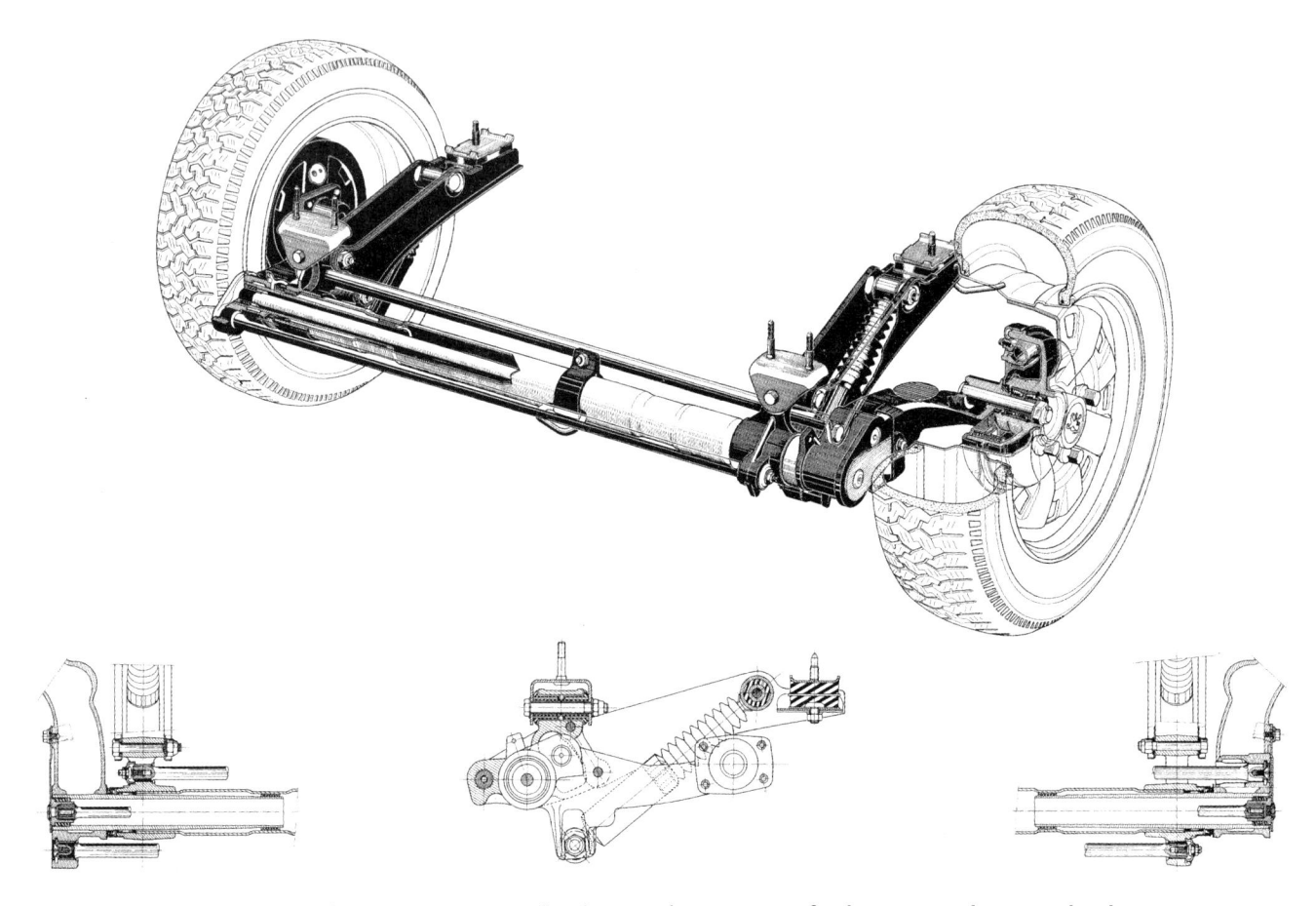

Rear suspension was compact, allowing maximum space for luggage and spare wheel.

The 205's rear suspension used a torsion beam system, which allowed maximum space for rear passengers and luggage. The nature of the beam's layout meant the 205's body was able to employ much narrower rear wheel arches, therefore minimizing their intrusion into the interior space.

The rear suspension was particularly compact, with a maximum height of just 215mm (8.5in). The suspension comprised two transversely mounted torsion bars, while more powerful versions, such as the 1360cc and diesel-engined cars, gained an additional anti-roll bar. Each end of the torsion bar was fixed to each of the rear trailing arms. A stub axle was attached to each suspension arm. The ends of the rear cross members were home to the torsion bar's housing and shock absorber mountings. On cars with the anti-roll bar, it was located inside the tubular cross member. Bump stops on these cars were fixed to the trailing arms and the rebound stops incorporated into the shock absorber.

That suspension set-up made the 205, even in low-powered versions, surprisingly good fun to drive. It gripped well and offered nimble handling without sacrificing too much in the way of comfort and those that tested it were quick to praise the car.

Following extensive corrosion testing (see below), the engineers at Peugeot were able to determine the best means to protect the suspension set-up. Each component was protected from the rigours of life on the road by the components being either galvanized, zinc-plated, sealed or protected by rubber gaiters.

The bonnet was designed to open almost vertically, allowing as much access to the engine bay as possible, with the aim of easing servicing.

42

AERODYNAMICS AND CORROSION PROTECTION

Once the 205's exterior design was signed off by Peugeot's management a team of engineers began an in-depth study to understand and improve the car's aerodynamics. All of the work on the 205's aerodynamics was completed using full-size models. This meant the engineers were able to determine the most efficient placement for the car's cooling intakes and the shape of the car's wing mirrors. Some design elements were lifted directly from the VERA car, having proven themselves sufficiently on the test car. These items included the position of the air intake in the car's front bumper, a bonded rear window and the shaping of the roof to create a lip along its rear edge. Some models, such as the GT and GTI, further accentuated the aerodynamic package with the inclusion of a spoiler.

Peugeot also considered the aerodynamics of the 205's interior. The ducting to move fresh air into a vehicle, be it for the engine or for passenger comfort, creates 'captive drag' and Peugeot's engineers worked hard to ensure the 205 had the smallest drag surface area possible.

In order to ensure an accurate model during testing, Peugeot loaded each 205 with the equivalent weight of two passengers and 60kg (132lb) of luggage. This made the car respond realistically in terms of road stance, performance and fuel consumption. The final results of Peugeot's efforts in the wind tunnel gave the diminutive 205 a drag coefficient of 0.35, an impressively low figure for a car in the 205's class.

The body was rust proofed at each stage of production, with 21 per cent of the panels being zinc-plated, 17 per cent galvanized on one side, and 4 per cent galvanized on both sides. The underside was protected by zinc-fused paint. Once the shell had been welded together it was then degreased and a phosphate coating was then applied to ensure good contact between paint and metal at the next stage. The shell was then fully dipped in a cataphoresis tank for electro-painting, while the underbody was then coated in stove-enamelled PVC.

Peugeot then subjected the 205 to accelerated corrosion tests in the lab. A test 205 was put through 24-hour test cycles. These would involve a car being driven for 24 hours before being placed in a test cell. Once in the cell, the temperature would be increased to almost 50°C (122°F), with a humidity of 95 per cent. This process would be repeated 120 times over six months. The car was then driven over 10 miles (16km) of gravel track, 600 miles (965km) of salted muddy track and 50 miles (80km) of salt water. Over the testing period, each 205 would complete 8,700 miles (14,000km) and 960 hours under testing, with Peugeot's engineers completing periodic inspections during the six months of the test.

This process allowed the prototype 205 to experience six years of life on the road in just half a year, after which it was stripped down to its component form and inspected. The information from this inspection was then used to create a computer model to determine which areas of the car were in need of improvement. The test also allowed Peugeot to evaluate the effectiveness of its anti-corrosion treatments, which included electroplated zinc and galvanized sheets, weldable paint, and a sealant-wax compound.

As the 1983 launch approached, Peugeot was confident it had done all it could to ensure that its new car would be able to cope with all the demands any environment could throw at it.

Production and Engines

Peugeot invested £55 million in its Mulhouse plant where production of the 205 would begin. The line was completely new and the press lines, responsible for producing the 205's body panels, were almost totally automated, requiring little human intervention. The line comprised 329 production units and was capable of producing up to 70 cars per hour. Each 205 shell required 2,572 welds to assemble the 477 components and 91 per cent of those welds were made automatically by the 41 robots that populated the line. The system was managed by 18 computers. The roof was also assembled automatically, while the completed shell and wheels were then painted electrostatically.

To meet the requirement for a broad range of engines, the 205 would come to market with a choice of five different engines, four petrol and one diesel. The petrol engines were 4-cylinder units with an alloy cylinder head and block, with a five-bearing crankshaft. The 205's gearbox was in the sump, beneath the engine.

The 954cc engine with a four-speed gearbox had previously been used in the older Peugeot 104 and Talbot Samba, though for the 205 it was reworked with new valve gear and the compression ratio was raised. The 1124cc had also been used in the Talbot and in some French-market 104s. It employed a single Solex carburettor. The 1360cc was also part of the XY7 engine family and had been developed for the 205. Developing either 59 or 79bhp, the 1360cc was the

■ M24: DESIGN AND DEVELOPMENT OF THE 205

ABOVE: **Mulhouse was subject to a £55 million investment and became home to the 205.**

The 205's production lines were heavily automated, with over forty robots populating the line.

M24: DESIGN AND DEVELOPMENT OF THE 205

direct result of Peugeot's VERA project. The VERA engine had a displacement of 1452cc but to keep costs to a minimum Peugeot used the camshaft, exhaust and inlet manifold from the XW7.

When it came to the diesel option, Peugeot once again looked within its existing family of engines, opting for a 1769cc unit based on the 1905cc XUD9 employed in the 305 GRD. The 205's ability to handle a range of power plants was showcased brilliantly with the 205 diesel. While the petrol engines featured a gearbox-in-sump layout, the diesel's gearbox used an end-on layout.

The diesel 205 enjoyed impressive fuel economy, with Peugeot reporting consumption of 72.4mpg (3.9ltr/100km) at 56mph (90km/h). The base 954cc petrol 205 received a 40ltr (8.8gal) fuel tank, the rest of the range featured a larger 50ltr (11gal) tank. Fuel consumption was impressive, with the 954cc base model returning 55.4mpg (5.1ltr/100km) at 56mph (90km/h), or 41.6mpg (6.8ltr/100km) on the urban cycle.

Each engine was mated to a gearbox best suited to that power plant's attributes, be it the XV8 and XW7's focus on economy or the XY7 and XY8's lean towards performance. Each petrol 205 used the same 180mm dry plate clutch and was cable operated.

The time for testing was over – the 205 was ready for launch.

Almost 500 components went into each 205 bodyshell.

M24: DESIGN AND DEVELOPMENT OF THE 205

ENGINE OPTIONS

Peugeot was keen to create a broad range of engine options for the 205. At launch the range included:

Base model	954cc	XV8	44bhp
GL	1124cc	XW7	49bhp
GR	1360cc	XY7	59bhp
GT	1360cc	XY8	79bhp
GLD and GRD	1769cc	XUD7	59bhp

Production of the 205 finally began in late 1982, when the first three hundred or so cars were built. JOHN EVANS

CHAPTER FOUR

TURNING POINT: THE LAUNCH OF THE PEUGEOT 205

The Peugeot 205 was unveiled to the UK press in October 1983, replacing the well regarded, if slightly dated, 104. The 205 was to be the first in a new generation of cars from the company, as PSA's management aimed to harmonize the vehicles produced by its Peugeot, Citroën and Talbot subsidiaries.

Road tests of the time mention that the 205 'sits in the range above the three-door Talbot Samara, but below the Horizon'. The early 1980s were a boom time for the small hatchback. More and more families had the financial wherewithal to add a second car to their household and cars like the 205, together with the Ford Fiesta, Austin Metro and Renault 5, found themselves increasingly popular, be it as a school-run taxi, shopping trolley or first car for fortunate sons and daughters.

In the UK, the new 205 would serve as a replacement for two cars, the old Peugeot 104 and the Talbot Samba, marking the beginning of the end for the Talbot brand. Many in the UK expected the 205 to be offered as a Talbot, given that the British brand enjoyed a bigger market share than Peugeot and a wider dealer network. And, from Talbot's point of view, it was, in Britain at least, the best known of the PSA brands. When the 205 came to market, Peugeot Talbot were able to boast around 500 dealers in the UK (many of which held joint Peugeot Talbot franchises) and over 9,500 across the continent of Europe.

At launch the cheapest 205 cost £3,895 for the most basic model, while the range-topping GT (note the absence of the all-important 'I') came in at £5,395. Mechanically, it followed the classic transverse layout as laid down by the Mini twenty years earlier, complete with its five-speed gearbox beneath the engine. Suspension was all-independent, with MacPherson struts at the front and a compact trailing arm and torsion bar at the back. Braking was handled by 9.7in discs up front and drums to the rear.

The five-door GT topped the range when the 205 launched in the UK in October 1983.

An original 205 GR from the car's UK launch programme.

47

TURNING POINT: THE LAUNCH OF THE PEUGEOT 205

SPECIFICATIONS: PEUGEOT 205 (1983–88)

	Saloon/XE/XL	GL/XL/XR	GLD/GRD/XLD	XS/SR/GR/GT
Engine				
Model	XV	XW	XUD	XY
Position	Front, transverse mounted	Front, transverse mounted	Front, transverse mounted	Front, transverse mounted
Block material	Alloy	Alloy	Iron	Alloy
Head material	Aluminium alloy	Aluminium alloy	Aluminium alloy	Aluminium alloy
Main bearings	5	5	5	5
Cylinders	4, in-line	4, in-line	4, in-line	4, in-line
Cooling	Water	Water	Water	Water
Bore and stroke	70 x 62mm	72 x 69mm	80 x 88mm	75 x 77mm
Capacity	954cc	1124cc	1769cc	1360cc
Valves	8	8	8	8
Compression ratio	9.3:1	9.7:1	23:1	9.3:1
Camshaft configuration	Single ohc	Single ohc	Single ohc	Single ohc
Camshaft drive	Chain	Chain	Belt	Chain
Carburettor	Single Solex carburettor	Single Solex carburettor	Single Solex carburettor	Twin carburettors (GT)
Maximum power	44.5bhp @ 6,000rpm	49bhp @ 4,800rpm	59bhp @ 4,600rpm	59/79bhp @ 5,000/5,800rpm
Maximum torque	51lb ft @ 2,750rpm	63lb ft @ 2,800rpm	80lb ft @ 2,500rpm	79/81lb ft @ 2,500/2,800rpm
Transmission				
Gearbox	4-speed manual	5-speed manual	5-speed manual	5-speed manual
Clutch	Diaphragm spring, single dry plate, cable operated	Diaphragm spring, single dry plate, cable operated	Diaphragm spring, single dry plate, cable operated	Diaphragm spring, single dry plate, cable operated
Ratios	1st = 3.882:1	1st = 3.882:1	1st = 3.308:1	1st = 3.882:1
	2nd = 2.296:1	2nd = 1.882:1	2nd = 1.882:1	2nd = 2.296:1
	3rd = 1.377:1	3rd = 1.377:1	3rd = 1.280:1	3rd = 1.502:1
	4th = 0.944:1	4th = 0.944:1	4th = 0.969:1	4th = 1.124:1
	Reverse = 3.568:1	Reverse = 3.568:1	5th = 0.757:1	5th = 0.904:1
	Final Drive = 3.563:1	Final Drive = 3.3.54:1	Reverse = 3.471:1	Reverse = 3.568:1
				Final Drive = 3.501:1
Suspension and Steering				
Front	Independent, MacPherson struts, coil springs, lower wishbones and anti-roll bar	Independent, MacPherson struts, coil springs, lower wishbones and anti-roll bar	Independent, MacPherson struts, coil springs, lower wishbones and anti-roll bar	Independent, MacPherson struts, coil springs, lower wishbones and anti-roll bar
Rear	Independent, trailing arms fixed to single beam, transverse torsion bars, telescopic shock absorbers and anti-roll bar	Independent, trailing arms fixed to single beam, transverse torsion bars, telescopic shock absorbers and anti-roll bar	Independent, trailing arms fixed to single beam, transverse torsion bars, telescopic shock absorbers and anti-roll bar	Independent, trailing arms fixed to single beam, transverse torsion bars, telescopic shock absorbers and anti-roll bar
Steering	Rack-and-pinion	Rack-and-pinion	Rack-and-pinion	Rack-and-pinion
Tyres	165/70/R13	165/70/R13	165/70/R13	165/70/R13
Wheels	13in, pressed steel, bolt-on disc	13in, pressed steel, bolt-on disc	13in, pressed steel, bolt-on disc	13in, pressed steel, bolt-on disc
Brakes				
Type	Discs front, drums rear	Discs front, drums rear	Discs front, drums rear	Discs front, drums rear
Size	Front 247mm, rear 180mm	Front 247mm, rear 180mm	Front 247mm, rear 180mm	Front 247mm, rear 180mm
Track	Front 1,350mm	Front 1,350mm	Front 1,364mm	Front 1,350mm
	Rear 1,300mm	Rear 1,300mm	Rear 1,314mm	Rear 1,300mm
Dimensions				
Overall length	145.87in (3,705mm)	145.87in (3,705mm)	145.87in (3,705mm)	145.87in (3,705mm)
Overall width	61.89in (1,572mm)	61.89in (1,572mm)	61.89in (1,572mm)	61.89in (1,572mm)
Overall height	53.74in (1,365mm)	53.74in (1,365mm)	53.74in (1,365mm)	53.74in (1,365mm)
Unladen weight	1,631lb (740kg)	1,642lb (745kg)	1,918lb (870kg)	1,720lb (780kg)
		1,720lb (780kg) (XR)		
Performance				
Top speed	88.9mph (143km/h)	95.7mph (154km/h)	96.3mph (155km/h)	110.6mph (178km/h) (XS/SR)
				101.3mph (163km/h) (GR)
0–60mph	18.8sec	14.6sec	15.1sec	10.6sec (XS)
				12.8sec (GR)
				15.1sec (SR)

TURNING POINT: THE LAUNCH OF THE PEUGEOT 205

Morocco played host to the 205's European launch and provided an ideal backdrop for the car to showcase its abilities. JOHN EVANS

READY FOR LAUNCH

The 205 would arrive in Britain in October 1983 but its European launch took place the previous January and did not actually take place in Europe at all. Instead, Peugeot headed to Morocco, where journalists from the UK's top fifteen car magazines experienced two full days of driving the new car. The UK launch took place across the Irish Sea, in the Republic of Ireland, and as with the Moroccan launch, the models offered included the Saloon, GL, GR and GT.

THE PRICE IS RIGHT

The 205 range comprised six models at launch in October 1983, from the basic Saloon to the sporting GT. Peugeot's price list at launch looked like this:

	Basic	Car tax	VAT	Total
Saloon	£3,126.43	£260.53	£508.04	£3,895
GL	£3,527.76	£293.98	£573.26	£4,395
GLD	£3,808.70	£317.39	£618.91	£4,745
GR	£4,009.37	£334.11	£651.52	£4,995
GRD	£4,290.31	£357.52	£697.17	£5,345
GT	£4,330.44	£360.87	£703.69	£5,395

Optional extras

Metallic paint with varnish coat (not Saloon)	£115.59	£9.63	£18.78	£144
Black paint	£65.03	£5.41	£10.56	£81
Electric front windows, central door locking and locking fuel cap (GT only)	£266.50	£22.20	£43.30	£332
Alloy wheels (GT only)	£189.44	£15.78	£30.78	£236

TURNING POINT: THE LAUNCH OF THE PEUGEOT 205

As demanded right from its inception, Peugeot launched the 205 with a broad range of engines, from the 954cc, 44bhp unit in the base 205 through to the 79bhp 1.4-litre GT. The base model covered the 0–62mph dash in 18.8 seconds, with a top speed of 83.2mph. The 1124cc GL shaved almost 2 seconds off that time, reducing it to 17 seconds, while adding 5mph to its top speed. The 59bhp GR covered the sprint in 14.8 seconds, topping out at 96.3mph. The fastest 205 at launch was the GT with the same 1360cc lump as the GR, albeit with 79bhp on offer. The five-door GT hit 62mph in 11.5 seconds, with a top speed of 105.6mph.

The motoring press responded well to the new Peugeot, with *Motor* awarding the 205 four out of five stars for its performance, praising the GR in particular for the 'feeling of effortlessness that characterizes the Peugeot's performance'. *Autocar* agreed, saying, 'We have covered a good number of miles in a 205 GT, been impressed by its peppy performance and recorded better than 40mpg over a 1,000 mile test distance.'

The 205 also found favour for its interior comfort. *What Car?* gave the 205 five out of five in its October 1983 road test, putting it ahead of the Fiat Uno, Austin Metro and Vauxhall Nova. 'The seats, though broad and long in the cushion, look thin at first. They soon prove soft and very comfortable in use, with much better support than is normally provided by Peugeot or, for that matter, most other small car manufacturers.'

They didn't stop there, with the 205 being complimented on its driving position and low running costs. The early press reports and road tests were almost unanimous in their praise of the 205 and it was clear that Peugeot had built a very good supermini, one that was more than capable of beating its rivals. Now all they had to do was sell it.

> **MOTOR'S REACTION**
>
> British magazine *Motor* awarded a full five stars in its launch road test, saying the Peugeot 'has a fine ride by any standards; for a small car it's little short of excellent. The 205's quality of ride wouldn't disgrace a large executive saloon.'

The base Saloon model featured a simple, clear control layout.

TURNING POINT: THE LAUNCH OF THE PEUGEOT 205

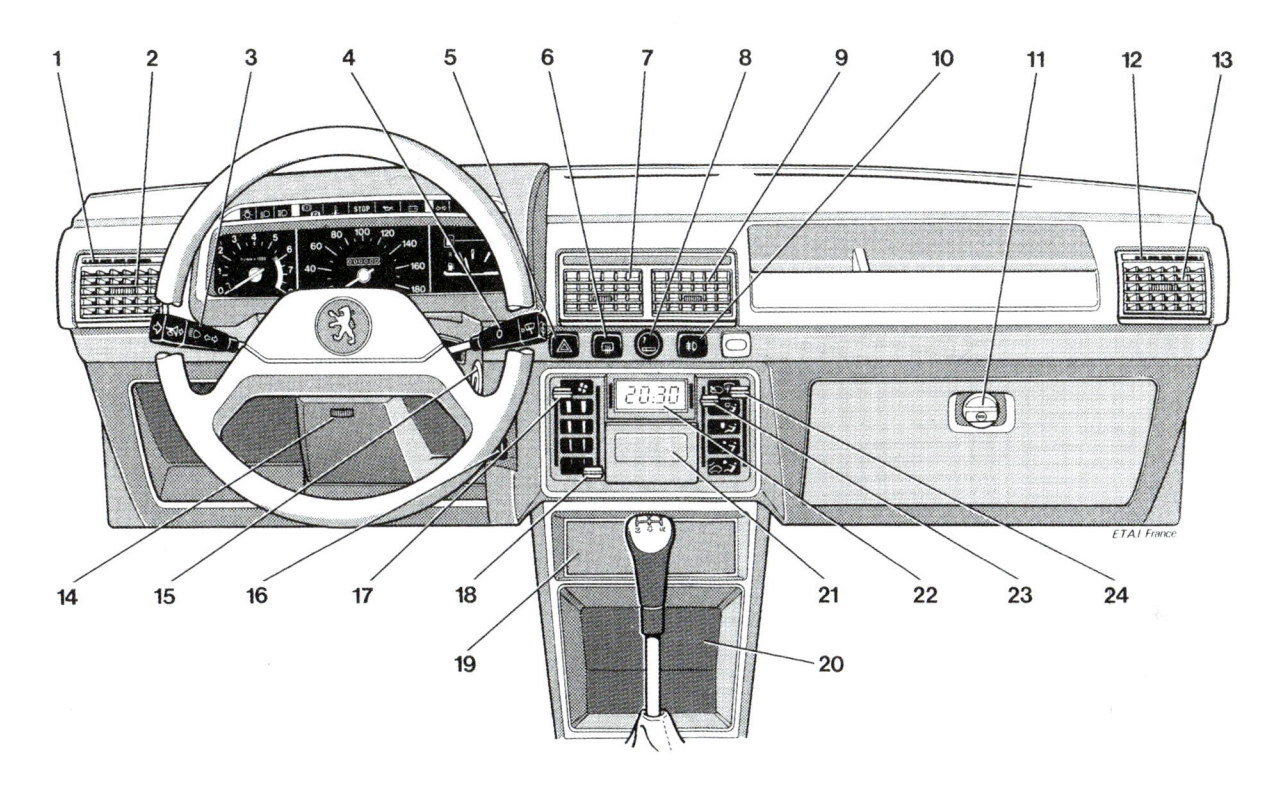

Compare this layout sketch to the Saloon interior. Note extras such as the clock and foglamp switch.

1. driver's airvent; 2. adjustment switch; 3. headlight, indicator and horn stalk; 4. wiper stalk; 5. hazard warning switch; 6. heated rear screen switch; 7. centre airvent; 8. cigar lighter; 9. centre airvent ; 10. rear fog lamp switch; 11. lockable glove box; 12. passenger airvent; 13. adjustment switch; 14. dash brightness adjustment dial; 15. ignition key slot; 16. choke (i think – the image doesn't show it clearly enough!); 17. heater temperature control; 18. fan speed control; 19. radio din slot; 20. storage cubby; 21. ash tray; 22. clock ; 23. fresh air/ recirculation switch; 24. ventilation level switch.

EXTENDING THE RANGE

The first extension of the 205's platform arrived in May 1984 when the GTI was unveiled in Spain. The GTI (see Chapter 5) would go on to become the iconic car of the 1980s and the lines of the 205 lent themselves well to the smaller, sleeker three-door body.

The GTI remained the only three-door 205 for almost eight months until in December 1984 it was joined by a wider range that closely mirrored that of the five-door. While the trim levels on the five-door range began with a G, the three-doors were christened 'X', so the new cars were named XE, XL, XLD and XR.

The three-door range would be enhanced in 1988 with the addition of the GTI-like XS. Externally it wore the same front bumper as the GTI, complete with driving lamps, with

The car that would define the 205, the GTI, arrived in May 1984.

51

■ TURNING POINT: THE LAUNCH OF THE PEUGEOT 205

A PERSPECTIVE ON PEUGEOT 205: A VIEW FROM THE LAUNCH

Sue Baker is a well-respected motoring journalist who has worked for a wide variety of magazines and newspapers during an impressive career. She also spent eleven years as a presenter on BBC television's iconic series *Top Gear* and its sister show *Top Gear Rally Report*. Here she recalls her time on both the European and British launches of the Peugeot 205, which she covered for *The Observer* newspaper.

My view of Peugeot was somewhat coloured by driving early diesels in their range, which were lumbering and painfully slow on start-up, taking about fifteen seconds waiting for the glow plug to warm up! Design-wise they seemed very workhorse, practical but not particularly elegant.

My first encounter with the Peugeot 205 was on the international launch in Morocco in early (February, I think) 1983. It was a fabulous launch trip organized by a very charismatic Italian PR – Corrado Provera – who was then Peugeot's French-based chief PR.

I think we stayed in Taroudant, with a route up through the Atlas Mountains. I recall being briefed at length about taking care on the fast ascents with some sheer drops. All the UK journalists managed the drive without mishap, but one car did go off the road and suffer some quite severe damage – driven by a young French PR man! They had a doctor travelling with the back-up crew, who had to give him some roadside first aid, but he was OK. They joked that it was all planned really to give them some crash test material!

I thought it was cute looking for a Peugeot, which up until then had mostly seemed rather stodgy and a bit dull. I remember thinking it was fun to drive, still a bit flimsy on build quality like its predecessors, and with slightly puny seats.

I liked the styling, it was neat and unfussy and quite smooth looking. It put Peugeot on the map, as an interesting alternative to the Metro, which was already established, and it seemed a bit more chic than the Vauxhall Nova, which was launched around the same time as the 205.

The UK launch of the 205 was later on in 1983, sometime in the autumn, and we went to Ireland. I remember thinking they were brave, because the roads were quite poorly surfaced and driving standards were poor. We came quite quickly round one corner to find a pony and trap stationary in the middle of the road while its driver chatted to someone leaning on a gatepost. On one wild rural road we came across an injured badger – the first I had seen for real – and lifted it out of the road to safety under a hedge. I don't recall where we stayed, but I do remember a rather naff 'medieval' banquet at Bunratty Castle. Splendid surroundings, but the food was dire!

Morocco was a fine location for the 205 launch, recalls *Top Gear* host Sue Baker.
JOHN EVANS

52

TURNING POINT: THE LAUNCH OF THE PEUGEOT 205

TOP: **The three-door range would be expanded by the end of 1984 with the arrival of the XE, XL and XR.**

BELOW: **Minor revisions were made to the 205 in 1988 with the fitting of a new dash boasting improved heating and ventilation and improved controls.**

53

TURNING POINT: THE LAUNCH OF THE PEUGEOT 205

SPECIFICATIONS: PEUGEOT 205 (1988 ONWARDS)

	XE/XL	GL/XL/XR	XS/SR/GR/GT	Automatic
Engine				
Model	TU9	TU1	TU3	XU5
Position	Front, transverse mounted	Front, transverse mounted	Front, transverse mounted	Front, transverse mounted
Block material	Alloy	Alloy	Alloy	Alloy
Head material	Aluminium alloy	Aluminium alloy	Aluminium alloy	Aluminium alloy
Main bearings	5	5	5	5
Cylinders	4, in-line	4, in-line	4, in-line	4, in-line
Cooling	Water	Water	Water	Water
Bore and stroke	70 x 62mm	72 x 69mm	75 x 77mm	83 x 87mm
Capacity	954cc	1124cc	1360cc	1580
Valves	8	8	8	8
Compression ratio	9.3:1	9.4:1	9.3:1	9.3:1
Camshaft configuration	Single ohc	Single ohc	Single ohc	Single ohc
Camshaft drive	Belt	Belt	Belt	Belt
Carburettor	Single Solex carburettor	Single Solex carburettor	Twin carburettors (XS/SR)	Single Solex carburettor
Maximum power	45bhp @ 5,200rpm	55bhp @ 5,800rpm	85bhp @ 6,400rpm	80bhp @ 5,600rpm
Maximum torque	54.3lb ft @ 2,400rpm	65.9lb ft @ 2,800rpm	85.4lb ft @ 4,000rpm	97.7lb/ft @ 2,800rpm
Transmission				
Gearbox				
Clutch				
Ratios	NA	NA	1st = 3.42:1 2nd = 1.95:1 3rd = 1.36:1 4th = 1.05:1 5th = 0.85:1 Reverse = 3.56:1 Final drive = 4.29:1	NA
Suspension and Steering				
Front	Independent, MacPherson struts, coil springs, lower wishbones and anti-roll bar	Independent, MacPherson struts, coil springs, lower wishbones and anti-roll bar	Independent, MacPherson struts, coil springs, lower wishbones and anti-roll bar	Independent, MacPherson struts, coil springs, lower wishbones and anti-roll bar
Rear	Independent, trailing arms fixed to single beam, transverse torsion bars, telescopic shock absorbers and anti-roll bar	Independent, trailing arms fixed to single beam, transverse torsion bars, telescopic shock absorbers and anti-roll bar	Independent, trailing arms fixed to single beam, transverse torsion bars, telescopic shock absorbers and anti-roll bar	Independent, trailing arms fixed to single beam, transverse torsion bars, telescopic shock absorbers and anti-roll bar
Steering	Rack-and-pinion	Rack-and-pinion	Rack-and-pinion	Rack-and-pinion
Tyres	165/70/R13	165/70/R13	165/70/R13	165/70/R13
Wheels	13in, pressed steel, bolt-on disc	13in, pressed steel, bolt-on disc	13in, pressed steel, bolt-on disc	13in, pressed steel, bolt-on disc
Brakes				
Type	Discs front, drums rear	Discs front, drums rear	Discs front, drums rear	Discs front, drums rear
Size	Front 247mm, rear 180mm	Front 247mm, rear 180mm	Front 247mm, rear 180mm	Front 247mm, rear 180mm
Track	Front 1,350mm Rear 1,300mm	Front 1,350mm Rear 1,300mm	Front 1,364mm Rear 1,314mm	Front 1,350mm Rear 1,300mm
Dimensions				
Overall length	145.87in (3,705mm)	145.87in (3,705mm)	145.87in (3,705mm)	145.87in (3,705mm)
Overall width	61.89in (1,572mm)	61.89in (1,572mm)	61.89in (1,572mm)	61.89in (1,572mm)
Overall height	53.74in (1,365mm)	53.74in (1,365mm)	53.74in (1,365mm)	53.74in (1,365mm)
Unladen weight	1,631lb (740kg)	1,642lb (745kg) 1,720lb (780kg) (XR)	1,918lb (870kg)	1,720lb (780kg)
Performance				
Top speed	88.9mph (143km/h)	95.7mph (154km/h)	110.6mph (178km/h) (XS/SR) 101.3mph (163km/h) (GR)	
0–60mph	18.8sec	14.6sec	10.6sec (XS) 12.8sec (GR) 10.6sec (SR)	

TURNING POINT: THE LAUNCH OF THE PEUGEOT 205

The tail lights and rear bumper were revised two years later, in 1990. GERARD HUGHES

alloy wheels offered at extra cost. Inside, the seats were reminiscent of the GTI, though trimmed differently. It also boasted an all-important rev counter – in the 1980s nothing said 'sporty' more than the addition of a rev counter. Power came from the 1360cc engine, with a twin-choke carburettor, mated to a five-speed gearbox. Top speed was in excess of 110mph (177km/h) with 85bhp and 85lb ft of torque. It offered much of the look and appeal of the GTI without the expense, a concept since copied by many a manufacturer.

At launch in 1984 Peugeot claimed the new three-doors were 'precisely matched to the exacting demands of today's busy roads'. In their words, the 'elegant' three-doors were a 'revelation'. They had a point – in its life time over two million three-door 205s would be built.

Though the 205 had undoubtedly become a huge success for PSA and played no small part in rescuing the company, Peugeot still looked to improve the 205 with a series of subtle revisions over its life. The first came in 1988 when the dashboard was revised with simpler heater controls and improved fresh-air ventilation while a more stylish centre console was introduced alongside a restyled steering wheel. That year the original X engines were replaced by TU engines. The TU units brought an increase in brake horsepower, up from 49bhp to 55bhp in the 1124cc engine, for example. Torque also got a healthy boost too, with, for instance, the 1124cc seeing an increase from 63lb ft to 66lb ft.

Externally the 205 remained largely as it had done when it arrived, the only changes being minimal revisions made in September 1990 when the orange front and side indicators were replaced by clear items and the rear lamps redesigned with the reversing lights moving down on to the back bumper.

MISSED OPPORTUNITY – THE 205 AROUND THE WORLD

The 205 would go on to become an iconic car across Europe, but curiously, for whatever reason, Peugeot's willingness to push the car in other markets seemed to be lacking. It took four years for the 205 to reach Australia, a market where Peugeot had enjoyed steady sales. When it did arrive in January 1987, it became the smallest Peugeot ever to be sold in the territory. Naturally enough, it was the GTI that led the way.

By 1987 the 205 was a double World Rally champ and

■ TURNING POINT: THE LAUNCH OF THE PEUGEOT 205

its motor sport success, combined with the fact that it was European, made it somewhat exotic in Australia and it quickly proved popular. Australia was struggling with a recession in the early 1990s so a cheaper model, the 205 Si, was added to the import list, but it was the GTI that had won the hearts and minds of Aussie petrol heads. In February 1994 the Australian market received its own special edition to celebrate its success 'down under', the GTI Classic, which went on sale boasting a similar look and specification to the GTI Griffe.

One market where the 205 never officially saw the light of day, but arguably could have thrived in, was the United States. Both Peugeot and Citroën had long struggled there and, rightly or wrongly, Peugeot had chosen the 405, not the 205, to spearhead its attempts to penetrate the US market during the 1980s. In 1986 Peugeot sold 14,336 cars in the United States; by 1990 that figure had plummeted to just 4,261. Could the 205 have helped Peugeot? Possibly. The 1990s were a curious time for the American car industry, with the big Detroit-based automakers trying, and failing, to come to grips with the increasing threat from Japanese rivals. European manufacturers all found themselves caught in the squeezed middle.

A few 205s, mostly GTIs, did manage to find their way onto American roads but the diminutive Peugeot was arguably robbed of success in one of the world's largest markets. There's every chance that US drivers would have taken to the 205. The VW Golf, initially marketed as the VW Rabbit in the United States, had found a niche there, a niche the 205 could have exploited had it had the chance.

In 1991, Peugeot announced they would be ceasing production of all their US-specification vehicles. They were not the only ones to do so. Ford and Renault did the same, while the Rover Group, who briefly entered the market with its 'Sterling' brand, also withdrew in 1991.

The 205 did much better in South America, a market where Peugeot had been more successful historically. The 205 found willing buyers in both Brazil and Argentina. So popular was the car in Argentina that the last models were sold there in 1998.

205 DIESEL – THE MARRIAGE OF DESIRABILITY AND FRUGALITY

Diesel had long been a popular alternative to petrol in mainland Europe so it was little surprise that Peugeot would choose to offer a diesel-fuelled version of the 205. In the UK, however, diesel cars, particular those in the 205's class,

The 205's incredibly economical diesel added another dimension to the car's appeal.
GERARD HUGHES

TURNING POINT: THE LAUNCH OF THE PEUGEOT 205

ABOVE: **The GRD badge would become a common sight on Britain's roads.** GERARD HUGHES

LEFT: **Once again the Fiesta led the way – opening the door for small diesel cars to enter the market.** FORD HERITAGE

were virtually unheard of. Traditionally the only diesel-powered cars on UK roads were typically large, European saloons and estates – the kind of thing one might expect to see occupying local taxi ranks.

One of the first cars to begin to alter the UK mindset was the VW Golf. The Golf showed British buyers that smaller, family-focused cars could also enjoy the benefits of diesel. Traditionally, small superminis had enjoyed impressive fuel economy due to their frugal petrol engines and low kerb weight. Diesel engines had an upper hand when it came to raw fuel economy but petrol engines boasted superior power and refinement. Diesels were thought of as dirty, noisy and slow. That perception was all set to change.

If a British driver was to look at the European market in the early 1980s they would have seen not only the likes of the Golf offered with a diesel engine but also smaller cars able to enjoy the economic benefits derived from diesel.

The Ford Fiesta was the first diesel supermini to arrive on the UK market, making its debut in August 1983. It made use of the same 1608cc engine that powered the Escort and Orion but in a supermini. It hit the headlines in the British press when it became the first car in its class to break the 70mpg barrier, with a claimed fuel consumption of 72mpg (3.93ltr/100km) at 56mph (90km/h).

The 205 would go further, at least according to the figures, with Peugeot claiming 72.4mpg (3.91ltr/100km) from the 205. In March 1984 *What Car?* put the new diesel 205 up against the Daihatsu Charade, which cost less and claimed even better fuel consumption. The Charade was powered by a miniscule 993cc, 3-cylinder diesel that developed 37bhp compared with the 59bhp found under the bonnet of the 205. *What Car?* were quick to praise the 205, welcoming how, 'with the wise installation of a big and powerful diesel engine in the 205, Peugeot have banished once and for all the idea that diesels are slow, smelly, rough and noisy. The 205 is as smooth and sweet-running as any petrol car.' The magazine went further, suggesting that the 205 diesel was an improvement on the already excellent petrol model, and complimenting it on its 'instant throttle response, terrific truck-like pulling power from the very lowest of engine speeds with a broad rev range that remains refined and smooth'.

The Peugeot trounced the Charade soundly, with the Peugeot scoring five out of five overall, and the Daihatsu recording just two from five. They summed up their findings by stating that 'the diesel 205 is actually a better car than the petrol model. It's not merely an advantage of economy, either. It scores where no other diesel has scored before: it is actually great fun to drive, with flexibility no petrol user could ever dream of.' It could have been argued that when placed head to head against a budget offering such as the Daihatsu the Peugeot would always outshine the Japanese car and that the comparison was a little unfair. A year later, *What Car?* pitted the 205 against the Charade for a second time, though this time it was joined by a sister Citroën, in the form of a Visa 17D, and the trend-setting Ford Fiesta. The Visa shared the same 1769cc engine, albeit mated to a four-speed gearbox. It made a strong case for itself – priced at £4,950 it was over £700 less than the Charade. The Fiesta, priced at £5,712, was the most expensive, closely followed by the Daihatsu at £5,699. The 205 XLD, at £5,320, was aggressively priced.

Once again, the 205 came out on top, closely followed by the Visa. In almost every category it was the Peugeot that won out. In performance it scored five out of five, with what was described as 'an overwhelming margin of superiority'. Ride and handling? Peugeot again. 'There's no competing with the 205's brilliantly smooth and stable ride,' said the magazine. The only category in which the Peugeot lost out was cost – scoring four out of five to the Fiesta's five. The reason? Simply put, What Car? found the Ford to be the most economical car they had ever tested. Combined with Ford's low-cost spares, cheap insurance, affordable servicing and enviable dealer network the Fiesta was all but unbeatable on a purely financial consideration. Despite that, the 205 won the test, with What Car? going as far as to describe the Peugeot as 'the best-ever small diesel', citing nothing could approach its mechanical sophistication even in the most basic trim.

The 205 diesel wasn't simply a great supermini, it played a huge role in redefining the British motoring public's perception of diesel as a fuel and brought about diesel's acceptance as an alternative to petrol. It brought diesel to the masses and paved the way for diesel to become Europe's most popular fuel.

Peugeot did not rest on its laurels. In 1991 the firm added a 'sports' diesel to the range in the form of the turbocharged GRDT. It used the same 1769cc diesel engine, essentially

The GRD Turbo added sporting performance to the diesel-powered 205 but lacked the out and out economy of the naturally aspirated version.

TURNING POINT: THE LAUNCH OF THE PEUGEOT 205

Petrol at £3 a gallon?

Petrol prices are heading for an all time high. A gallon of four star looks like topping £3.00p before too long. Petrol prices have never risen so fast before and as the crisis worsens motorists may face even steeper rises.

The Automobile Association urged motorists to drive slower and to switch to a more economical fuel.

JUST WHEN THE MOTORING WORLD SEEMS TO HAVE GONE MAD

Some words of sanity from Peugeot

Now may seem the worst possible time to be thinking of buying a new car. However, it is the very best time to take a look at a way of motoring which saves you money every time you drive, because Peugeot have two major offers available on their diesel range.

DIESEL TECHNOLOGY MEANS ECONOMICAL MOTORING

Today's diesels save you money in many ways. As you notice every time you visit a filling station, diesel is consistently cheaper than petrol – at the moment it's more than 35p/gallon cheaper than 4-star* – and the difference in price is increasing all the time. Then there is the lower fuel consumption of diesel cars – for example a 205 GRD can return up to 72.4mpg at a constant 56mph. The servicing costs are lower because diesels are inherently more robust and the engines last longer. Consequently second hand prices hold up well; if you sell a car with, say, 60,000 on the clock you know there's a lot of life left in it and can price it accordingly.

PEUGEOT DIESELS MEAN PERFORMANCE WITH REFINEMENT

Gone are the days when a diesel was only suitable for buses or tractors. Peugeot, more than any other manufacturer, has led the way in building cars which match diesel reliability with performance and power. Diesels are less powerful, litre for litre, than petrol engines, so Peugeot have developed larger capacity diesels which maintain a similar power output to the equivalent petrol engine in the same model. Peugeot diesels are refined, smooth and impressive. ("For the enthusiastic driver the 309 GRDT is pure bliss" – Diesel Car, June 1990).

DIESELS AND THE ENVIRONMENT

Diesel fuel contains no lead. The more efficient combustion of diesel fuel means that, in general, the diesel engine emits approximately 1% of the level of carbon monoxide emitted by a normal petrol engine, about 70% less hydrocarbons, and 20-30% less of the "greenhouse gas" carbon dioxide, and about the same level of nitrogen oxides. Finally, a well designed, well maintained engine and use of the newer, more advanced diesel fuels will minimise other exhaust emissions. All in all, diesel is a considerably cleaner fuel than petrol.

MAJOR OFFERS ON PEUGEOT DIESELS

For some motorists, the higher purchase price has been a barrier preventing them from making the switch to a diesel car. Peugeot are delighted to announce two important offers to help overcome the barrier:

FREE £200 INTRODUCTORY BONUS

For a limited period, all Peugeot 205 and 309 diesels are available with a £200 Introductory Bonus. It works like this: Claim your Diesel Bonus Voucher by calling the FREEFONE number below. Then, if you buy and register your new 205 or 309 diesel before December 17th 1990 your dealer will validate the voucher and return it to Peugeot's Head Office. You will then receive a cheque for £200 direct from Peugeot, so the Bonus will not affect the deal you make with your local Peugeot dealer – so you are likely to save even more.

TO CLAIM TODAY, SIMPLY CALL
0800 300 705

PLUS FLEXIBLE FINANCE**

Peugeot are offering a number of attractive finance packages, including a low 10% deposit option. The table below gives an example of how much easier it is to own your new Peugeot diesel. Ask your dealer for details.

	205 XLD
ON THE ROAD PRICE	£8,520.00†
LOAN PERIOD	48 MONTHS
FLAT RATE/APR	7.9%/15.3%
DEPOSIT (10%)	£852.00
MONTHLY PAYMENT	£210.23
FINANCE CHARGES	£2,438.04††
COST SAVING VS APR 23.0%	£1,282.80†††
TOTAL COST	£10,958.04

For economy with power and refinement, choose a Peugeot diesel – motoring for the nineties.

PEUGEOT DIESELS
FUEL FOR THOUGHT

PEUGEOT. THE LION GOES FROM STRENGTH TO STRENGTH

Peugeot were not slow to market the diesel's unique appeal.

■ TURNING POINT: THE LAUNCH OF THE PEUGEOT 205

BRINGING THE 205 TO MARKET – THE VIEW FROM PEUGEOT TALBOT

John Evans was the public relations manager for Peugeot from 1982 to 1987 and recalls that period of Peugeot history fondly.

I joined Peugeot in April 1982. I'd been a political correspondent and a motoring journalist. We were launching the 505 estate – a huge car! Peugeot had just been integrated into Talbot. What a lot of people might not be aware of is the fact that Talbot was the dominant brand. Talbot was in Coventry, while Peugeot had relatively small offices in West London. We were the minor brand. When I joined we were in the process of moving to Coventry.

Talbot were struggling, their approach was simply to stack them high and sell 'em cheap. They just wanted to ramp up production and push as many units out to dealers as possible. Peugeot had a very different atmosphere. Nobody believed we were going to do any serious business. At that time our range included the 104, which had its fans, but had not been particularly successful, we had the 305 which was a great little car but never really found its audience. Then of course we had the 505 and Estate and the much-missed 604.

Talbot launched the Tagora around the time I joined and it died a death. Peugeot wasn't really well known in the UK and lots of people within the company thought that Talbot would remain the dominant brand. My first trip to France changed my mind. I could see then that Peugeot was the future and Talbot was something of a hangover the management of PSA didn't really want. Peugeot demanded a very different approach to sales to Talbot.

The Talbot Tagora was a flop, recalls John Evans. JOHN EVANS

Word got out that a replacement for the 104 was coming. As soon as I saw it I thought 'Wow! That looks fantastic!' – everyone in the UK thought the 205 would be a Talbot. Nobody believed there would be any volume in Peugeot.

In August 1982 I took six members of the Car of the Year jury over to France to see a 205. They could look at it, sit in it, but that was it. They were there to be examined. After they saw the car they were given a presentation about the car – it gave very little away, confirming the car would be a five-door, but not much more. They were stunned – it was nothing like the other stuff Peugeot made.

We were given very clear info on the car, it was not to be sold like a Talbot, and it was to be aimed at the prestige end of the market. I went back to France in December 1982 for

The Moroccan launch was a special one for John. JOHN EVANS

60

TURNING POINT: THE LAUNCH OF THE PEUGEOT 205

The 205 had many of the roads to itself allowing the journalists driving it to see just how good the new baby Peugeot was. JOHN EVANS

a recce and then we got the dates for when journalists would get it. My boss, Brian Llewellyn was very much a Talbot man and didn't really get too involved in the 205 launch, he left me to it.

On 26 January 1983 I went out to Morocco for the launch. We had a GL, GR and GT, all five-doors. Peugeot even managed to get the roads closed so we were able to drive the 205s flat-out. I remember at one point we were in the middle of nowhere, flying along and suddenly there was a chap stood in the middle of the road, flagging us down to tell us to turn left. As we got closer we realized it was a police officer – Peugeot had hired him to ensure we all made this left turn! I thought, 'What a company to work for – they're hiring the police to direct us!'

Once the European launch was done I then had to plan the UK launch. I wanted to do something a little bit different, so I thought about going to Ireland to do it. Ireland was friendly to our budget and not somewhere the press would have had

continued on page 60

The GT was the model used on the launch. Here one takes a rest in the Moroccan countryside. JOHN EVANS

61

TURNING POINT: THE LAUNCH OF THE PEUGEOT 205

continued from page 59

the chance to visit. The launch ran from 10 to 24 September 1983 and we based it at Dromoland Castle in Shannon and the journalists drove down to the Dingle Peninsula.

We had around 120 journalists through the car and we were getting really good reviews. We did one week for the national and local press and the second week was for those that needed a bit more time with the car, TV for example, the likes of Top Gear, and Peugeot Talbot came out too for a day. I was there for three weeks in total. Even those who had been concerned about the 205 not being a Talbot began to see the sophistication. The first cars went to dealers in April 1983.

The Fiat Uno launched at the same time and was a great little car but the 205 won hearts. With the 205 we weren't just launching a car, we were relaunching a brand.

In August 1983 we were told there was going to be a diesel version, so we went to Mulhouse. Nobody had driven a diesel like it. I even ran a left-hand-drive example in the UK for a while so the journalists that hadn't gone to Mulhouse could try the car for themselves.

Once we'd finished the launch activities we took the journalists outside and handed them the keys to a normal looking 205 and said, 'Go and try this' – they came back astonished. What they didn't realize was we'd given them a five-door 205 but with the engine and suspension from a GTI. We asked them not to write about that car as we wanted them to sample the full GTI soon. Amazingly nobody breathed a word!

Later, John would travel to the Irish Republic for the car's UK launch. JOHN EVANS

The T16 was shown to the press in April 1984 and I took journalists over to France, to Paris, to Poissy. The first year, with Ari Vatanen and Terry Harryman, the car showed it was a threat. Ari was a lovely guy but of course had that terrible accident in Argentina. Timo Salonen won the World Rally Championship in the second year, he was brilliant to talk to. Usually smoking, he was so very laid-back. The third year Juha Kankkunen won it. The only car that really gave us a run for our money was the Lancia Delta and then of course at the end of the year they banned Group B, which was a terrible shame. Of course Ari came back and did very, very well in the Paris–Dakar. I did PR for the UK works team. We had Louise Aitken-Walker and Ellen Morgan in a Group A 205 GTI and they competed in the British Rally Championship. They did really rather well for themselves, they came 16th in the RAC Rally that year.

In August 1984 we did the diesel launch in London. We gave each journalist a can with six gallons of fuel in it. We put in a little auxiliary tank with a tap they could turn so they wouldn't run out of fuel. We sealed up the fuel tank so they couldn't put more in! We told them to leave London and drive to the Gleneagles Hotel, near Perth. People were getting 50–52mpg, which today is common but back in the 1980s that was phenomenal. It was a lovely little car. The engine was beautiful.

After the diesel, we then had the GTI launch, which took place in Spain. I remember L. J. K. Setright set off like a maniac. I was convinced he was going to crash. The guy sharing with him got out after twenty minutes – he flagged me down beside the road and said that the way Setright was going he was going to kill himself.

The GTI was the first car to get a press like the Golf GTi. If you've got one now you've got a great car. It was a fantastic product and we just couldn't sell enough of them.

We lost Car of the Year that year by just a single vote. When the results came out we saw that Setright was the only guy not to give us any votes. He gave the maximum to the Fiat Uno. He just wasn't a Peugeot guy. We got a wigging from Peugeot in France when they found out because they thought perhaps we weren't doing our job properly. They wanted to know why he hadn't given us any votes. But that was Setright – he wasn't to be persuaded.

December 1984 saw the three-door launch. It was quite a small affair really, essentially they were the same cars just with two fewer doors!

In April 1986 we got an Evo 2 T16. I remember Pentti Airikkala did some testing with us and he was always quite vocal about how well he could have done with the T16 had he

TURNING POINT: THE LAUNCH OF THE PEUGEOT 205

transplanting the set-up from the British-built 309. The GRDT gained alloy wheels, the same seats as the GTI and the same three-spoke steering wheel as its legendary brother. Unlike the GTI, though, the GRDT was offered in five-door form, adding practicality to its sporting appeal. The turbo-assisted engine developed 116lb ft of torque, a figure close to that of the 1.9 GTI, meaning the GRDT had plenty of grunt. With 78bhp available it boasted a power-to-weight ratio of 84bhp/ton, endowing the diesel turbo with some impressive performance figures. However, the downside to increased power was a decrease in fuel consumption. While the naturally aspirated diesel had been praised by the motoring media for its delightful balance of performance and economy, the case for the diesel turbo faltered somewhat, with the official combined consumption at 56mph (90km/h) being listed as 61.4mpg (4.6ltr/100km), down 11mpg on the original diesel's 72.4mpg (3.91ltr/100km).

During a road test in 1991, *Autocar* felt the – by now – eight-year-old 205 had been overtaken by the revised Rover Metro as the segment leader when it came to combining ride and handling, but for sheer driving enjoyment the Peugeot could 'still trade punches with the best'. By 1991 the 205 had gained power steering and the magazine found that, despite the addition of assistance, the Peugeot retained an impressive level of feel through its steering wheel. Though the 205 was now beginning to show its age it was still praised for its 'mighty mid-range punch, great throttle response and admirably muted voice'. However, when compared with other rivals, the diesel turbo's fuel consumption and high cost (almost £12,000 according to the road test) meant that the previously almost unbeatable 205 had become tough to recommend.

Perhaps the biggest compliment payable to the Peugeot 205 is just how little it changed after launch. Some rivals, such as the Mini Metro, were significantly reworked and some – like Ford, with the Fiesta – replaced their car with a completely new model. While it is true that the dashboard was replaced in 1988, and items such as indicator lenses and tail lights were replaced, the 205 remained virtually identical to the car whose design was finalized back in 1981.

Peugeot put over 100 journalists in the 205 during the Irish launch and received plaudits from the media in return. JOHN EVANS

had the chance to drive it in the World Rally Championship. The car was ultimately driven by Mikael Sundström in the RAC Rally. Our Group B car never really achieved much. I suspect our rally programme in general was a great source of frustration and probable disappointment to Des O'Dell, who of course had done so well with Talbot.

In June 1986 we did the CTi launch. We had a weekend to run the cars in, which was no hardship – they were such great little cars, they looked superb. The press launch ran the cars across Wales, from Cardiff up to Chester.

By the end of 1986 we'd completed all of the 205 launch activities. We'd done it. It was a great product, all the bits were well known and the car sold well immediately.

I left Peugeot in September 1987 for a job with Mercedes Benz but I continued to run 205s for ten years afterwards!

63

CHAPTER FIVE

ARRIVAL OF THE GTI: THE BIRTH OF A LEGEND

When the Volkswagen Golf GTi arrived in Britain in 1979 it changed for ever the way in which hatchbacks were viewed. Before those three letters were grafted onto the Golf's tailgate there was little choice when it came to quick, nippy cars as at home on a winding B-road as they were in the city centre. In terms of performance, there was at least a broad range of sports cars, but few of them were family friendly. So while Volkswagen were not the first company to make a go-faster version of an everyday car, it was the Golf GTi that caught the public's imagination.

Small, front-wheel-drive hatches were now seen as so much more than second cars for shopping and the school run. These were legitimate sporting vehicles, offering the performance of your typical MG or Triumph, but with a hefty dose of real-world usability. The introduction of the Golf GTi changed the car market almost overnight and put paid to many of the sports cars that had once been so popular.

A string of copycats followed but it was the 205 that took the Volkswagen concept, refined it and moved the game to the next level with the launch of the 1.6 205 GTI. The Golf had grown in size when the Golf Mk2 arrived in 1983 and had arguably lost its edge. The VW was now busy fighting a fierce battle with the likes of the Escort XR3i and Vauxhall Astra in the larger hatchback, or C-sector, market. The Golf's growth left a gap in the market and smaller hot hatches began appearing, such as Ford's Fiesta XR2 and the badge-engineered MG Metro from Austin Rover.

The Golf GTi had shown that a hot hatch would be a big seller. It reignited the niche of practical performance cars.
VW GROUP UK

ARRIVAL OF THE GTI: THE BIRTH OF A LEGEND

By the time of the 205's launch in February 1983 Peugeot's plans for more sporting variants were well underway, though few would have predicted the impact the car would have. Work had been progressing on a rally car since December 1981 and when former World Rally Championship co-driver Jean Todt became director of Peugeot racing in 1982 he set about the formation of a new rally team, Peugeot Talbot Sport. The new team made public its plans for rallying with the announcement of the 205 T16 in 1983, together with the road-going 205. The T16 utilized a turbocharged, mid-mounted, 1.8-litre engine and, despite its similar silhouette, was a very different creature to its road-going brother, given that, at the time, the sportiest 205 on offer was the 1.3-litre, five-door GT.

In order to meet homologation regulations (the process whereby a car is approved to compete in a certain class or race series), 200 mid-engine, four-wheel-drive T16s were built, yet the rally-bred machine was never intended to be anything more than a limited-run build, being too raw and too expensive to ever be considered a mainstream model. Still, those 200 cars had done their job; people now looked at Peugeot in a new way and the market was now primed for a mass-market, sporting 205.

The Golf grew as the 1980s dawned, leaving a gap for the Fiesta XR2 to exploit. FORD HERITAGE

The sporting 205 at launch was the twin-carb GT but it lacked the raw power of rivals.

65

ARRIVAL OF THE GTI: THE BIRTH OF A LEGEND

SPECIFICATIONS: PEUGEOT 205 GTI (1984–1992) AND CTI (1985–1992)

	1.6 CTI/GTI	**1.9 CTI/GTI**
Layout and chassis	Front engine, front-wheel drive, monocoque chassis	Front engine, front-wheel drive, monocoque chassis
Engine		
Model	XU5J XU5JA (1986 on)	XU9JA
Position	Front, transverse mounted	Front, transverse mounted
Block material	Aluminium alloy	Aluminium alloy
Head material	Aluminium alloy	Aluminium alloy
Main bearings	5	5
Cylinders	4, in-line	4, in-line
Cooling	Water	Water
Bore and stroke	83 x 73mm	83 x 88mm
Capacity	1580cc	1905cc
Valves	8	8
Compression ratio	9.8:1	9.6:1
Camshaft configuration	Single ohc	Single ohc
Camshaft drive	Toothed belt	Toothed belt
Ignition	Bosch Multipoint	Bosch Multipoint
1984–86	LE2 Jetronic	LE2 Jetronic
1986–92	LU2 Jetronic	M1.3 Jetronic
Maximum power	104bhp @ 6,250rpm 115bhp @ 6,250rpm (1986 on)	130bhp @ 6,000rpm 122bhp @ 6,000rpm (1992 on)
Maximum torque	99lb ft @ 4,000rpm	118.7lb ft @ 4,750rpm
Transmission		
Gearbox	(to 1988) BH 3/5, (post-1988) BH 1/5	(to 1988) BH 3/5, (post-1988) BH 1/5
Clutch	Diaphragm spring, single dry plate, cable operated	Diaphragm spring, single dry plate, cable operated
Ratios	1st = 3.251 2nd = 1.850 3rd = 1.360 4th = 1.609 5th = 0.865 Reverse = 4.063	1st = 2.923 2nd = 1.850 3rd = 1.360 4th = 1.069 5th = 0.865 Reverse = 3.688
Suspension and Steering		
Front	Independent, MacPherson struts, coil springs, lower wishbones and anti-roll bar	
Rear	Independent, trailing arms fixed to single beam, transverse torsion bars, telescopic shock absorbers and anti-roll bar	
Steering	Rack-and-pinion	Rack-and-pinion
Tyres	185/60/14	185/60/14
Wheels	14in alloy, bolt-on	15in alloy, bolt-on
Rim width	5.5in	5.5in
Brakes		
Front	247mm (9.7in) diameter ventilated discs with Bendix or Girling single piston sliding caliper	
Rear	247mm (9.7in) self adjusting drums with leading and trailing shoes on 1.6, solid discs with Bendix single piston sliding caliper on 1.9	
Dimensions		
Track	Front 1,382mm Rear 1,339mm	Front 1,382mm Rear 1,339mm
Overall length	145.87in (3,705mm)	145.87in (3,705mm)
Overall width	61.89in (1,572mm)	61.89in (1,572mm)
Overall height	53.74in (1,365mm)	53.74in (1,365mm)
Unladen weight	2,061lb (935kg) (CTI) 1,874lb (850kg) (GTI)	2,061lb (935kg) (CTI) 1,874lb (850kg) (GTI)
Performance		
Top speed	118mph (190km/h) (CTI) 121.7mph (196km/h) (GTI)	127mph (204km/h)
0–60mph	9.7sec (CTI) 9.1sec (GTI)	7.8sec
Fuel Consumption	56mph: 47.1mpg (6ltr/100km) 75mph: 36.2mpg (7.8ltr/100km) Urban: 30.7mpg (9.2ltr/100km)	56mph: 47.9mpg (5.9ltr/100km) 75mph: 36.7mpg (7.7ltr/100km) Urban: 29.1mpg (9.7ltr/100km)

ARRIVAL OF THE GTI: THE BIRTH OF A LEGEND

Car of the Year jurors were teased with these GTI development mules in late 1983, early 1984. Looking identical to a normal 205 they boasted the engine and suspension set-up from a GTI. Needless to say they were impressed. JOHN EVANS

In creating the 'hot' 205 Peugeot opted to follow the same mantra set by Volkswagen with the Golf GTi, a formula arguably laid down by BMC's Mini Cooper back in the 1960s. It is a simple strategy that is well known to almost every car enthusiast. Take a small, simple front-wheel-drive hatchback and replace its engine with a more powerful, livelier alternative. Of course there was much, much more to the genesis of the GTI than a simple engine swap. The base-model 205s had been praised for their ride and handling so the basis for a credible Golf GTi alternative was there from the Peugeot's launch in 1983. However, few at Peugeot could have expected the 205 GTI not only to become an alternative to the Volkswagen but also, arguably, to better it.

Peugeot's decision to press ahead with the GTI would prove to be a masterstroke for the company and its overall image. It brought about a sea change in both the company's fortunes and the public's perception of it. By the early 1980s the hot hatch was well on its way to becoming an established part of the motoring landscape. Peugeot knew that a combination of alloy wheels, three-digit bhp figures, sporty sculptured seats and a smattering of interior goodies were what were required for its sporting 205.

The GTI debuted a little over a year after the 205's unveiling and unsurprisingly Peugeot chose to take their styling cues from the T16. Priced at £6,245, it offered Golf-rivalling performance and even sharper handling, all in a supermini-sized package. Despite this it was still over £1,600 cheaper than the Golf GTi, a lot of money in 1984. Though it was more expensive than class rivals from Ford and MG it offered considerably more power than either of those competitors and combined that power with a fine-handling chassis.

Compared to the standard 205, the GTI grabbed your attention immediately. At the time it was the only three-door variant offered in the range and that in itself made it stand out, its sporty looks emphasized by a colour palate that included Cherry Red, Alpine White and Graphite Grey. A new front bumper with chin spoiler housed a pair of driving lamps, the ride height was lowered, and 14in Italian-made Speedline alloys with low-profile Michelin tyres replaced the standard steel wheels, echoing the style of those on the rally machine. The doors gained extra cladding, with contrasting red piping running from front to rear, while sporty '1.6' and 'GTI' badges adorned the car's hindquarters and tailgate. Under the bonnet the 1580cc XU5J engine was the largest engine to have been fitted to a road-going 205 at that time and developed 105bhp and 99lb ft of torque using Bosch L-Jetronic fuel injection.

Inside, there was much that any 205 driver would have found familiar, though the GTI specification added oil pressure and temperature gauges, more supportive seats and – as was the fashion of the time – red carpets. The GTI was generously equipped for a new car in 1984, and prospective

The 1.6 GTI made an instant impact when it was launched. GERARD HUGHES

67

■ ARRIVAL OF THE GTI: THE BIRTH OF A LEGEND

An early **GTI** interior shows sports seats and a new steering wheel. Red was an obvious choice for the carpets.

LEFT: **Alloys drew inspiration from those fitted to the Turbo 16 rally car.** GERARD HUGHES

The 1.6 engine covered the 0–60 dash in 8.6 seconds, with a top speed of 116mph (187km/h). *Car* called it 'raunchy, rapid and indecently refined'.
GERARD HUGHES

ARRIVAL OF THE GTI: THE BIRTH OF A LEGEND

SETRIGHT'S VIEW

Legendary motoring writer L. J. K. Setright was complimentary about the cars 'great lightness and sweet gearchange' but questioned Peugeot's decision to chase its rivals, rather than focusing on what he considered Peugeot to be, a producer of more comfort-focused cars, not live-wire hot hatches. He disliked the GTI's large alloy wheels and 'tacky' plastic trim. Setright, as ever, stood out in the crowd, being one of the few journalists to express a dislike of the GTI. He would later underline his dislike of the GTI by giving his votes to its chief rival, the Fiat Uno, in the Car of the Year poll.

owners were impressed. Less than ten years earlier it was unusual to find a basic push-button radio fitted as standard, yet here was a small, relatively inexpensive hatchback with a level of kit previously commonplace on more executive-class cars. Despite the three-door configuration, the GTI retained a spacious back seat with room for two adults comfortably; the sporting additions did little to compromise the 205's natural practicality.

PUTTING IT TO THE TEST

The 1.6 left the majority of road-testers of the day impressed. Peugeot chose to host the GTI's launch in Spain. The 1580cc engine was regarded as 'sparkling', covering 0–60mph in 8.6 seconds, while in May 1984 *Car* spent 2,000 miles at the

The three-door 205 was wonderfully well-proportioned and the shape has aged remarkably well. GERARD HUGHES

69

ARRIVAL OF THE GTI: THE BIRTH OF A LEGEND

wheel of the then-new hot hatch, regarding it as 'raunchy, rapid and in some ways indecently refined'.

The GTI was met with almost universal praise. Here was a genuine sports car from a manufacturer with little previous pedigree in the sector. Peugeot made big comfortable saloons, and the occasional pretty coupé, not hot hatches. Well, now all that had changed.

With its top speed of 116mph (187km/h), the GTI was put on a par with larger hot hatches such as the XR3i and Astra. It wasn't just quick on the straights though, as the chassis, too, received equal plaudits. It was light and agile, with excellent front-end grip, well contained body roll and quick, responsive steering, evoking memories of the Mini Cooper S from twenty years previously. The 205 was certainly lively and was known to even be a little tail-happy, being particularly prone to lift-off oversteer.

When *What Car?* compared the 205 with the Metro and the Ford, it was the 205 that came out on top, recording a full five stars as opposed to three stars for its peers, with strong praise reserved for 'strong road holding, agile steering and terrific performance from a refined engine'; refinement that the Ford and Metro were found lacking.

Fiat had the 205 GTI firmly in its cross hairs with the Uno Turbo. The Peugeot would prove to be the better car. FIAT UK

One of the key components to the GTI's success was Peugeot's ability to rework what was already at its fingertips – there was very little that was actually 'new' on the new car. This was not a bespoke, purpose-developed sports car, but the GTI quickly proved to be much more than the sum of its parts. The XU5J engine had been in use for a number of years prior to the arrival of the GTI, having seen service in a variety of Peugeot and Citroën cars, such as the Citroën BX, none of which could be regarded as exciting. It was hardly the kind of engine you would expect to find at the heart of a performance car. Peugeot's plundering of its parts bin meant the GTI cost little more to produce than the other 205s available, and this had the benefit of making it cheap to run and cheap to repair.

The GTI was a fantastic car to drive, but its drivability was just one aspect of its appeal. As a child of the 1980s the 205 was born into a style-conscious, materialistic decade. Britain in the 1980s was a time of excess and everything about you had to make a bold, brash statement. The 205 GTI boasted more kerbside appeal than any of its rivals and owning a car with those three famous letters on the boot lid was a genuine achievement. So while Ari Vatanen was wowing rally fans worldwide, the GTI was winning fans on the road and within the first year almost 2,000 GTIs had been sold.

What Car? then set about pitting the car against a second set of European rivals in the form of the Fiat Uno Turbo and Renault 5 Turbo.

There were a number of parallels between the 205 and the Uno: both produced 105bhp and both used the same Bosch fuel injection. The turbocharged Renault was the fastest of the trio and was considered to have the best ride in its class, offering a more composed ride than either the 205 or the Uno.

Despite that, the 205 won the day, with the Uno soundly beaten into third place. It may have matched the 205 in terms of horsepower, but *What Car?* described it as uneven, with a bumpy ride and 'uncompromisingly hard' while the magazine was also critical of its handling, labelling it 'vague and lifeless'.

The 205 was the most expensive of the trio but was still considered the one to own. The competition was getting wise to the all-conquering Peugeot. The Renault ran it close, yet it was the GTI that remained at the top of the class. *What Car?* concluded that, 'Somehow Peugeot have contrived to combine looks, performance, character and top quality road behaviour in one very desirable package. The GTI has its faults, of course, but taken overall, it's a winner all the way.'

ARRIVAL OF THE GTI: THE BIRTH OF A LEGEND

STAYING AHEAD OF THE COMPETITION

The success of the GTI opened the floodgates for hot hatches in the UK and a string of copycats followed. In the mid-1980s every manufacture, from Austin Rover to Yugo, produced their own take on the 205 formula with varying success and an automotive arms race began to develop. Body kits became the automotive equivalent of shoulder pads as each manufacturer sought to outdo the other. Of the cars that came in that period, some were good, most were garish, but all ate away at the GTI's market share.

In May 1986, not long after the millionth 205 had been built, the company set about revising and expanding the GTI range, tweaking the 1.6 for improved performance and paving the way for a further model, the 1.9. Before the 1.9 arrived, the 1.6 was subjected to its first revision since its launch. Headline power increased from 105 to 115bhp, thanks to a re-profiled camshaft, larger valves and an improved cylinder head, though the engine's torque remained the same. The suspension on the 1.6 had been modified a year previously and had gone a long way to answering criticism from some quarters that the car was too harsh. While performance had been increased, so had price, with the 1.6 GTI now costing £7,490 before anything had been ticked on the options list.

ABOVE: **The T16 provided near limitless promotional possibilities for the new GTI.**

RIGHT: **December 1986 saw the 1.9 GTI join the 205 range.**

71

■ ARRIVAL OF THE GTI: THE BIRTH OF A LEGEND

GTI – THE RIVALS

During the 1980s it seemed that every manufacturer was rushing to join the hot-hatch party. Some of the cars were instantly dismissible, others became almost as iconic as the 205. It was these that would become the GTI's main rivals.

Golf GTI

The Golf GTI is arguably the best known of the 205's rivals. When it arrived at the tail end of the 1970s it kick-started a new generation of small performance cars. The Golf had been created by a group of keen Volkswagen engineers looking to see what could be done to create a sporting version of the firm's new water-cooled wonder. By the time the 205 GTI arrived, the Volkswagen had moved upmarket with the 1983 Mk2. The Mk2 grew larger than the original but VW had been careful to ensure the car retained a similar look to the Mk1. It arrived in Britain in 1984 and quickly became one of Britain's most popular cars in its near ten-year lifespan. The Golf's growth left a gap in the market for a smaller hot hatch, such as the 205. Despite this movement, the later 1.9 205 GTI could still be considered a rival to the VW.

MG Metro

The plucky Brit was developed as cheaply as possible with the dual intention of keeping the MG name alive and offering a sporting alternative to the relatively humble Austin variant. The Metro offered a spirited drive but, with its roots going back to the Mini Cooper S of the 1960s, was somewhat outdated by the 205 with its five-speed gearbox, higher top speed and quicker 0–60. With only a 1275cc, sub-100bhp engine at its disposal, the MG was always going to struggle when going toe-to-toe with the 205; even in turbocharged form it would be bettered by the Peugeot. The nearest competitor in terms of power from the Austin Rover stable came in the form of the MG Maestro 2.0 EFi, a car that was considerably larger than the 205 and more on a par with Ford's XR3i and Volkswagen's Golf rather than the diminutive 205.

Fiat Uno Turbo

The Uno had pipped the 205 to the 1984 European Car of the Year title and remained one of the 205's key rivals during its early years. Fiat responded in 1985 with the Uno Turbo. Its 1.3-litre, turbocharged engine developed almost as much power as the 1.6 GTI and Fiat took the fight to Peugeot by pricing it as closely to the Peugeot as possible. In 1989 Fiat revised the Uno range. The Turbo gained a Garrett T2 turbo as well as Bosch fuel injection and improved aerodynamics. The changes meant the Fiat enjoyed a boost in power, upping it to 118bhp. While the Uno offered similar straight-line speeds to that of the 205 it could not compete with the Peugeot in terms of ride, handling and refinement.

ARRIVAL OF THE GTI: THE BIRTH OF A LEGEND

Opel Corsa SR/Vauxhall Nova GTe/Gsi

Arriving in 1987, the sporting Corsa/Nova featured a 1.6-litre, multi-point fuel-injection engine developing 96bhp. The development work was completed by Opel's tuning partner Irmscher and for the UK a 1.4-litre, 80bhp model was also offered, badged as the Nova SRi. The Nova would be one of the lesser players in the class and the Vauxhall would never approach the sales of the 205. Before the arrival of the GSi, British buyers were offered the Nova Sport, a car created by Vauxhall UK in order to homologate the Nova for sub-1300cc Group A rallying. It was on the rally stage where the Nova would enjoy its biggest success, becoming a popular choice with the amateur rally driver, something that continues to this day.

Renault 5 GT Turbo

Renault had dabbled with performance versions of the 5 going back as far as 1976 with the Renault 5 Alpine/Gordini Turbo (Alpine in Europe/Gordini in the UK). It developed 110bhp and used a 1.4-litre engine with a Garrett T3 turbo. Renault also created the mid-engined 5 Turbo, a car that enjoyed much success on the rally stage. The closest rival to the 205 came in 1985 with the launch of the Renault 5 GT Turbo. It used the same 1397cc engine and used a T2 turbo and developed 114bhp. The 5's scant kerb weight made it a quick car, capable of covering the 0–60 sprint in under 8 seconds. Unlike the 205 its performance was hampered by turbo lag. Renault revised the car in 1987 with power increased to 118bhp. The Renault 5's long life would come to a close in 1991 when the GT Turbo was discontinued, replaced by the iconic Clio 16v.

Fiesta XR2 and XR2i

Ford's first go-faster Fiesta was the Supersport, which launched in 1980, only to be replaced shortly after by the XR2 in 1981, beating the 205 GTI to market. It boasted a 1600cc engine but its power was restricted as Ford's marketeers did not want the Fiesta to compete for sales with the larger Escort XR3i. The original, 94bhp XR2 was replaced in 1989 by the Mk3 XR2i. The XR2i developed 103bhp, meaning it still lagged behind the GTI in terms of power. The Fiesta RS Turbo arrived in April 1990 with a top speed of 133mph (214km/h), 131bhp and 135lb ft of torque, meaning that – on paper at least – it was a match for the 1.9 GTI. On the roads it was quite another matter, with wayward handling and poor steering. In 1992 the Fiesta gained a 16v engine, the Zetec, and the Turbo was replaced by the RS1800. In 1994 the XR2i was dropped.

ARRIVAL OF THE GTI: THE BIRTH OF A LEGEND

The 1.9 gained larger wheels and a top speed of 127mph (204km/h).

In December 1986, as the T16 was taking its second World Rally Championship title, the revised 1.6 was joined by the edgier, more powerful 1.9. Now the 205 GTI was no longer considered a junior hot hatch. Instead, it was ready to go head to head with the Lancia Delta, Renault 5 Turbo and a host of other 1980s hot hatches. It became the fastest road-going version of the GTI, bar the 200 Turbo 16s.

The 1.9 was unveiled to the French motoring press on 15 December 1986, with the UK media invited to sample the car in the New Year of 1987. Peugeot's PR machine of the time said the 1.9 was aimed at a different kind of customer to the 1.6, the company having identified a need for an ultimate hot hatch with a 'no compromise' performance.

Boasting 130bhp and a top speed of 127mph (204km/h), the 1.9 GTI set a high-water mark for performance Peugeots. A wealth of changes were made to the power unit. While the bore remained the same as on the 1.6, stroke was increased and the compression ratio lowered (from 9.8:1 to 9.6:1), resulting in a healthy boost in torque, rising from 98lb ft to 119lb ft. The gearbox got higher ratio gears, giving the newer car longer legs for cruising and helping it achieve that higher top speed. The 1.9 received larger diameter alloys, with 15in alloys replacing the 1.6's smaller items. Inside, a leather-trimmed steering wheel was fitted as standard, while options included a sunroof, electric windows and central locking.

These factors meant the 1.9 was capable of 0–60 in less than 7.8 seconds, something none of its rivals, bar the Renault 5 Turbo, could match. It employed larger shock absorbers (30mm as opposed to 25mm) and was stiffer sprung than the 1.6, losing some refinement in the process. The 1.9 was considered more predictable than the smaller-engined GTI, creating a neat, neutral balance with stacks of tractability. The 1.9's track was reduced by 10mm at the front but increased by 11mm at the rear to incorporate the new rear discs demanded by the more potent engine, meaning it stopped as well as it went. Despite the increased performance the 1.9 was still capable of offering decent fuel economy, with Peugeot's figures recording 48mpg (5.9ltr/100km) at 56mph (90km/h). Of course finding someone willing to drive their GTI at 56mph was a little more challenging.

The word was out and the 205 GTI was fast becoming the hot hatch to own. In a little over two years Peugeot's reputation had been transformed and the 205 (helped in no small part by the GTI) and the company quickly had a best-seller on its hands. By 1986 the 205 range had made it into the top ten best-selling cars in Britain for the first time, helped in no small part by the GTI, which was selling 7,000 cars a year in Britain and accounting for 20 per cent of total 205 sales (as opposed to just 11 per cent in its native France).

For a company with little previous sporting pedigree, Peugeot scored big with the GTI and, unsurprisingly, enthusiastic customers flocked to dealers. Some were new to Peugeot, keen to sample the faster 1.9, while others traded in their 1.6s for the new car and, for a time, used values exceeded those of factory-fresh examples. It was such a success that the French motoring press quickly began refer-

ARRIVAL OF THE GTI: THE BIRTH OF A LEGEND

Even Ford's brand-new Fiesta XR2i, launched in 1989, could not match the 205 GTI's finely poised handling.

ring to the car as the 'sacré numéro' (sacred number), such was the effect the 205 had on the company's fortunes.

The revisions to the 1.6 and the addition of the 1.9 kept the 205 at the head of the hot-hatch pack for the remainder of the decade, though the arrival of the 1.9 brought about a long-running debate over which was the better car, the smaller 1.6 or the 1.9. With its 15bhp advantage in power over the 1.6, combined with a boost in torque, the 1.9 was the better car on paper. It was quicker on the road, too. But for its extra pace it lacked some of the frenetic energy the 1.6 had in spades; it was more laid-back, with its taller gears and softer, more civilized suspension, and extra torque making fewer demands on the driver.

As new rivals came onto the scene, such as the Mk3 Ford Fiesta, the 205 remained ahead of its opponents, even in the form of the 1.6. When *Autocar* compared the two in October 1989 the road test fell in favour of the Peugeot: 'Few owners will be trading in their 205s for the XR2i. The Fiesta has impressive specification, but on the road the 205 is on a higher plane. When the Peugeot feels crisp and responsive, the Ford feels vague and dull-witted. The XR2i ultimately lacks clarity of purpose and the ability to entertain.' So with the 1980s drawing to a close, the 205 continued to dominate the small hot-hatch segment – as it would until the final GTI was built in 1996.

TUNING

Wherever there's a successful car an army of specialist tuners and tweakers will follow and the 205 GTI was no different. With so many people buying 205s, owners sought to mark their cars out as something individual, something special and unique to them. A variety of body kits and spoilers were soon on offer, some from Peugeot themselves, others from third-party companies keen to cash in on the GTI's popularity.

Some took a more in-depth look at the GTI and sought to make improvements to the original formula. Among the most highly regarded of these was the German company Gutmann Automobiltechnik. Gutmann's engine kits were extensive, ranging from a simple cam and engine control unit upgrade to engine exchange programmes and turbo conversion kits capable of boosting the 1.6's output to a phenomenal 148bhp, while Gutmann's modifications to the 1.9 increased output from a basic 130bhp up to 180bhp.

Three hundred special Gutmann models were also built by the tuner, who swapped the 1.9 GTI's cylinder head for that of the 309 GTI while also remapping the engine and installing an oil cooler, an uprated air filter and a new exhaust system. The result was a 1.9 GTI that now developed 158bhp. The company also made modifications to the

■ ARRIVAL OF THE GTI: THE BIRTH OF A LEGEND

Gutmann specialized in tuning components, but also built 300 bespoke Gutmann GTIs.

The Gutmann tuned engine gained a remap, an oil cooler and improved induction and exhaust. The result was 158bhp.

ARRIVAL OF THE GTI: THE BIRTH OF A LEGEND

ABOVE: **The Gutmann's rear badging was similarly subtle and remains in keeping with Peugeot's original design theme.**

LEFT: **Unique 15in alloys were used to distinguish the Gutmann from the regular GTI. The suspension was also lowered.**

205's handling, lowering the suspension by 30mm as well as upgrading the brakes.

Visually, the Gutmann set itself apart by wearing unique 15in alloy wheels as opposed to the standard Peugeot items. Gutmann also added subtle badges to the car's front and tailgate.

Inside, the Gutmann featured a unique leather steering wheel and custom gear knob, while a badge bearing the company's name was attached to the dash. The faces of the dials were also retrimmed, in white.

In the UK, the tuning charge was led by Turbo Technics, specialists in turbocharging naturally aspirated engines. The company began trading in 1981 and soon began offering turbo conversion for both the 1.6 and 1.9. The conversion used a Garret T25 turbo and increased the 1.6's power to 160bhp and the 1.9's to 175. Heady stuff for the 1980s.

Another key developer of the 205 was French outfit Dimma, who developed a wide range of body kits and styling accessories to totally transform the look of the car. From twin headlight conversions to large whale-tail spoilers, Dimma allowed customers to modify the appearance of their car in any number of ways. The company was best known for the production of its famous 'Lionne Sauvage' kit, which aped many of the T16's aggressive features. It added broad, pronounced rear arches, a more stylized front bumper and a large tailgate-mounted spoiler. The benefit of hindsight may make some of these extensively modified cars look dated, however they were a key part of the 205's growing popularity. Dimma-kitted cars are an unusual sight today but remain popular within the owners' community.

Jean Todt was so impressed with Dimma's work that he gave the company and its kits Peugeot's official approval. Some thirty years on, the company still produces the kit as well as a variety of kits and accessories for other French cars.

The GTI's success would become a double-edged sword. The car's potent reputation quickly made it a popular choice for that new craze of the late 1980s, joyriding. As more and

The Dimma name became synonymous with modified 205s. DIMMA/TERRY PARKHURST

77

■ ARRIVAL OF THE GTI: THE BIRTH OF A LEGEND

A distinctive steering wheel and white dials set the Gutmann off.

ARRIVAL OF THE GTI: THE BIRTH OF A LEGEND

A revised 205 GTI interior with new wheel and heater controls (note the non-standard stereo unit). GERARD HUGHES

more GTIs were stolen, insurance premiums rose higher and higher. Suddenly, performance cars had become an expensive hobby. People began looking more at insurance groups and less at performance figures when it came to buying a car and the GTI's sales began to drop away.

Towards the tail end of the decade Peugeot revised the car, adding a new dash with updated heating controls and a three-spoke steering wheel. As the 1990s dawned the 205 received a further face-lift, with the aim of giving the car a fresh look for the new decade. Clear indicators replaced the original units while revised tail lamps moved the reverse lamp onto the rear valance. Elsewhere black trim replaced the original grey and a slightly larger exhaust was fitted.

It seemed the sun was beginning to set on the GTI. A steady decline in sales led to the 1.6 being discontinued in September 1992, almost a decade after its launch. The introduction of European emissions standards in 1992 gave rise to catalytic converters becoming standard in October 1992, dropping power on the 1.9 GTI to 122bhp and lowering the amount of noxious chemicals the car emitted. Elsewhere Peugeot aimed to improve the car's security and reduce the number of stolen GTIs by introducing a key-pad engine immobilizer, which required the driver to enter a predetermined pin number before starting the vehicle. Although the system worked well enough, it was awkward and somewhat time-consuming in practice and wasn't carried over to future models.

Seats were also updated but remained comfortable yet supportive.

79

■ ARRIVAL OF THE GTI: THE BIRTH OF A LEGEND

With increasingly tight emissions regulations and rising insurance costs, the 1980s favourite hot hatch's days were numbered. Although the 205 remained in production in Europe until 1996, the GTI disappeared from the price lists in 1994, by which time some 300,000 GTIs had been built.

While new GTIs were no longer coming off the production line, a loyal fan base had built up around the car. The reputation it had established ensured that it became a true cult classic, a fact underlined when *Car* magazine declared the 205 GTI the Car of the Decade.

LOOKING BACK

Thirty years on from its launch, it is easy to dismiss the GTI as just another car from a decade when everyone made a go-faster version of their shopping trolley. However, to do that underestimates the huge impact the 205 GTI had on not just Peugeot's image in the UK, but culturally too. The 205 took the hot-hatch recipe, refined it and became a beloved automotive icon along the way. It was arguably the last truly involving performance supermini, one free from the electronic aids that are part and parcel of today's cars, and by looking as good as it drove the GTI found favour with more than just your average petrol head.

As it moved from new car to used car, a new generation of drivers began to find the appeal in the car and in the 1990s it became a huge part of the modification and cruise scene. Magazines like *Max Power*, *Redline* and *Fast Car* became the indispensable guides to a new breed of 205 owner, packing information on the best engine modifications, body kits and, as importantly, sound systems. The 205 GTI had found a new audience – a new breed of fan that had perhaps been too young or had not been able to afford the car when new. The 205 was now within the grasp of a much wider range of owner who began to put their own spin on the car. One popular modification was to swap the XU5J for the more powerful Mi16 1.9 from the larger Peugeot 405 saloon. In standard trim it developed in excess of 160bhp and, like the original 205 engine, was readily tuneable. Some owners went further, shoehorning in Cosworth engines that saw rear-wheel and four-wheel drive replace the GTI's front-wheel drive.

These more potent engines gave even more power in their basic form. The advances in tuning technology have meant that some modified GTIs surpassed 200bhp, showing just what is capable from a resourceful owners' community.

As well as becoming a popular car for modifiers, the GTI also became a common sight at club-level motor sport events and track days, the car's natural sporting nature lending itself ideally to hill climbs, sprints, rallycross and rallying.

Today, while many of its hot-hatch contemporaries have been forgotten, original-specification GTIs are becoming highly prized classics and values are increasing. Some seek low-mileage, original-specification examples while other owners seek to extract more power from their cars and push the development of the GTI further and further.

The 205 GTI gave Peugeot an appeal and desirability the company might never have expected, and while other Peugeot superminis have gone on to wear the iconic badge, none have bettered the 1980s icon. While each and every one has been compared to the 205, none has been so well received, so highly praised and so warmly regarded as the original 205 GTI.

The 205 GTI was the iconic car of the 1980s and has matured into an ultra-desirable classic.
GERARD HUGHES

CHAPTER SIX

GROUP B, RALLYING AND THE 205 T16

As the 1980s dawned the world of rallying was due for arguably its biggest revolution since the sport's inception. When Audi debuted its all-wheel-drive Quattro on the Jänner Rallye in Austria it set rallying on a path of rapid development and massive popularity.

Rallying had first become truly popular during the 1960s, when the all-conquering Mini Cooper became the sport's poster boy. The Mini's light, front-wheel-drive layout caused something of a stir and, for a while, it was the dominant force on the rally stage. However, rear-wheel-drive cars began to fight back, with Ford's Mk1 Escort leading the charge. The Mini suffered from a lack of development and the Ford was quick to take advantage and, as the 1970s wore on, faster rear-wheel-drive machines such as Renault's Alpine, Lancia's Ferrari-powered Stratos and Fiat's 131 Abarth came to dominate the field.

When PSA completed the takeover of Chrysler Europe in 1979 and resurrected the Talbot marque it became involved briefly in Formula One, becoming sponsor of the Ligier team, which was rebranded Talbot. The team enjoyed some success, finishing fourth in 1981, with two wins by Jacques Laffite. The company's real success, though, came on the rally stage.

In its inaugural year in the World Rally Championship (WRC), Tony Pond took the Talbot factory team's Lotus Sunbeam to a fourth-place finish on the 1979 Rallye Sanremo. Things improved the following season with Henri Toivonen and Guy Fréquelin piloting the Talbots. Toivonen made

Talbot Sunbeam Lotus had been a rally winner for Talbot and, by extension, Peugeot.
AUTHOR

81

■ GROUP B, RALLYING AND THE 205 T16

history at the RAC Rally by becoming the youngest driver to win a world rally. In 1981, the Talbot enjoyed consistent podium finishes and although Fréquelin and co-driver Jean Todt narrowly lost the drivers' title to Ari Vatanen, Talbot captured the WRC manufacturers' crown.

Jean Todt was born in Pierrefort, France, in 1946. A lifelong fan of motor sport, Todt took part in amateur events, borrowing his father's Mini Cooper. However, he decided his future lay in navigating rather than driving. As a co-driver, the Frenchman competed in over fifty WRC events and gained a fierce reputation for his fastidious organizational skills in a broad variety of cars, from NSUs to Ford Escorts. Having won the manufacturers' championship in the Talbot he retired from competition.

The introduction of the Group B regulations in 1982 saw many manufacturers, Peugeot included, re-evaluate their plans for the sport.

Four-wheel drive had been deemed legal in 1979 by the Fédération Internationale du Sport Automobile (FISA) – the section of the Fédération Internationale de l'Automobile (FIA) charged with regulating motor sport – and it was a then little-known German company by the name of Audi that would first take advantage of the revised regulations. Audi's development engineer Roland Gumpert had been working on a four-wheel-drive, off-road vehicle for the company and felt the benefits of the system to a rally car were obvious. The management at Audi took some convincing, but Gumpert was determined to prove his theory.

To begin with many teams ignored four-wheel drive, believing the systems to be too heavy and too complex for use in competition, but the Audi would prove them wrong. With its use of four-wheel drive, the Quattro broke the mould, the Audi boasting levels of grip its rivals could not hope to match. It was powerful, too, with a 2-litre, turbocharged, 5-cylinder engine.

Audi's success was not simply limited to the rally stage. The Quattro's triumphs had a huge impact on Audi as a whole, massively improving the public's awareness of the brand.

FROM NAVIGATOR TO TEAM PRINCIPAL

Since retiring from competition, Todt has managed a variety of teams competing in motor sport and in October 2009 he became president of the FIA. Today, he is one of the most respected men in world motor sport, having enjoyed

Jean Todt (left) would become the figurehead around which the new Peugeot Talbot Sport team would be built.

82

GROUP B, RALLYING AND THE 205 T16

The mid-engined, rear-wheel-drive 305 was liked by test drivers but ultimately too old-fashioned in practice.

tremendous success as the general manager of Ferrari's Formula One team. The seeds for this success were sown back in 1981 when he moved from the car to the garage.

Before Todt's involvement, there had been a proposal to take a mid-engined, rear-wheel-drive version of the Talbot Horizon onto the World Rally stage and Lotus built a prototype. Peugeot, however, had several other projects in development that could have led to a new World Rally car. None of these made it beyond the drawing board, except for one, a V6-powered 305.

The car was put together quite quickly and before long it was being put to the test by Timo Mäkinen. Mäkinen had famously won the 1965 Rallye Monte Carlo in a Morris Mini Cooper S and was now working for Peugeot, test driving their rally machinery. The Finn came away from these test sessions impressed, but the Quattro's success put paid to that idea – the V6 305, like the Horizon, was simply too old-fashioned when faced with the newcomer from Germany.

The Group B cars were very different animals to the rally cars that had gone before them. Group B cars were right at the cutting edge of automotive engineering, rivalling even Formula One in terms of development budgets as teams sought ever-increasing ways to push their car through each stage as fast as they could.

For the 1982 season, the FIA took the decision to revise the rules for rallying, specifically appendix J, which dealt with the number of vehicles required for homologation. Previously, rally and race cars had been visibly and mechanically linked to their production equivalents but Group B would change much of that.

The introduction of Group B halved the number of vehicles required by the manufacturer from 400 to 200, freeing manufacturers to push the development of more powerful, technically advanced cars. In order for their chosen vehicle to become homologated a manufacturer would be required to build those 200 identical vehicles within a twelve-month period. This lower figure made homologation less of a challenge and manufacturers could develop more technically advanced vehicles, safe in the knowledge that they would more than likely be able to sell the majority of 200 vehicles the regulations demand they produce.

Peugeot's management had demanded that the new rally car should appear as similar as possible to a vehicle from Peugeot's road-going range. Naturally, the focus fell on the upcoming 205 and the formation of a new team. Jean Boillot approached Todt with the idea of forming a new motor sport division within the company, with the as-yet-unreleased 205 at its heart. As the 205 had been developed under the

83

GROUP B, RALLYING AND THE 205 T16

designation of M24, it was logical that the future World Rally Championship winner should be referred to internally as M24 Rally. By October 1981, Todt was in place to organize and manage the new team.

One of Todt's first tasks was to name the team. Todt was keen to feature the word 'sport', since it was almost universally understood. He also wanted to include the Talbot name, since Talbot were the current world champions. And so, Peugeot Talbot Sport was born. The team's iconic livery featured the blue and yellow of Peugeot, the light blue of Talbot and red to underline the sporty nature of rallying. Todt also set about reorganizing the disparate motor sport departments within Peugeot, shutting down Peugeot's previous rally department and moving the competitions department to a location just outside Paris. The ever forceful Todt recalled in his book *Peugeot 205: The Story of a Challenge* how 'Those who disagreed had no right of appeal – I had the full backing of Boillot.'

As the replacement for the Sunbeam was still in its infancy, Todt decided to allow the Talbot team to continue rallying during 1982. Todt had huge respect for Talbot's Des O'Dell and, despite a reduced budget, maintained a production programme for Fréquelin and a similar, UK-based season for Swedish driver Stig Blomqvist. With these initial details decided upon, Todt was then visited by Bernard Perron, who at the time was working on special project vehicles for Peugeot. Perron expressed his dislike of the 305 project. Todt listened and shortly afterwards appointed Perron head of project design on M24 Rally.

Todt declared there could be no more experiments and that the car they were developing had to win Peugeot the World Rally Championship. With many of the pieces now falling into place, Todt defined the key characteristics of the car:

- Four-wheel drive
- Mid-engine layout
- Longer wheelbase
- Wider track

In creating the T16 Peugeot would create a world first in rallying: a four-wheel drive, transverse, mid-engined car. The results would be breathtaking.

Once Perron was on board he was joined by Armand Froumajou from the planning department, as well as former Talbot Lotus boss Des O'Dell. Englishman O'Dell became,

The heart of the 205 T16 – the XU8T.

84

GROUP B, RALLYING AND THE 205 T16

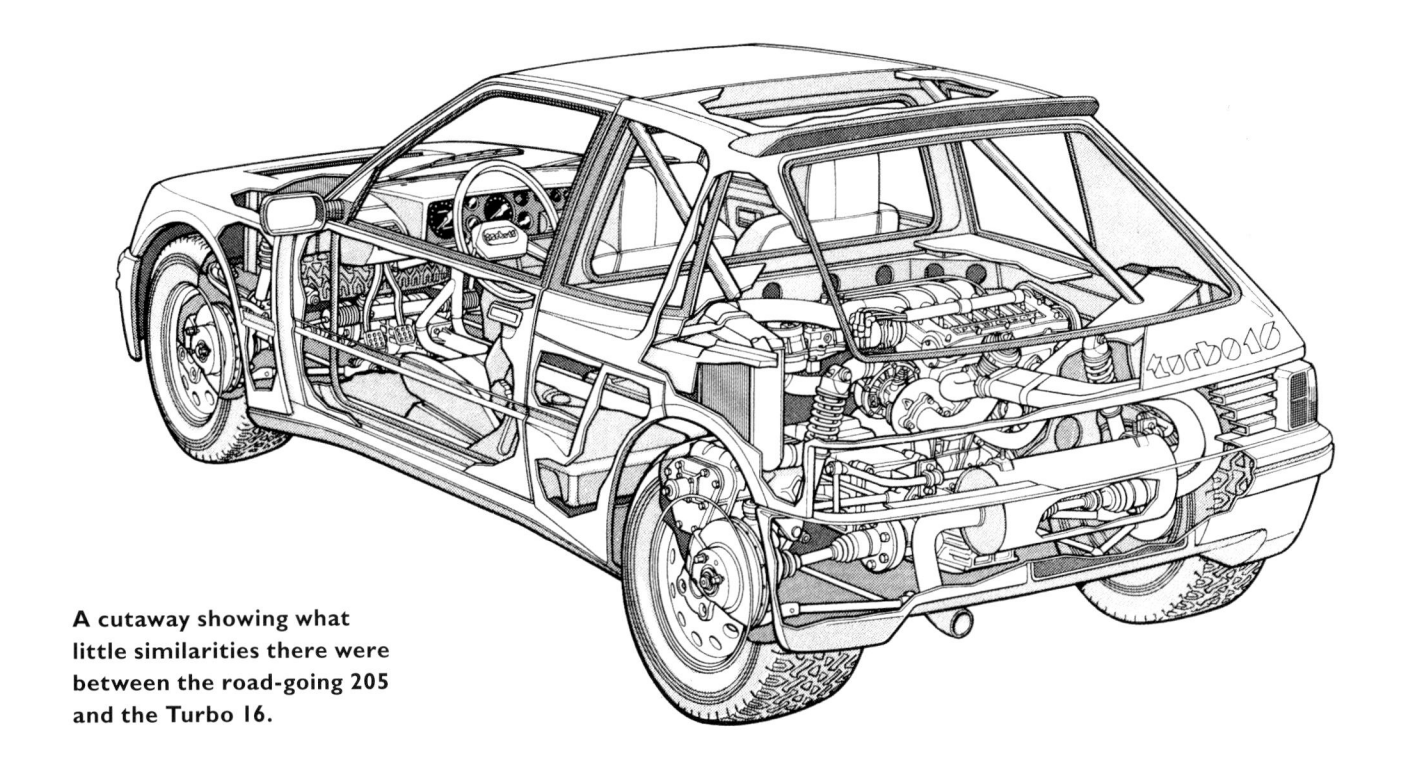

A cutaway showing what little similarities there were between the road-going 205 and the Turbo 16.

according to Todt, the first technical director of Peugeot Talbot Sport.

Working at the company's La Garenne factory, the engineer's first task was to create a prototype bodyshell with sufficiently widened and lengthened track while retaining the silhouette of the 205. This proved relatively straightforward. The team then began to deal with the important question of what engine should power the new car.

Any thoughts of a new, bespoke unit for the car were quickly abandoned. The project had already demanded significant investment from Peugeot and the company simply could not justify the expense of designing, developing and building an entirely new engine. Engineer Jean-Claude Vaucard and technical director O'Dell felt the car should use a large, naturally aspirated engine and lobbied strongly for the PRV 'Douvrin' V6.

The PRV engine was co-developed with Renault and Volvo (hence the PRV name) and had originally been conceived as a larger V8. The fuel crisis of the early 1970s led to those plans being re-evaluated and the PRV was instead born as a V6. It powered a wide range of cars, from the Renault Alpine to the DeLorean DMC-12, and made its debut in 1974 in the Peugeot 504 and Volvo 242. By 1982 it was approaching ten years old. Others within the team were keen to see the car embrace a new generation of engines PSA were close to unveiling in the Peugeot 305 and Citroën BX.

This new engine, the XU, was chosen for the M24 Rally. The next step was to determine what the XU would be capable of. Peugeot's engineers deemed that the XU would be turbocharged and feature four valves per cylinder, thus requiring a new 16-valve cylinder head. At 1775cc and turbocharged, the XU8T – as it was now known – developed 200bhp and 188lb ft torque. A new induction system was also developed by the team, with the aim of easing the load on the turbo, reducing the amount of heat build-up and keeping complexity to a minimum. By February 1982 the XU8T was confirmed as the engine for the new car.

With the engine chosen, the team's next task was to identify the correct gearbox for the car. A company the size of PSA Peugeot produced a wide variety of transmissions and the team carefully investigated and assessed each one. The engineers considered that whatever gearbox they were to use might one day be needed in the road-going 205. The gearbox needed to be capable of withstanding the levels of torque developed by the XU8T. After much research, they found what they were looking for – a Citroën unit, the SM.

■ GROUP B, RALLYING AND THE 205 T16

The first road-going T16s are shown to the world's motoring press. JOHN EVANS

The SM gearbox took its name from the car it was used in, the Maserati-powered SM. It also saw applications in the Lotus Esprit. It was strong and more than suited to the rallying application, having evolved steadily since its introduction in the 1970s.

As 1982 dawned Todt worked furiously to put in place a schedule and a budget for the M24 Rally. He formed a promotions department for the team, as well as a committee including engineers Jean-Claude Vaucard and Hubert Allera, and Bernard Perron. The committee reported directly to Peugeot president Jean Boillot, who retained the right to veto any or all aspects of Todt and the committee's work. Todt's aim was that both the conventional, road-going 205 and its rally-ready brother would be unveiled together, instantly giving the new car a strong link to its more mundane road-going version.

Midway through 1982, the entire project hung by a thread as Peugeot's financial woes continued to mount. These pressures forced Boillot to take time away from the company as he considered not only his own future but also that of the rally car. Boillot was able to negotiate Talbot's exit from Formula One and also garner the support of the company's management. With the full backing of PSA's corporate management for the M24 Rally, Boillot accepted all of Todt's proposals and the project began to gather serious pace.

After a twenty-minute meeting between Todt and Boillot, the car had its name: the Peugeot 205 Turbo 16.

The small production run of the T16 made it too niche for one of the company's main plants so the company looked for a partner to handle the building of the car. Peugeot went with Heuliez, a company based in Cerizay, in western France. Founded in 1920, Heuliez had worked previously with Peugeot, their relationship dating back to 1925, and by November 1982 the first car was in production. Heuliez would handle construction of all of the 200-plus T16s.

As 1982 gave way to 1983 things were progressing smoothly. However, with the first test of the T16 just two days away, Todt found himself lacking the most vital component – a driver for the car. Stig Blomqvist had been under contract to Peugeot Talbot Sport and had enjoyed some success in the Talbot during 1981, securing third place in the RAC Rally, but now signed for Audi Sport. Todt had expected Blomqvist to remain with the team and envisioned the Swede leading the T16's test programme and, in time, WRC events.

The ever-pragmatic Frenchman turned instead to countryman Jean-Pierre Nicolas. Nicolas had rallied successfully during the 1970s, and Todt had served as his co-driver on

Jean-Pierre Nicolas was the first man to test the 205 and compete in it.

several events. An accident in 1978 led to him hanging up his helmet. Following his retirement he took up a management position with Renault in Marseille. Tucked away in the south of France, Nicolas was oblivious to the developments going on at Peugeot.

Nicolas found his job with Renault fairly mundane and was curious when Todt contacted him and asked him to meet him in Paris that night. Nicolas agreed, and got on the next available flight to the French capital. Todt offered Nicolas the position of test driver for the 1983 season, asking him to leave his job with Renault – and to give him an answer by the following morning. Nicolas agreed, excited by the car, Peugeot's plans and the opportunity to get behind the wheel of a rally car once more. The following morning, he was presented to the media as the 205 T16's test driver.

In February 1983 the Turbo 16 was ready for its first drive. The first test took place at Peugeot's Mortefontaine test track, near Paris.

Todt arranged for the T16 to be presented to the world's media outside Peugeot's Paris headquarters alongside a standard five-door 205, as originally envisaged. Todt was warned that the T16 might not be ready and that it might be necessary to 'simulate' the car's movements for the video presentation Peugeot intended to shoot. When the car arrived, it was still unclear whether it would run or not – thankfully the engineers had succeeded, at least in part.

Nicolas and Boillot climbed inside the car not knowing quite what to expect. The XU8T fired into life and all was well, except for one issue. The car's clutch didn't work. The engineers gathered around and pushed the car, allowing Nicolas to get the car into gear and drive alongside the production 205 long enough to capture those now iconic images.

Todt had completed the first part of his vision. The 205 Turbo 16 was here. Now the real hard work could begin.

TESTING TIMES

The T16's debut had come too late for Peugeot to make the 1983 season, so while Audi and Lancia battled it out on the world stage, Peugeot focused on preparing the T16 for the first rally of the 1984 season, the Rallye Monte Carlo, due to take place the following January.

The first prototype tests began in earnest with the team from La Garenne joining Nicolas at the Mortefontaine test track to ensure everything worked as it should on the T16.

Testing proved to be a challenge for the PTS team and the T16 showed itself to be worryingly fragile.

Unfortunately, it didn't. The Peugeot's road from concept car to rally winner was a decidedly rocky one. Nicolas planned a circuit at the test track that would challenge the T16 but after five laps the car had all but fallen apart. So far, all the 205 had shown was its fragility. There were some signs of encouragement, though, since Nicolas found the car to be incredibly quick, with sublime handling. He considered it to be every bit as good as the Audi Quattro that Peugeot had brought along to the test for back-to-back comparisons. Todt, on the other hand, was concerned. Rivals at Audi had commented that they believed the T16 would fail; that its design was too unorthodox. Todt secretly questioned himself and his decisions while the production of the 200 homologation T16s got underway.

As that first prototype rally car headed back to the La Garenne factory for strengthening, Nicolas's testing continued, this time at the wheel of one of the road-going T16s. The problems continued, with Nicolas finding the new car to be unstable at the back, as well as reporting problems with the steering. Working steadily on the issues revealed by Nicolas, the T16's gremlins were exorcized one by one until, in August 1983, the team's competition cars were delivered from La Garenne to the Peugeot Talbot Sport headquarters.

Some weeks earlier, all of the T16s had been gathered together for a press shoot. Peugeot was keen to show the world that it had hit its homologation number, and that there really were 200 T16s. The cars looked fantastic, and the image became iconic. Peugeot demonstrated the T16 to the assembled press in both Paris and at Mortefontaine – another player in the Group B drama had taken to the stage.

■ GROUP B, RALLYING AND THE 205 T16

The T16 would quickly prove itself and that famous red, blue and yellow livery would be etched into the mind of rally fans worldwide. ARTCURIAL

GROUP B, RALLYING AND THE 205 T16

The T16's bespoke design ensured ease of access to the engine and suspension components, something vitally important during a time-restricted rally service. ARTCURIAL

Now that the twenty 'Evolution' T16s had been handed over to the PTS technical department their first task was to up the power output to 320bhp. Nicolas quickly became accustomed to the new power and as things progressed Peugeot opted to test the car on gravel, looking to replicate rallying conditions. The test proved to be a disaster. The car ran badly, the gearbox refused to change gear smoothly, and key mechanical components, like the hubs and suspension wishbones, failed.

The team worked tirelessly to cure these new faults. As 1983 drew to a close, they were able to begin to fine-tune the car, making it ready for its World Rally debut. Nicolas continued his hard work, focusing on getting as much grip from the car as possible. He and the team experimented with the levels of power delivered to the front and rear wheels, eventually settling on a two-thirds rearward bias.

At last, in October 1983, the Peugeot 205 T16 was driven in competition for the very first time at the Sarlat Rally. This first run was a world away from the glitz and glamour of a World Rally event, but the T16 proved itself, coming second overall. Everything was falling into place and the T16 was set to enter the World Rally stage at the French round, the Tour de Corse, in May 1984. One question remained. Who would drive it?

ENTER THE FLYING FINN

From the moment he joined Peugeot, Jean-Pierre Nicolas had known he was not the man to lead the 205's charge for World Rally victory. Todt had been considering who would be Peugeot's lead driver for quite some time. With Blomqvist essentially contracted to Peugeot Talbot Sport (albeit driving for Talbot in the UK), Todt had been hopeful that the talented Swede would become lead driver of the new Peugeot. However, Blomqvist had opted to join Audi for the 1982 season. Fréquelin, with whom Todt had driven to the manufacturers' title in 1981, had joined Opel and was fully focused on the French National Rally Championship. Undeterred, Todt narrowed his options down to four: the young and talented Henri Toivonen (who had driven previously for Talbot), Markku Alén, Walter Röhrl and Ari Vatanen.

GROUP B, RALLYING AND THE 205 T16

SPECIFICATIONS: PEUGEOT 205 TURBO 16 (1984), PARIS–DAKAR (1987–1989), RALLY E1 (1984–1985) AND RALLY E2 (1985–1986)

	Turbo 16 Road Car	Rally E1 and E2
Engine		
Model	XU8T	XU8T
Position	Mid-mounted, transverse, 20 degree rearward inclination	Mid-mounted, transverse, 20 degree rearward inclination
Block material	Aluminium alloy	Aluminium alloy
Head material	Aluminium alloy	Aluminium alloy
Main bearings	5	5
Cylinders	4, in-line	4, in-line
Cooling	Water	Water
Bore and stroke	83 x 82mm	83 x 82mm
Capacity	1775cc	1775cc
Valves	16	16
Compression ratio	7:1	7:1
Camshaft configuration	Twin ohc	Twin ohc
Camshaft drive	Toothed belt	Toothed belt
Carburettor	Bosch K Jetronic injection	Bosch K Jetronic injection
Maximum power	197bhp (Rally E1) 340bhp (Rally E2) 450bhp	197bhp (Rally E1) 340bhp (Rally E2) 450bhp
Maximum torque	188lb ft (Rally E1) 332lb ft (Rally E2) 369lb ft	188lb ft (Rally E1) 332lb ft (Rally E2) 369lb ft
Transmission		
Ratios	1st = 2.923:1 2nd = 1.944:1 3rd = 1.407:1 4th = 1.129:1 5th = 0.969:1 Reverse = 1.154:1	NA
Final drive		
Suspension and Steering		
Front	Double wishbones with coil spring, telescopic Bilstein shock absorbers and antiroll bar	
Rear	Double wishbones with coil spring, telescopic Bilstein shock absorbers and antiroll bar	
Steering	Rack and pinion with hydraulic power assistance	
Dimensions		
Overall length (T16)	150.39in (3,820mm)	150.39in (3,820mm)
Paris–Dakar	162.20in (4,120mm)	
Overall width (T16)	66.93in (1,700mm)	66.93in (1,700mm)
Paris–Dakar	70.87in (1,800mm)	
Overall height (T16)	53.31in (1,354mm)	53.31in (1,354mm)
Paris–Dakar	51.18in (1,300mm)	
Weight (T16)	2,524lb (1,145kg)	2,524lb (1,145kg)
Paris–Dakar	2,866lb (1,300kg)	
Performance		
Top speed	130mph (209km/h)	N/A
0–60mph	7.8sec	4.3sec (Rally E1) 3.3sec (Rally E2)

GROUP B, RALLYING AND THE 205 T16

THE CHOSEN FEW: THE 200 205 T16s

In order to see the T16 homologated, it was necessary for Peugeot to build 200 examples for the general market. The road-going T16 was detuned in comparison with the rally car, developing 200bhp and 188lb ft of torque. *Autocar* magazine tested the £25,000 car in June 1984 and was largely positive about the car and its abilities, calling the T16 'the next generation of all-wheel-drive sports saloon' and that the Peugeot 'drove marvellously'.

205 T16 (Road car)
Price in 1984: £25,000
Power: 200bhp @ 6,750rpm
Torque: 188lb ft @ 4,000rpm
Top speed: 130mph (206km/h)
0–60mph: 7.8sec

■ GROUP B, RALLYING AND THE 205 T16

Alén had driven for Fiat since 1974 and had joined Lancia in 1982 and had committed his long-term future to the Italian manufacturer. Toivonen was consistently linked in the motor sport press to the Peugeot team, but nothing came of those rumours, while Röhrl was in the processes of swapping his rear-wheel-drive Lancia 037 for an Audi Quattro.

Todt met with the three Finns at the Rallye Sanremo in September 1983 and over three separate breakfasts discussed the forthcoming 1984 season. By the end of the day, Vatanen had agreed to join Peugeot Talbot Sport.

Vatanen had won the World Rally Championship in 1981 in a Ford Escort RS1800 but after taking championship glory his career stalled during 1982 and 1983, when he struggled at the wheel of an Opel Ascona. Vatanen's flamboyant driving style made him a huge favourite with the fans. While Röhrl was clinical, almost machine-like while driving, watching Vatanen at the wheel of a rally car was akin to watching a concert pianist in full flow; a car to Vatanen was like an instrument and the Finn excelled at playing it. Vatanen was joined in Peugeot's first year by Nicolas, who, having been at the heart of the T16's development and testing, knew the car better than anyone.

Ari Vatanen had won the 1981 World Rally Championship and was a firm favourite with rally fans.

WORLD RALLY DEBUT

Finally, after a frantic last-minute rush to ensure the 200 road-going and twenty 'Evolution' cars were complete, the

Jean-Pierre Nicolas on the 1984 Acropolis Rally – neither T16 would complete the event.

GROUP B, RALLYING AND THE 205 T16

205 T16 was ready for its World Rally debut. On 3 May 1984 the T16 took to the stage for the first time on Corsica's twisting mountain roads. Vatanen was quick to find a rhythm with the car, finishing the first stage in fifth. The Finn got quicker, dismissing the times set by Röhrl in the Audi, and took the lead by the end of day one. The second day did not go quite so well for Vatanen. In heavy rain he crashed out, leaving Nicolas to bring home the surviving T16. The Frenchman battled his way to a fourth-place finish. The T16 had performed all but flawlessly in its first event. From here, things could only improve for Peugeot Talbot Sport.

The 1984 season moved quickly, and the team soon found themselves in Greece, for the Acropolis Rally. This marked the first time the 205 had rallied on gravel and Vatanen took a short while to adapt to the different surface in the new car. He pressed on and by the second day took the lead, only to be scuppered once more, this time by mechanical failure. First his 205's fuel pump failed, then the distributor

The T16's engine bay was meticulously detailed. ARTCURIAL

The T16's debut season had been cause for celebration, but the car's real story was just beginning. ARTCURIAL

93

■ GROUP B, RALLYING AND THE 205 T16

belt broke and the car's turbo failed. Once again Nicolas was left to continue alone, but his 205 failed the following day, when the rough terrain damaged the car's underside, resulting in brake failure.

Peugeot did not contest the next two rounds of the championship in New Zealand and Argentina as Todt considered it unnecessary to travel to these events in what was essentially a development year for the car, its drivers and the team. The decision gave PTS almost two months to focus on its next event, one that Vatanen was determined to win, for it was his home round, the 1000 Lakes Rally. Vatanen headed to Finland with the team to test and set up the Peugeot's suspension and ensure the team was ready for the event. Back in France, a new, faster 205, the 'Evolution 2', was being readied for the 1985 season.

Nicolas did not enter the 1000 Lakes, so the T16's chances came down to Vatanen, and Vatanen alone. Expectations were high, and two days before the start of the event competitors were invited to test their cars over one of the rally's stages. The 205 revealed itself to be totally inept on the undulating stage – it was only Vatanen's skill that kept the car from leaving the road. This was a disaster for the team. With the start of the rally rapidly approaching, they fought to rework the car's suspension, devising new shock absorbers almost overnight.

As the rally began, Lancia took the lead. The team was prepared for the worst, but as each stage came, Vatanen began to dominate the rally, posting faster and faster times and leaving the Audis and Lancias far behind him. They had done it: the T16 had won its first World Rally event. Vatanen said at the time, 'The car was very good, and is very good. I am sure it will have a bright future.'

As August rolled into September, the World Rally teams headed south to Italy for the Rallye Sanremo. A year earlier Vatanen had agreed to join Peugeot, but now the team was looking to replicate its success in Finland. Nicolas returned for the Sanremo, which was to be his final event, as he had opted to retire from competition – for the second time – at the end of the 1984 season. In contrast to the short, two-day 1000 Lakes, this was a long, arduous event lasting for five days. Vatanen dominated proceedings from the off, setting records on thirty-one of the rally's fifty-four stages.

The penultimate round of the championship saw the competition head to the Ivory Coast, a round from which Peugeot withdrew following some disastrous pre-event testing. The team instead prepared for the last round of the year, the Lombard RAC Rally of Great Britain.

> ### THE BIRTH OF GROUP B
>
> The FIA introduced the new Group B regulations in 1982, redrawing the World Rally landscape at a stroke. Prior to 1982 Group 4 had been the main class for rally cars and required the manufacturer to produce at least 400 examples of their intended rally car. The FIA's Group B regulations merged the old Group 4 with Group 5 and halved that number, giving manufacturers an almost free reign in the design and development of their cars. The new regulations proved hugely popular. Manufacturers flocked to the championship, chasing race wins, public relations glory and victory over their rivals. Spectators fell in love with these high-powered, high-adrenaline cars and rallying surpassed the popularity of even Formula One. Drivers like Walter Röhrl and Peugeot's Ari Vatanen became household names. In just four years the power output of the typical rally car doubled from 250bhp to almost 500bhp. However, Group B's time was short-lived. A series of incidents, including several fatalities, led the FIA to ban Group B in 1986. Rallying changed and learned from the tragedies that had occurred during the Group B era. Despite the dark shadow those incidents cast on the sport, the Group B cars are remembered today for the right reasons: as legendary, iconic cars from a time when rally cars pushed the sport to its absolute limit.

With Nicolas retired, Vatanen piloted the sole 205, dominating proceedings from start to finish – the only issue being a broken windscreen when the Finn left the road after a brief lapse in concentration.

The 1984 season had been a great success for Peugeot Talbot, with the team winning three of the six rallies it entered. Todt was pleased, though he demanded improvements for the 1985 season.

GOING FOR GLORY: THE 1985 WORLD RALLY CHAMPIONSHIP

With Jean-Pierre Nicolas moving on to become head of Peugeot Talbot Sport's promotion department, Todt's immediate concerns for the 1985 season were who would partner

GROUP B, RALLYING AND THE 205 T16

The PTS 'family' photo for 1985. Pictured are Jean-Pierre Nicolas (front row, far left), Jean Todt (brown trousers), Timo Salonen, Bruno Saby and at the end, nearest the 205, Ari Vatanen.

Vatanen and how many cars the team should run. After much deliberation, Todt opted to run a three-car team: two to compete for the entire season, with a third car to act as support for the long endurance rallies, such as the Safari.

Todt was keen to bring Walter Röhrl into the team, seeing the clinical German as the ideal counterpart to the flamboyant Finn. Röhrl was popular throughout Europe, which would aid Peugeot's promotional push in countries like Germany, and, just as important, Todt believed Röhrl and Vatanen could work well together. In the end, Röhrl decided not to join Peugeot, so Todt continued his search, narrowing it down to a trio of Finnish drivers: Markku Alén, Henri Toivonen and Timo Salonen.

Alén's financial demands were deemed too high by Todt, and he remained with Lancia for the next two years. Toivonen had driven for Talbot in 1981 and played no small part in the team's WRC constructors' title but Vatanen was unsure how he would work with the younger man. When Toivonen won the 1980 Lombard RAC Rally in a Talbot Lotus Sunbeam he had become the youngest ever driver – at 24 years 86 days – to win a World Rally event. However, negotiations between Peugeot and Toivonen became drawn out and eventually the young Finn would sign for Lancia.

The final Finn was Timo Salonen. Salonen was less well-known than the other drivers on Todt's shortlist but he had enjoyed considerable success in the rather dated and somewhat uncompetitive Nissan 240RS. He clearly had ability and enjoyed an excellent relationship with Ari Vatanen so he was chosen to drive the second T16.

Peugeot Talbot Sport's 'Flying Finns' – Timo Salonen and Ari Vatanen. Salonen was usually seen smoking.

95

■ GROUP B, RALLYING AND THE 205 T16

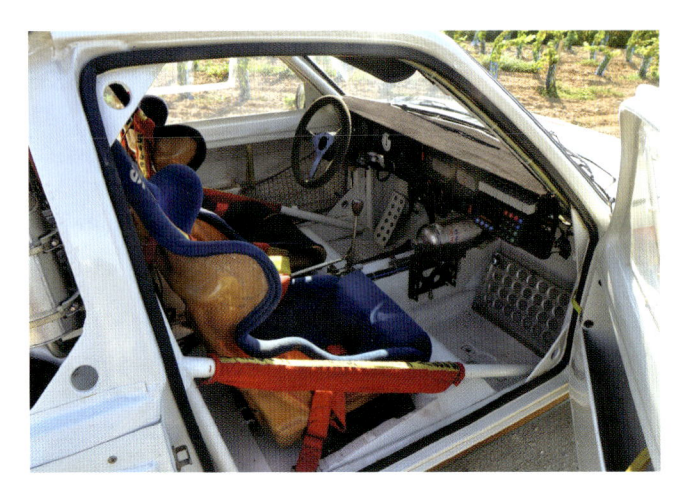

The cockpit of a works T16 (left) – compare this with that of the 200 homologation cars.

The question remained who would drive the third car. Todt initially considered hiring Michèle Mouton, who was at the time the best-known female rally driver in the world. Being French, she was an ideal fit for Peugeot. Todt had concerns that Mouton's fame might overshadow the team's achievements but Jean Boillot was keen for her to join PTS so Todt made her an offer. Audi made a similar offer and, having enjoyed success previously with the German outfit, she opted to compete once again in the Quattro during the 1985 season.

Todt had two other French nationals to consider: Guy Fréquelin, with whom Todt had driven during Talbot's 1981 WRC title victory, and Renault driver Bruno Saby. Negotiations with Fréquelin were brief: he wanted to compete in the entire championship and remained under contract to General Motors, having driven for Opel in the 1984 French National Championship. Saby, on the other hand, was willing to accept the part-season proposal and was highly rated by the recently retired Jean-Pierre Nicolas.

So, as the 1985 season began, Peugeot Talbot Sport were ready, not only with two new drivers but also with a new car. The Evolution 2 took the T16 and revised it further, increasing the power from 335bhp to 424bhp. Peugeot extracted the additional power from the engine courtesy of a new turbocharger, revised engine management and a new water-cooled intercooler. Outside, the most striking difference

Vatanen would win the 1985 Monte Carlo Rally despite a series of setbacks.

The Peugeot Talbot Sport service bay during the Monte – a hive of activity for drivers, crew and mechanics.

96

GROUP B, RALLYING AND THE 205 T16

Vatanen raises a toast as he celebrates another victory, this time in Sweden.

was the prominent rear spoiler. The Evolution 2 would miss the start of the season, however, and ultimately make its debut on the Tour de Corse, as the previous T16 had done.

The 1985 season opened in Monte Carlo on 26 January. Drama was never far away from the Peugeot team. Vatanen crashed and then suffered an eight-minute time penalty after a mistake checking in at the end of the stage. The Finn valiantly battled back, putting in one of the finest drives ever on the Monte, winning twenty-one stages. Despite the setbacks, Vatanen won the event, with team newcomers Salonen and Saby finishing third and fifth respectively.

The snow and ice of the Swedish Rally would feel very much like home for Vatanen and Salonen, whose Scandinavian sensibilities paid off. Vatanen led the rally consistently from start to finish, while Salonen, still acclimatizing to the 205, again finished third.

Swapping snow for sunshine, the Peugeot team headed to Portugal for the next round. After two rallies Salonen was now starting to get to grips with the T16 and during pre-event testing proved his abilities further still, outperforming Vatanen. Portugal was not to be an enjoyable round for Vatanen. He suffered a puncture on the first stage, then a suspension joint failed. His rally was over, leaving Salonen to continue the charge alone. Salonen would eventually take his first WRC win in Portugal, but not before breaking a gearbox and a steering rack. Todt had told Salonen to back off and take second place, but the Finn wanted to win. When Walter Röhrl's Audi began to experience difficulties, Salonen took the lead and held on to it.

Three rounds in and Peugeot had taken all three wins. As the team prepared to travel to Africa for the Safari Rally, spirits were high. In the month between Portugal and the

Portugal meant another Finnish victory in the 205, though on this occasion it was Salonen, not Vatanen, who took the top step on the podium.

97

■ GROUP B, RALLYING AND THE 205 T16

The 1985 Safari would not be a success for Peugeot as the T16 struggled with the harsh environment. Only Salonen would finish, albeit outside the points.

Safari, the team were frantically busy, some tasked with finishing the new Evolution 2 T16, others set to work strengthening the Peugeot in order to cope with the harsh terrain of the rally.

Despite their best efforts, the 205 struggled to adapt to its first forays into Africa. Vatanen's car suffered head-gasket failure, Saby's car broke its chassis and Salonen's finish was a disappointment. Fellow Finn and future Peugeot driver Juha Kankkunen would instead win the rally in a Toyota Celica. Luckily for Peugeot, Audi failed to score any points. The team collectively dusted itself off and moved on. The destination this time was Corsica.

Corsica had been the scene of much excitement and joy for Peugeot the previous year. Sadly they were not to enjoy the same good fortune on their return to the island. The Evolution 2 was still very much untested and so the team opted for Saby to drive the new car, while Vatanen and

Bruno Saby was chosen to pilot the new Evolution 2 T16 as it made its World Rally debut in Corsica.

98

GROUP B, RALLYING AND THE 205 T16

The Evolution 2 was much more dramatic visually – note the large rear spoiler and broad air dam at the front of the car.

PTS mechanics get to grips with Saby's car during the Tour de Corse.

Salonen would remain in the Evolution 1. In the end, who drove what was of little significance. Salonen retired with an electrical fault and Vatanen lost almost half an hour after suffering two punctures. The Finn fought back and was on course for another epic comeback when he crashed violently, his T16 rolling over several times, leaving the road and falling down a ravine. Incredibly, both Vatanen and his co-driver escaped serious injury.

The entire event however was overshadowed by the death of Lancia driver Attilio Bettega. The 32-year-old was killed instantly when his Lancia 037 hit a tree, shattering his seat. It was to be the first of several incidents that would come to mar Group B. Lancia withdrew from the event, while others, perhaps surprisingly, continued. Finally, in subdued circumstances, Bruno Saby would finish second in the Evolution 2.

Salonen overcomes injury to his hands to take victory on the Acropolis Rally.

99

■ GROUP B, RALLYING AND THE 205 T16

The team's doctor tends to Salonen's hands, which had suffered severe blistering, during the Acropolis.

Bettega's death caused many to question rallying, but the season continued with the Acropolis Rally. Vatanen struggled in Greece – the rear suspension bolts could not cope with the rough Greek terrain and he ultimately retired when the steering column on his 205 broke. Peugeot's great rival Audi fared no better, with Röhrl retiring too. Victory would be fought over by two drivers, Salonen for Peugeot and Blomqvist for Audi. In the end, the Swede would bow to the Finn, with Peugeot taking another victory, the first for the Evolution 2. Salonen battled through the pain barrier to win the Acropolis, with Peugeot's team doctor coming to his aid to deal with the blisters on his hands.

It was a one-two finish for Peugeot in New Zealand with Salonen first, closely followed by Vatanen.

100

GROUP B, RALLYING AND THE 205 T16

Blomqvist by one second. As the second stage drew to a close, Vatanen's car failed to arrive at the finishing line. At first, the team thought Vatanen had suffered a puncture, so the team's helicopter retraced the car's route. There had been a serious accident. The Peugeot had hit a dip and rolled end over end. Vatanen's seat snapped, rendering his safety harness redundant. Co-driver Terry Harryman had suffered broken vertebrae, while Vatanen was unconscious. The pair were flown to the nearest hospital, where Vatanen's condition was so serious he was rushed to intensive care.

The accident had almost killed him. His knees were crushed, his leg and back broken. He fractured eight ribs and punctured a lung. Once stabilized, Vatanen was flown back to Europe, where he was reunited with his wife in Paris, before flying home to Finland. Despite the gravity of Vatanen's accident, Peugeot continued to compete in the rally. As the critically injured Vatanen arrived back in Europe, Salonen was winning the Argentinian Rally, with Reutemann finishing third.

Vatanen would spend almost two years recovering from his injuries, both physical and mental. Instead of battling Audis and Lancias, Vatanen would now focus on battling the depths of depression. In typical Vatanen fashion it was a battle he would win, and though he would never again compete in a Group B World Rally event he would return to motor sport and to great success.

Despite almost losing Vatanen, the team continued and headed for Finland and the 1000 Lakes. With Vatanen out, Peugeot needed a replacement driver and found one in the Swede Kalle Grundel, who had been driving for Peugeot of Germany. Four rounds of the 1985 season remained, and

Victory on his home rally, the 1000 Lakes, meant that Timo Salonen was the World Rally Champion – Todt's mission was a success.

As if to underline the rollercoaster nature of Group B rallying, New Zealand saw Peugeot's fortunes improve considerably. The T16 excelled on New Zealand's twisting, undulating roads and for the first time Peugeot enjoyed a one-two finish, with Salonen taking victory, closely followed by Vatanen.

From New Zealand, the team made its way to Argentina where Audi would launch a new improved Quattro. Saby did not travel to Argentina. Instead, former Formula One champion and Argentinian Carlos Reutemann would compete in the third car, giving Peugeot plenty of local support.

As the rally began, Vatanen was at his best once again, setting the fastest time, leading teammate Salonen and rival

Timo Salonen and co-driver Seppo Harjanne – the 1985 World Rally Champions.

101

■ GROUP B, RALLYING AND THE 205 T16

GROUP B RALLYING – THE CARS

The Peugeot 205 T16 competed against a wide variety of rivals from a broad range of manufacturers. Group B enjoyed huge popularity with motorsport fans and a level of media coverage on a par with Formula One. The 205 T16 was one of the big challengers for championship honours alongside the likes of the Audi Quattro and the Lancia Delta but every manufacturer wanted a piece of the Group B action.

Audi Quattro
Debut: 1980
Engine: 2110cc, 5-cylinder, turbo
Transmission: Six-speed

The Quattro was largely responsible for the birth of Group B. In a stroke, the Quattro made the previously successful rear-wheel-drive cars, such as the Ford Escort, obsolete.

Lancia 037
Debut: 1982
Engine: 1995cc, 4-cylinder, turbo
Transmission: Five-speed

Development of the 037 began in 1982, almost as a direct response to the success of the Audi. Its first season was a struggle, but Lancia succeeded in taking the constructors' championship in 1983. Placed up against the Quattro and 205 T16 it proved uncompetitive. It was succeeded by the Delta S4 in 1985.

Lancia Delta S4
Debut: 1985
Engine: 1759cc, 4-cylinder, twin-charged (turbo and supercharged)
Transmission: Five-speed

The Delta S4 was Lancia's response to the Peugeot 205 T16 and an effort to return to the top of world rallying. It bore little resemblance to the road-going Delta. Like the Peugeot, it was mid-engined and four-wheel drive. The S4 quickly proved itself, winning the 1985 Lombard RAC Rally on its competitive debut. The legacy of the S4 however, will forever be tinged with tragedy following the fatal crash of Henri Toivonen and Sergio Cresto in 1986.

MG Metro 6R4
Debut: 1985
Engine: 2991cc, 6-cylinder, naturally aspirated
Transmission: Five-speed

Austin Rover took a somewhat unusual approach to Group B. While rivals went for smaller forced-induction units, Austin Rover opted for a large, naturally aspirated engine, choosing a twin ohc 3-litre V6, capable of developing between 250 and 410bhp depending on specification. The MG was late arriving in Group B and although it enjoyed a successful run in the 1985 Lombard RAC Rally its 1986 season was beset with technical issues and the Metro failed to complete a single event. The troublesome V6 would eventually prove itself, powering the Jaguar XJ220 supercar.

Ford RS200
Debut: 1986
Engine: 1803cc, 4-cylinder, turbo
Transmission: Five-speed

Ford had taken its time to get into Group B, initially planning to base its entry around the Mk3 Escort. Called the RS1700T, it was powered by a 1.8-litre, turbocharged engine with rear-wheel drive. Continual teething problems and the rapid development of all-wheel-drive rivals saw the car become outdated before it even entered a rally. Ford switched to develop the RS200. Unlike many rivals, the RS200 was not based on a regular car from Ford's range, instead being custom-designed for rally success. The RS200 came third in the 1986 Swedish Rally but at the following WRC round, in Portugal, an RS200 would crash into a crowd of spectators, killing three people.

GROUP B, RALLYING AND THE 205 T16

The 1985 Lombard RAC Rally proved to be an event to forget for Peugeot Talbot Sport as all three T16s retired from the event.

PTS were in a strong position to win their first world title. Grundel was somewhat naïve and left the road early on. Todt was furious. The Swede improved, however, and brought his T16 home in a respectable fifth place. Salonen, on the other hand, was flawless. The Finn drove a near-perfect rally and took the win.

Todt's team had succeeded. Peugeot were world champions, scoring 142 points. Their nearest rivals, Audi, finished second on 126. The gap in the drivers' championship was even wider, Salonen scoring maximum points on five out of the nine rallies he contested, finishing 52 points clear of Blomqvist in the Audi.

With the title secured, Peugeot opted not to enter the Rallye Côte d'Ivoire, returning for the final round in Britain. Despite their newly crowned world champion status, the Lombard RAC proved to be something of a damp squib for Peugeot Talbot Sport, with all three T16s retiring – Salonen due to a loss of oil pressure, and Grundel and newcomer Mikael Sundström both suffering accidents.

1986: THE END OF GROUP B

The 1986 season began with Timo Salonen as world champion. Saby would continue alongside him while Juha Kankkunen filled the place of the still-recovering Ari Vatanen. Michèle Mouton also made her debut in a Peugeot 205 T16, though this car was privately entered by Peugeot's German subsidiary.

As the 1986 season began Michèlle Mouton found herself at the wheel of a Peugeot Deutschland-backed T16.

Mouton would go on to enjoy great success in domestic German rallying in the car as well as contesting certain stages of the World Rallying Championship.

103

■ GROUP B, RALLYING AND THE 205 T16

With Vatanen still recovering, another Finn signed on for Peugeot Talbot Sport – Juha Kankkunen. His first victory came in Sweden.

Starting in Monaco, it quickly became apparent that the Group B game had changed, thanks to one car – the Lancia Delta S4. The S4 was both supercharged and turbocharged. Driven by Henri Toivonen and Markku Alén, the S4 was a devastatingly quick car, developing 560bhp. Toivonen showed just how quick the S4 was, winning the Monte Carlo Rally, with the Peugeots of Salonen finishing second, Kankkunen fifth and Saby sixth.

From Monaco the WRC moved to the snow of Sweden. The Swedish Rally saw Peugeot return to the top of the podium, with Kankkunen taking his first win in the T16. Alén came second in a Delta S4 leaving the two teams tied for the lead in the championship. Salonen retired after his T16 suffered a loss of oil.

While the likes of Audi, Peugeot and Lancia had dominated the championship for the past six years, Ford had been strangely absent, not having had a world champion since Vatanen in 1981. They opted to return in 1986 with the RS200. The RS developed over 400bhp and Ford were keen to make up for lost time. The RS made its debut in Sweden, driven by Stig Blomqvist and former Peugeot driver Kalle Grundel. It was fast – Blomqvist retired with mechanical problems, but Grundel brought the RS home in an impressive third.

As the teams set off for Portugal it seemed that Ford would become a force to be reckoned with. However, the next round saw the first of a pair of tragedies that would ultimately lead to the demise of Group B rallying.

The Portuguese rally showed, in the worst way, just how popular Group B rallying had become. Massive crowds lined the roads, diving away at the last minute, giving the drivers little margin for error. It was an accident waiting to happen.

GROUP B, RALLYING AND THE 205 T16

On a fast mountain section local driver Joaquim Santos lost control of his RS200 and crashed into a crowd of spectators. Three people were killed and thirty were injured. That night, Henri Toivonen demanded action to ensure spectator safety. Shockingly, the rally continued, though the works teams from Peugeot, Audi, Austin Rover, Ford and Lancia all withdrew.

Rallying continued and the season moved on to Kenya, where Kankkunen finished fifth as the Finn continued to dominate the championship. Peugeot and Lancia were still neck and neck for the drivers' and manufacturers' titles.

In Corsica, a Peugeot won again, though this time it was Bruno Saby at the wheel as team leader Salonen crashed out and Michèle Mouton suffered gearbox failure. After the end of day one, Lancia occupied three of the top four places, with Toivonen in the lead and Saby a close second. The next day, Saby overhauled Toivonen, only for the Finn, together with American co-driver Sergio Cresto, to put in a string of fastest stage times, showing incredible pace in his Delta S4.

On stage eighteen, however, he somehow missed a turn, sending the Lancia plummeting down a cliff. The S4's design placed the driver's and co-driver's seats over the car's petrol tanks. During the accident, the car caught fire, killing the trapped pair. The rally was immediately suspended. The Lancias of Markku Alén and Miki Biasion withdrew and when the event resumed the following day Saby cruised through the remaining stages to a subdued win.

The FIA responded to one of the darkest moments in WRC history by immediately banning all Group B cars from the 1987 season onwards. Rallying would never quite be the same again – Audi withdrew from the sport and changes were made immediately, reducing the length of stages and events overall. Manufacturers who had only recently joined the WRC, such as Ford and Austin Rover, saw their investment all but wiped out.

A month later, the championship continued, moving to Athens, though many had lost their appetite for the sport. Juha Kankkunen would win the Acropolis Rally, with Bruno

Kankkunen won again in Greece as he began to assert his grip on the championship.

■ GROUP B, RALLYING AND THE 205 T16

Peugeot were joined by Stig Blomqvist on their returned to Argentina, the scene of Vatanen's brush with death.

Saby finishing third. Champion Salonen's hopes of retaining the title were beginning to fade, following his retirement with suspension issues on his T16. Kankkunen then recorded his third victory of the season, in New Zealand, to give him a clear lead at the top of the drivers' table.

The Peugeot team returned to the scene of Vatanen's accident the previous year, looking to move another step closer to securing a second championship. Following Ford's re-evaluation of their Group B campaign, Stig Blomqvist joined the Peugeot team for the trip to South America, and it was the Swede who gave the team their best position in Argentina. Kankkunen retired with suspension trouble, while Saby's engine expired, forcing him out of the rally. After three days in Argentina, Lancia's Miki Biasion and Markku Alén took first and second place respectively, and the championship swung back in Lancia's favour.

Salonen and Kankkunen dominated the 1986 1000 Lakes, while a recovering Ari Vatanen joined fans to take in the action.

106

GROUP B, RALLYING AND THE 205 T16

San Remo ended in controversy for the team when all three T16s were excluded from the event on a technicality.

Peugeot would fare much better in the next round, however, as the WRC returned to Finland and the 1000 Lakes Rally. Peugeot dominated the event, with Salonen and Kankkunen coming first and second and Blomqvist finishing fourth, thus securing the WRC manufacturers' title for Peugeot.

The major teams chose not to travel to Africa for the Rallye Côte d'Ivoire, so the battle between Lancia and Peugeot for the drivers' championship had to wait until October's trip to Italy for the Rallye Sanremo. With the return of Vatanen and Italian driver Andre Zanussi joining the team, there were four Peugeots taking part in the rally, aiming to keep the Lancias in check. Salonen crashed out and then – towards the end of the event, with Kankkunen challenging the Lancias hard – the remaining three 205s were surprisingly excluded from the event, the rally's stewards deeming that the 205 was using a type of aerodynamic skirt that broke the rules. It was the end of Peugeot's rally and Lancia cantered to a one-two-three finish. Peugeot launched an appeal, demanding the result be stricken from the record. Meanwhile, Kankkunen led the championship by just three points with two rounds to go – the championship would go down to the wire.

The 1986 Lombard RAC Rally began in the south-west of England, in Bath. Peugeot fielded three cars, with Mikael Sundström returning to the team following his drive for the team in the 1985 RAC. Kankkunen said at the time, 'I'm only interested in Alén's times, because we have to fight with him for the points.' The Finn suffered disaster near the end of the rally, badly rolling his T16 during the forest stages, dropping three minutes – an eternity in rallying. Kankkunen battled on and recovered remarkably well to finish third, closing to within five seconds of Alén. Salonen would find only his second win and third podium of the year. Sundström, who had enjoyed great success in the Scottish Rally Championship, finished fourth. The battle for the driver's title was down to two men – Alén for Lancia and Kankkunen for Peugeot.

Kankkunen spent most of the 1986 RAC Rally chasing Marku Alén. He rolled his car and finished third, with Salonen winning the event.

107

■ GROUP B, RALLYING AND THE 205 T16

The T16 proved itself tough enough to tackle the rigours of the Safari Rally.

GROUP B, RALLYING AND THE 205 T16

Alén led the drivers' championship by a single point, while there was just a nine-point gap between Lancia and the leaders, Peugeot. The championship headed to the United States for the final round. Many of the works teams opted to miss the Olympus Rally, so the battle came down to the two Finns. Alén soon found a lead, getting some 36 seconds ahead of Kankkunen. At the end of the rally both Alén and Kankkunen celebrated victory and had to wait three weeks until the outcome of Peugeot's appeal over the dispute on the Rallye Sanremo.

FISA ruled in Peugeot's favour. The Sanremo results were annulled, Alén's points were taken away and Kankkunen won the title with 118 points from Alén's 104. Salonen finished third, with Saby in seventh place. Peugeot retained the manufacturer's title with 137 points, 15 more than Lancia in second place. Kankkunen and Peugeot were world champions, but Group B was over. Without rallying, what would become of the 205 T16?

FROM WRC TO PDR

Peugeot had invested heavily in the T16 and its rally programme and when Group B was banned it took legal action against the FIA. That action was unsuccessful, but the end of Group B was not to be the end of the T16's motor-sport success.

Todt decided to repurpose the T16 to compete in long-range endurance rallies, principally the Paris–Dakar Rally. The Paris–Dakar was first run in 1979, its foundations having been laid a year earlier when Frenchman Thierry Sabine became lost in the desert and thought that the terrain might provide the ultimate setting and challenge for an endurance rally.

The Paris–Dakar saw not only the 205's return to competition, but also the return of fan-favourite Ari Vatanen. Vatanen would be joined by Shekhar Mehta and Italian Andrea Zanussi. Kenyan Mehta had come to prominence driving for Datsun and won the 1981 African Rally Championship. His experience rallying across Africa made him an ideal choice for Peugeot, providing back-up for the returning Vatanen.

In order for the T16 to compete in the Paris–Dakar, a number of revisions were made to the car. First, it grew longer, its wheelbase gaining a 300mm (12in) extension to bring the Peugeot's length to 2,880mm (113in). Its track was also widened by 100mm (4in). The longer, wider T16 was reinforced with a stronger roll cage, while it now tipped the scales at 1,300kg (2,866lb).

With huge expanses of Africa to traverse, the T16 needed increased range so it was fitted with an extra 190ltr (42gal) fuel tank, with two tanks under the driver's and navigator's seats. The extra tank allowed the Peugeot to carry over 400ltr (88gal) of fuel, giving it a range of 500 miles (800km) – enough for it to cover the longest rally stages without the need to refuel.

The suspension was suitably reinforced to cope with the harsher African terrain – each wheel featured a double spring/shock set-up and the suspension geometry was also revised.

Power-wise, the Paris–Dakar T16 was less powerful than its World Rally-winning brother, developing 360bhp at 8,500rpm. It also received shorter gear ratios, with the exception of sixth, which was left as it was in the World

Two years, two champions: 1985's Timo Salonen and Seppo Harjanne and 1986's Juha Kankkunen and co-driver Juha Piironen.

■ GROUP B, RALLYING AND THE 205 T16

The Paris–Dakar Rally would represent a very different challenge for Peugeot Talbot Sport and the 205 T16.

The 1987 event marked Ari Vatanen's return to motor sport – he was joined by Shekhar Mehta and Andrea Zanussi.

Rally T16, allowing the car to reach a top speed of 143mph (230km/h). This new version of the T16 was christened 205 T16 GR, with the GR standing for 'Grand Raid', eluding to the fact that the Dakar is more properly known as a 'rally raid'.

Following several weeks' testing in October 1986, the new 205 T16 was ready for its first endurance event. On 1 January 1987, it made its debut on the Paris–Dakar Rally. The event was Vatanen's first in competition following his near-fatal accident in Argentina and began with a qualifying stage in Paris, which would determine the starting order once the cars reached the African continent.

The Paris stage did not go as Peugeot and Vatanen had hoped. The Finn hit a bank and suffered suspension failure, and the car limped across the finish line on three wheels while a gaggle of spectators clambered onto the 205's rear in an effort to counterbalance the car and keep its front end up.

110

GROUP B, RALLYING AND THE 205 T16

ABOVE: **In order to survive in the desert, the T16 was elongated and gained a larger fuel tank.**

ABOVE: **Winning the Paris–Dakar added another victory to Jean Todt and the PTS team's long list of honours, one fought for in the most gruelling manner.**

RIGHT: **Just as it had dominated World Rallying, the T16 took the Paris–Dakar in its stride and brought Vatanen back to the sport he loved so dearly.**

111

■ GROUP B, RALLYING AND THE 205 T16

A few weeks later, on 22 January, Ari Vatanen added another victory to his long, long list of motor-sport successes. After travelling over 13,000km (8,000 miles) through France, Algeria, Niger, Mali, Mauritania and Senegal – 8,315km (5,155 miles) of them in competitive mode – he had won the Paris–Dakar.

Later in 1987 the Vatanen, Mehta, Zanussi trio headed to America for the Pikes Peak International Hill Climb. Dating back to 1916, this prestigious hill climb in Colorado quickly became a gathering place for manufacturers looking to maintain or increase their exposure after the banning of Group B cars from the WRC.

Peugeot's Pikes Peak cars were prepared with larger spoilers, front and rear, in order to increase grip on 'The Race to the Clouds', which at the time was run over gravel rather than the tarmac of today. They were also lighter than the rally equivalent, shedding about 140kg (308lb), and more powerful, developing almost 600bhp.

As with the World Rally Championship, the 1987 Pikes Peak Hill Climb boiled down to a face-off between Vatanen in the Peugeot and Röhrl in the Audi. The Finn would lead the German in qualifying, completing the half-distance sprint four seconds faster than Röhrl. At the time, Vatanen told the media: 'After testing we've done a lot of work. The mechanics have worked extremely hard to improve the car and so

TOP: **With the Dakar mission accomplished, Vatanen and Peugeot turned their attention to the United States, to Colorado and the Pikes Peak Hill Climb.**

LEFT: **Vatanen would climb the hill fastest in practice but his old sparring partner Walter Röhrl would get the better of him. Vatanen would finish second, teammate Zanussi third.**

112

GROUP B, RALLYING AND THE 205 T16

Peugeot headed back into Africa in 1988, with Juha Kankkunen piloting a 205 T16 and Vatanen the new 405 T16.

Vatanen led the event until, incredibly, his car was stolen. This left Kankkunen and the T16, on its last major international motor sport event, to take victory.

The two Finns, Vatanen and Kankkunen, formed a formidable alliance on both the Paris–Dakar and at Pikes Peak.

113

has Jean-Claude Vaucard. It's due to their efforts that the car is considerably better than it was a week ago. We were able to go much, much faster. The car is very rewarding now.'

Despite the efforts of all at Peugeot Talbot Sport and Vatanen himself, victory would elude the Finn that year. Röhrl posted a Pikes Peak record to beat Vatanen's time by seven seconds and teammate Zanussi's by eight. Audi took first place that year, with Peugeot's T16s finishing second, third and fourth. Peugeot would return to Colorado in 1988 when Vatanen would enjoy victory not in a 205 but in a 405, setting a new course record as well as starring in the iconic *Climb Dance* cinematic short that detailed his success.

The 205 T16's final victory would come on the 1988 Paris–Dakar Rally, with a win for Juha Kankkunen, who was competing in the endurance event for the first time. However, this year's story was all about teammate and fellow countryman Ari Vatanen, who had won in 1987 and was now driving the new Peugeot 405 T16. The team was completed by former Formula One driver Henri Pescarolo.

Vatanen and the 405 quickly gelled and the Finn was well on his way to victory when, incredibly, his car was stolen – taken from a football stadium in Bamako, the capital of Mali, while the team slept. Jean Todt was contacted with ransom demands but thankfully the car was found intact. With minutes to spare, Vatanen and co-driver Bruno Berglund made it to the start line and were able to continue. However, Vatanen would still be robbed of victory. Since his car had not been on the start line half an hour before his allotted start time, the 405 and Vatanen were struck from the rally, with second place Kankkunen and the 205 taking the victory by default.

FROM 'A' TO 'N' – THE 205 GTI IN MOTOR SPORT

While the 205 T16 is rightly remembered as being the leading light of the 205's motor-sport career, it should also be remembered that the more humble GTI also campaigned in rallying and circuit racing.

When the FIA redrew the motor-sport groupings in the early 1980s, Group A was born. In order to qualify as a Group A car 2,500 cars of that model had to be built in a single year – something that the Peugeot achieved easily with the fiercely popular GTI. Group A allowed many private teams to compete in rallies and races without the huge financial demands of the Group B supercars.

The 205 GTI enjoyed much rallying success in its own right. AUTHOR

The GTI also found itself a popular choice for Group N competitors. Group N – or 'showroom class' as it became known – allowed for limited modifications to the cars, meaning that the budget for a rally campaign was reduced further still.

Peugeot Talbot UK ran several Group A 205s alongside their own T16 and enjoyed some impressive results with the car. While the UK T16 programme met with little success the GTI proved quite different. The car was driven by Louise Aitken-Walker, with Ellen Morgan serving as co-driver. The pair soon proved that even the near-standard 205 was a capable rally car, finishing in sixteenth place overall on the 1985 Lombard RAC Rally.

In Britain, Peugeot launched the GTI Rally Club in 1988 with three drivers, including, most notably, Colin McRae, who was chosen to compete in the 205's first forays into British rallying. Peugeot UK's tentative steps into British rallying went well and the following year it was expanded with the creation of the GTI Rally Challenge. Thirty Peugeots contested the championship, with a mix of 205 and 309 GTIs competing for the prize of a works-assisted drive in a 309 GTI on the RAC Rally that November.

For the 1990 season, Peugeot upped the ante quite considerably. The winner of the Peugeot Challenge – now split into two classes, the Super Cup for those who had entered previously and the GTI Challenge for newcomers – would get a works drive not only in the RAC Rally but also in the following season's British Rally Championship. That year saw the emergence of Richard Burns, a future World Rally Champion. Hinting at future successes, the nineteen-year-

RALLYING THE GTI – LOUISE AITKEN-WALKER

Louise Aitken-Walker's motor-sport career began in 1979 when she was entered into Ford's 'Find a Lady Rally Driver' contest by her brothers. The Scot succeeded in beating 2,000 competitors to the prize. In a hugely successful and varied career she won dozens of rallies, finished fourth in the 1989 British Touring Car Championship and was crowned the 1990 Ladies World Rally Champion. Today she works in the motor trade with her husband, Graham, and was inducted into the Scottish Sports Hall of Fame in 2002. She began rallying for Peugeot in 1987.

Louise Aitken-Walker and Ellen Morgan led Peugeot UK's charge in their 1.6 GTI. Here the car is undergoing testing prior to its debut. JOHN EVANS

Aitken-Walker had earned herself an enviable reputation prior to joining Peugeot and still speaks fondly of her time with the team. LOUISE AITKEN-WALKER

In 1987 I was looking for a drive and it was between Peugeot and Audi. The Audi deal was more of a development drive than the Peugeot and I felt the 205 would suit me better, that the Peugeot would be easier for me to adapt to, so I signed for Peugeot.

Peugeot, and Talbot before them, were a team I'd liked and respected. They'd done well in British rallying with the Talbot Sunbeam with people like Toivonen driving for them. I thought they'd commit to the programme so that helped me make my mind up. Before the 205 my first thought of Peugeot would have been of a taxi. A big, comfortable, slightly old-fashioned saloon with sofa-like seats and nothing crisp about it. In the 1970s they were big, old cars. I remember Andrew Cowan in a Chrysler; even that was big. They got it sorted with the 205. As a road car it was properly trendy. I had both a 1600 and a 1900 – one of the perks of being a Works driver is a free car. I loved them, it was great, a properly nippy wee thing.

I always competed in a 1600 GTI. The T16 was a big, huge, powerful car and I wasn't prepared to drive a car like that at that stage of my career. Peugeot UK had some very good drivers driving for them, the likes of Mikael Sundström, Kalle Grundel. They all had 1900cc 205s and 309s and not one of them ever beat me.

I remember we didn't get a lot of time to do testing. I think it was on the Mintex, when we finished second overall to Pentti Airikkala, we'd not long tested the car and went straight into competition.

My best time was on the RAC Rally, I remember we were in sixth place overall, on a World Championship event. I was thinking, 'If we can finish here it'll be amazing!' Someone up ahead of us had hit a pile of logs and spread them across the road. Well we ended up hitting one and it burst the oil cooler pipes, forcing us to retire.

My whole experience with Peugeot was amazing. It's like a horse – if it's suited to you, you're unstoppable. It was like that with the 205 – it suited me so well. It suited me down to the ground and I got so much confidence from that car. The Peugeot team were fantastic as well. They set the car up for me exactly how I wanted it, which a lot of teams don't do – they'll work with the lead driver and feed back from there, but at Peugeot I got the car I wanted. All of my time with Peugeot was just great fun.

People are still rallying 205s today. It just goes to show what a great car the 205 was and still is.

Despite her teammates driving more powerful 1.9-engined cars, Louise consistently outperformed the likes of Mikael Sundström and Kalle Grundel. LOUISE AITKEN-WALKER

■ GROUP B, RALLYING AND THE 205 T16

The GTI became a popular car on European rally stages, as shown here with this Italian 205.

old won the 1990 GTI Challenge and the works drive for the 1991 season. The competition grew further in that season, with over 100 entries battling to get the better of Burns. They failed, however, as the young Englishman dominated the competition once again.

The rules were revised for the 1992 season with the aim of making the GTI more competitive but the 205's time on the rally stage was beginning to draw to a close. The 205's baby brother, the 106, was making itself known on the national rally circuit and Peugeot UK's involvement in motor sport was moving away from the rally stage to the race circuit.

The final Peugeot Challenge was run in 1993 and that year's RAC Rally saw the last works-backed 205 being entered into the event. Trevor Smith's GTI was the best-placed 205, finishing twenty-eighth, while the Norwegian duo of Bernt Kollevold and Bjorn Lie finished forty-seventh in their Rallye. The remaining 205s, both GTIs and crewed by Jacques Jonquières and Jacques Phelippeau, retired, as did the all-British team of Nigel Heath and Tim Hely. In 1994 the 205 was superseded by the 306.

The 205 had introduced a wealth of drivers to the world of rallying. Future champions like Colin McRae and Richard Burns took some of their first steps in the sport and enjoyed their first success at the wheel of a 205 GTI. While the T16 had become a global superstar in the few brief years of Group B, Peugeot UK's national programme had been a fantastic success. Peugeot's support of and interest in grass-roots rallying would continue for years to come.

TIME WITH THE LEGEND: AN INTERVIEW WITH ARI VATANEN

Ari Vatanen was born in Tuupovaara, Finland, in 1952. He developed a love for driving from an early age and his passionate, full-throttle driving style made him a huge favourite with the fans, not only in his Finnish homeland, but also right across the world.

In a career that ran from 1974 to 2003 he drove for Ford, Opel, Subaru, BMW and Mitsubishi. He was crowned World Rally Champion in 1981, piloting a Ford Escort RS1800 to the world title. When he joined Peugeot Talbot Sport he was tipped by many as one of the favourites for the title once again. As history records, however, fate would have other plans.

The Peugeot 205 remains a very special car to Ari Vatanen. From his breathtaking debut in the 205 to his life-changing accident (and the fear that he had contracted AIDS following three blood transfusions) and his eventual victories in the Paris–Dakar, his years with Peugeot had a huge impact on his life and career.

Adam Sloman: Why did you opt to join Peugeot Talbot Sport?
Ari Vatanen: You know that it was publicly known that Jean Todt had four drivers on his list. Walter Röhrl, Markku Alén, Henri Toivonen and myself. And he asked me, I stopped in Paris on the way to the Acropolis Rally, must have been 1983, and I saw Jean for dinner in a restaurant. At the time I was still one of the four. In 1983 I won the Safari with Opel. Jean Todt was at the start of one of the sections. I decided, for once, I would be wise and clever. I said to myself, 'I won't start away from the line like Vatanen is supposed to. I won't go, you know, with my wheels spinning because that's not the wise way to go – it doesn't look good and it isn't necessary. So I started really gently, I paid real attention, I started like a grandma. Jean was there getting a feel for things. Two months after that I met Jean. He probably took me on false grounds. I was only acting, just to impress him. I managed to disguise my real nature! Then I came to see Jean. We knew each other, we had a fight in 1981 to the title. Another co-driver of mine, Dave Richards, both stopped after that rally and went on to great success but that's another thing. I always remember one English mechanic who had been something to do with Talbot who said to me 'Oh Ari, you mustn't go to Peugeot! You know those French people!' It was very typical of that Anglo-French rivalry, and one of the first questions ringing in the back of my mind when I saw Jean Todt regarding the project. I asked 'Is it true you will only use French components and French people at any cost?' he said 'No Ari, we use whatever it takes to win!' This was his first answer to me and it reassured me. I soon became very convinced about the project. It was new, it was unconventional. New people to me, new country to me, everything was new to me. And that appealed to me. I sort of half guessed what was to come. I had no hesitations after that initial statement from that English mechanic!

AS: What was your initial reaction to the Peugeot 205 T16?
AV: Er, very, very first reaction was not particularly impressive. The engine wasn't running properly and didn't give full power or run cleanly. The wishbones were far too weak, we bent them immediately. The engine didn't give good power. I thought 'Oh dear, oh dear' but they put these things right

Ari joined Peugeot in 1984 – he admits he did his best to impress Jean Todt.

■ GROUP B, RALLYING AND THE 205 T16

He gelled almost immediately with the 205. 'I was absolutely convinced we could do well,' he recalls.

so fast. When I went to the Corsica Rally I was really, really confident that we would do well. I was absolutely convinced we would do well. And as I say, I have to say a lot for Jean-Claude Boillot, we speak at least once a month still today. Jean had such a human approach to things. The mechanics were so enthusiastic. Jean Todt brought them croissants in the morning.

AS: So it was more like a family, then?
AV: Absolutely. Absolutely. I didn't speak any French at the time; only Carlos Barras, the Portuguese driver, had been to Talbot and he spoke quite good English and the engineers, their rusty school English all came back quite soon so we were able to converse with the engineers and Jean Todt, but not much the mechanics. But still, we had this mutual understanding and they of course tried their best because they realized the stakes were high. We had kind of a devotion and it's all about helping one another. This confidence and confidence in the team grows exponentially when you see that everybody is trying the best. You motivate one another, you inspire one another. You spark off of one another.

At the end of the second stage of the Corsica Rally the entire board of directors were there to see. When Mr Boillot, as the head of Peugeot, nor the president of PSA, nor the Peugeot family, supported Jean Todt's programme, they said 'OK, it's on your head. It's your responsibility.' You have

The T16 experienced some early teething problems, but these were soon overcome, something Ari puts down to Peugeot Talbot Sport's 'brilliantly enthusiastic' mechanics.

Ari says the team was inspired by one another and credits Jean Boillot for giving Jean Todt a free rein over the team.

As the team became more successful, a strong sense of unity began to develop. 'We had a devotion that was all about helping one another,' says Ari.

to bear in [mind] the situation Peugeot was in at that time. They had the Talbot operation, there were many reasons why Peugeot was doing so badly. He took this gamble, but it was a gamble that paid off. The 205 was the first new Peugeot and motor sport awoke people. They followed up with other models and it saved the company. He [Boillot] gave a free hand to Jean Todt.

AS: After your accident did you ever consider not returning to motorsport?
AV: Well, it was an incredible nightmare, the accident. My psychological problems and I was convinced I had AIDS. Once your mind turns 180 degrees nothing rational stays with you anymore. So when I was in that state of mind I thought that my life was finished. I saw nothing but black in front of me. Once I came out into daylight from that tunnel, that deep hole, it became obvious, almost automatic that I would go back to rallying because your will to live is stronger than anything else. Once I saw life in its proper colours, the real colours, there was no question, no pros or cons. Would I rally again? Of course. When I awoke from that nightmare at the 1986 1000 Lakes rally, two weeks later I was testing for the Paris–Dakar, jumping a T16 something like 67 metres over flat ground. It was a very long-lasting accident.

AS: Was there ever a time when you were driving again that fear became an issue for you?
AV: No, no, no. If you start to question the entire foundation, if existential questions come to your mind then it is time to give up. Of course you get frightened when you have a close shave, sure, momentarily. You take a deep breath and think 'Ooh – that was close' but not otherwise, no. You are happy to get into your car. And then it takes over. In a way, when it goes well you're just a passenger, you drive, but you're still a passenger. You go in the flow, that flow, that emotion. You go by the seat of your pants. You don't think about it. Like a pianist who plays with her eyes closed. Her mind is somewhere else, her fingers stay on the keys but her soul is somewhere else. That's how driving is when it's at its best. There is no place for fear. No place for it. It's totally incompatible with the world you are in. It's detached from the real world.

AS: Do you think you would have a chance to win the WRC in the T16 had it not been for your accident?
AV: If and if and if and if! The way it happened was meant to be I suppose. Now I can say light-heartedly that I am the only driver to win every World Championship I've driven, because I only got to drive in one full World Rally Championship and I won it! In '81. Even Sébastien [Loeb] cannot say that! So of course 1985 was supposed to be my championship year and it started off like that and then I look at the pictures of the accident. My daughter, her boyfriend is from Patagonia, she came back recently and brought back an Argentinian sports paper from 1985 and it had a picture of the accident. I am lying on the ground, right after the accident, my leg badly broken, you don't see my upper body, which was totally broken, I had blood coming from my bottom, I was dying. When I see that picture it brings tears to my eyes. I see that photo and think, 'My, I am still here. After that!' I can't complain, I can't. It's a miracle that I am still here.

■ GROUP B, RALLYING AND THE 205 T16

Though not Vatanen's car, this image shows how his accident, and a nightmare that blighted his life for two years, began.

AS: So from that point of view then, it doesn't bother you that you were robbed of your chance to win?
AV: No. Not at all. No, no. It would have been too perfect a story. Now it's real life. The way it turned out to be it's not a polished version – it's not the Hollywood version, it's the real version.

AS: Looking back, the field seemed so strong, with so many talented drivers.
AV: I have a lot of respect for Walter Röhrl, who was so methodical in his approach. Understeering car, beautiful lines, in a way the opposite to me. Of course people then say he never had the nerve to compete in 1000 Lakes but I really respected him. Then there was Markku Alén who was great. I had some fantastic fights with Markku. Hannu Mikkola, who was a little bit older than me and at Audi. Miki Biasion and Didier Auriol – you name it, they were all there. For some their heyday lasted longer than others – I've had battles with all of them. In Group B of course you also had Henri Toivonen.

AS: What was the first thing you drove after your accident?
AV: The very first thing? I had still not come out of my nightmare – I was still in that terrible world. At the practice for the '86 1000 Lakes, I met up with Salonen and Kankkunen. Salonen came to test a few weeks before the 1000 Lakes and I went to that session. It was like a confirmation that I was a lost cause, I was still sick in my mind. I was so frightened. I was driven by Salonen and tried to drive myself. I was frightened being next to him and I was frightened to drive. I was not yet fit. My mind was not well. Only a few weeks later, my brother-in-law took me by helicopter to the 1000 Lakes. I was hiding from people. I was convinced that I had AIDS and everybody knew – it was in my mind. I couldn't face people. He said 'Let's go to see some rallying. We'll be in a distant field so you won't see anyone.' I overcame my fears. Before then I wouldn't have gone – I couldn't have stood to see people. I awoke from the nightmare, it was like a big relief. You know if you have a bad dream and you wake up, well imagine that on a bigger scale. Suddenly I realized, all the thoughts I had about AIDS, and they weren't true. I awoke there and then and realized the fear was not true. That rally, the spectators, it's like a man who's been condemned to death has suddenly been given a reprieve. A few weeks after that we were testing for Paris–Dakar. All those African events, it was like a human school. I forgot your original question! I got lost talking about my feelings!

GROUP B, RALLYING AND THE 205 T16

Paris–Dakar was a cathartic experience for the Finn. 'It was like a wonderland – you can hardly believe it's all true.'

AS: Do you think Group B put success ahead of driver and spectator safety?
AV: Well spectator safety is a question of country. It's a question of culture. Some countries, like Portugal where the people are so enthusiastic, or in Monte Carlo, people were literally on the road. That was the result of that period of life. That was how people expressed themselves. Luckily not everybody is as dour as Finns are, or as reserved as the English are. Luckily we have people who are hot-blooded, who are passionate. We need passionate people. We need to forgive those people. They endangered themselves and our sport, but they showed how passionate they were about us and our sport. In a way, that's all part of that special period. Afterwards you can say it was a crazy period. But then say it was madness. We need to do things in life that are not reasonable, in order to push the frontiers. We must progress in life. Thanks to technology, science and research you open up the world to new possibilities. Group B, in a lot of ways, was part of that human progress. There's no progress without risk. So you realize, 'Yes we made a mistake' but whatever we find out on the way to that mistake can then be used and channelled in a more purposeful way. But you must push boundaries in order to make discoveries. You could see Group B in that light.

AS: Your philosophy towards driving is more of an artistic one as opposed to say a clinical approach favoured by someone such as Walter Röhrl. Why and where does that come from?

AV: Why is your handwriting like it is? Because it reflects your personality. Your driving style is an extension of your personality. It's an extension of what you are. There are no two Adams, no two Aris alike. Even identical twins are different. So that's the whole beauty of life, that we are all different. What I am trying to say is when I've had accidents there were times when I should not have gone off the road. Like in Portugal – we were leading by six minutes and I went off the road. Downright stupid, but that's me. People come up to me, like yesterday at the train station, and remember what I did. If I had lived this very professor-like lifestyle, never made a mistake, they wouldn't. Because they themselves make mistakes. I am not a perfect human being – such a thing does not exist – but if you give the image of being perfect in your profession people may respect you, but they won't love you, because they know themselves they fall far short of perfection in their own lives. Colin McRae was an example of that same style – people can identify themselves with it. You rise from the ashes of your mistakes. That's real life. Maybe you might be better as a driver if you are more clinical. Statistically you might be better if you have more wins but does it make you a better human being? You don't learn from victories. You learn from failures, from mistakes. When everything goes wrong, that humbles you. You realize how small you are. You learn from death. You learn how fragile life is. In life you have to confront everything life gives you. People respect successful drivers, but they don't love

Swede Bruno Berglund would serve as Ari's co-driver in the desert.

121

■ GROUP B, RALLYING AND THE 205 T16

Victory was never far away from Todt and Vatanen during their time at Peugeot.

them. People respect Schumacher, for example, but they don't love him like they do a Senna or someone who perhaps made more mistakes. They don't love people who are too perfect, too polished, and too machine-like.

AS: Of the other Group B cars, were there any you look at and think 'I'd have loved to have had a go in that'? MG Metro 6R4, for example…
AV: Nothing against the Anglo-Saxons, but definitely not Metro! [Laughs] Definitely not! It was funny that they built that car when all of the best cars were already out. They turned up late and built a car like that. Anyway, that's another story! Not really. No. I was afraid of Lancia, in a way, because I didn't think Lancia were very safe, particularly the 037 – I admired how much faster Walter and Henri went in them. Audi was not my kind of driving style with the way it understeered. But Peugeot to me was like the Escort. A little bit unstable in the jumps, which is of course how my accident happened in Argentina. It's an emotional attachment that makes it so special.

AS: How did it feel getting back to competition in Paris–Dakar?
AV: Oh incredible. I was living again. I was alive. I thought I was going to die. I thought my whole family was going to die. I thought they were all infected with AIDS. I went to see an Egyptian psychiatrist, near Maidenhead where we lived at the time. I started to tell him about all my AIDS fears. He said to me, 'Ari, we agree to disagree.' If he had been Finnish, or English, whatever, I don't think I would have listened to him but he had that Arabic human approach. He wouldn't hear a word of it. He knew I lived in a false world and I couldn't be talked out of it. He said, 'Ari, I can send you for tests in New York, in Tokyo, but you won't believe it. So we will agree to disagree.' I wondered if the laboratory

GROUP B, RALLYING AND THE 205 T16

technicians might have made a mistake or got distracted or wondered if it was all a conspiracy because this is what the sick mind tells you. Then I just awoke.

With that backdrop, I came literally from death – imagine how broken I was. I was a desperate case. Then came the psychological fear. Then I am standing next to the Eiffel Tower, on the Paris–Dakar start line. You cannot believe how I felt. And then I won that rally! But winning was just like a bonus. I was living again. And then to discover Dakar, and the beauty of Dakar, and the vastness of it. Ah! It was unreal. It was like a wonderland – you can hardly believe it's all true. It's absolutely mind-blowing. You're just surfing on the wave of life. The big wave just takes you!

After 13,000km Rita [Ari's wife] was waiting for me. We rolled the car, we got lost – there was one incident, there's a railway line in the middle of the Sahara. It goes from an iron mine to the sea. We were warned not to go near it, because there was a lot of metal in the sand. I don't know how but I found it, and had three punctures and no spares. I was leading the rally by an hour and a half, maybe two hours at that time. I said 'Oh they warned me! I wasn't on a main track.' I thought I'd blown it.

My teammate Shekhar Mehta was miles away. We waved but he did not see me because in the desert you don't see what's to the side, you are concentrating on what is ahead of you. Shekhar had the spare tyres for me. I thought, 'I've blown it. I've lost it on the edge of a victory.' What happened? Andrew Cowan came along – he was the only car that was on the same track as me. I said, 'Andrew, please – now try to catch Shekhar, stop him and send him back.' And would you believe, Andrew Cowan wasn't one of the fastest drivers in the world but he caught Shekhar, told him I was in trouble and sent him back. Half an hour later, Shekhar came back. I couldn't believe it. We took all his wheels and left him there in the middle of the desert and that saved the day. We went to Timbuktu and to places that are now too dangerous, so that rally was just incredible. Jean Todt sent him a lot of expensive wine as a thank-you afterwards. That event meant so much for Peugeot. For me the main thing was I [was] back in life. I was living again.

The desert provided Vatanen with much inspiration and had a huge impact on him, personally and professionally.

123

■ GROUP B, RALLYING AND THE 205 T16

'That event meant so much for Peugeot. For me the main thing was I [was] back in life. I was living again.' ARI VATANEN.

AS: How do you reflect on that period now? How would you sum up that period, or your time with the 205?
AV: Fondly. It was a special period. I am very privileged. But I mean success would not have done it. Success would have made me more blinkered. It was probably the best period in my life, with Rita standing by me. She learnt of my accident from television. From a smiling lady on a news programme. Of course they didn't realize how badly I was injured. And then eighteen months later I was competing again. For me, it was physical and mental pain, but for Rita, I can't imagine what that anxiety must have been like. I was so sick, I was screaming at her. In '85 I remember screaming at her, 'Why

124

GROUP B, RALLYING AND THE 205 T16

have you bought Christmas presents? We are all dying!' Can you imagine, she had to live like that? And then on the prologue for Paris–Dakar Shekhar Mehta, who started before me, came in after me. They were saying 'Ah, again Vatanen has gone off the road!' She must have been thinking 'This is not true' but I drove so slowly, because I knew how long Paris–Dakar is. I got overtaken by Mehta, and then my front wheel collapsed! The ball joint was missing a circlip. The whole thing collapsed. I couldn't turn right! People were on the opposite side of the car trying to balance me and help me round. I lost so much time. I was 278th or something. Rita was there thinking, 'No. This is not true.' They found several ball joints with no circlip. I said to Jean [Todt], 'Jean, this time, please believe me, this time it was not my fault!'

To go from so close to death to then come back and lose so many minutes on Paris–Dakar, it was unbelievable. We had more than our fair share of drama! It's the setbacks in life that weld you together.

AS: How do you feel about your son, Max, rallying?
AV: I bought him an Opel Rekord Estate in the nineties, it was there waiting for him, but he was never interested. A few years ago when he got his licence, we were sat in the sauna. It's a very Finnish thing, you can speak openly, there's nothing to hide behind. Suddenly Max says out of the blue, 'Dad do you think it's too late for me?' It brought tears to my eyes. Had we lived in Finland it might have been easier, but it's taken a little while. He has dreams, obviously, life is about dreams, but dreams by definition are unreasonable – but they have to be. It's a long shot to turn it into a professional career, it's far more difficult and expensive these days to become a professional driver, there are so few places these days and he has started so late, but if your kid starts rallying it's extremely expensive, it involves friends, family, extended family, it's a massive undertaking. It's very intense. And of course there's the worry and anxiety when you're at the end of the stage waiting for your son to come through. It's like what Rita went through. She thought it was all over, she thought 'That's it, it's over for our family' and now Max is out there doing it. But, *c'est la vie*. That's life – you can't divert someone from their path in life. But we will see, to be in it should be enough. Very few can be the next Loeb, or Vatanen. There are few places and thousands trying. But you are doing something purposeful, you are chasing your passion. When your heart and mind is in it, it's all encompassing. It's not just about winning. You're investing everything you have and more into it. You're not just ticking over in life, you live flat-out.

Results are only numbers at the end.

'It's not just about winning. You're investing everything you have and more into it. You're not just ticking over in life, you live flat-out. Results are only numbers at the end.'

CHAPTER SEVEN

SPECIALS AND VARIANTS: FROM COMMERCIALS TO THE CTI

One of the strongest indicators of a model's success is its ability to spawn variants and expand into other, broader market segments. The 205 did just that, being offered not only in three- and five-door varieties but also as a convertible and in two commercial variants.

WORKING FOR A LIVING

Peugeot had long offered commercial variants of its cars. Cars such as the 305 Estate were easily repurposed for commercial service and right into the 1980s Peugeot continued to produce a full range of light commercials that included the 305 van and 504 pick-up. Small vans continued to be popular, particularly in urban areas, and the likes of Austin Rover had found a van version of its Metro quite successful, as had Ford with their Fiesta van.

From 1985, Peugeot began offering a van based on the three-door 205. It was known as the 205 Service in mainland Europe, but in Britain it was simply the 205 van. The conversion saw the rear window replaced by steelwork, while the rear seats gave way to create a useful load bay, offering 1.2

The 205 Service was the first attempt at a 205 for the light commercial market.

SPECIALS AND VARIANTS: FROM COMMERCIALS TO THE CTI

Thanks to a reworked and extended fibreglass rear, the XA gained improved load capacity.

The Fourgonette, or 205F, did away with much of the 205's bodywork to create a much more useful van.

cubic metres of space, while being able to carry up to 340kg (750lb) of goods.

Keeping things simple, the 205 van was offered with just two trim levels, Standard or GL, and a simple engine choice, either a 1124cc petrol unit or a 1769cc diesel. The standard van used a four-speed gearbox, with the petrol version developing 50bhp. The GL gained a fifth gear, more comfortable, car-like cloth trim and a wash/wipe function for the rear screen. Despite its simplicity, by 1993 it was being offered in seven different colours, four of which were metallic.

In Europe, the situation was a little different. In 1986 the 205 XA launched. Built by French coachbuilders Durisotti and later Gruau, the XA was based on a three-door but with a raised fibreglass body section grafted on to the rear. It got a larger tailgate as well, which gave improved access to the load bay. Gruau's version was named the VU, and the firm would go on to offer a version that retained the rear seat. In 1991, when the 205 range was face-lifted, the XA was refreshed too. It became the 205 XA Multi and was offered with a 1.1, 1.7 or 1.9 engine.

The XA was joined by the 205 Fourgonette in 1990. The Fourgonette, or 205F as it became known, was based on the five-door and was a more complete van conversion, ditching much of the original 205 bodywork. Intended to replace the Multi, the F was larger than the coach-built vans and shared a chassis and a vast number of components with the Citroën C15 van. Engine choice was the same as that of the 205 van, with either a 1.1-litre petrol or 1.8-litre diesel offered. Both commercials remained available alongside one another until the Multi was discontinued in 1993. The 205F would last until 1997 when it was replaced by the Peugeot Partner and Citroën Berlingo.

Gruau also developed a prototype pick-up version of the 205, based on a GTI. This particular 205, however, never saw production.

A MORE PRACTICAL PEUGEOT

One variant that could have added further sales to the 205's already impressive sales figures was an estate. Peugeot had a fine reputation for producing estate cars and at the 1984 Turin Motorshow the company's long-time partner, Pininfarina, showcased the Verve, an estate concept based on the five-door 205. Riding on standard GTI alloys and finished in silver, the roofline was raised by around 40mm (1.5in) while the tailgate glass was set flush to the side windows. Inside, the Verve featured tan leather trim and, in the back, a roof-mounted refrigerated storage box. This was a neat feature for a show car, but the cost of such an item in the mid-1980s would quite likely have been prohibitive for a mainstream production vehicle. The motoring press at the time seemed confident that the car would see production but Peugeot chose not to pursue the development of the 205 Verve.

■ SPECIALS AND VARIANTS: FROM COMMERCIALS TO THE CTI

Pininfarina's 205 Estate, named the Verve, was created in 1984 but it did not lead to a production version. PININFARINA

Another 205 estate surfaced in 1988, this time christened the 205 Nepala. It took a rather different approach to the process of converting hatchback to estate. Shown in Brussels, it featured a separate fibreglass section, incorporating a revised tailgate and windows as well as a new back bumper, grafted onto the rear. Only one Nepala is thought to have been built and it is believed to still exist in Belgium.

Alhough the 205 never did gain an estate variant, Peugeot clearly felt the idea had merits. Every 2-series car since the 205 has been offered as an estate.

DROP THE TOP

By far the most popular and successful variant of the 205 has to be the convertible. Peugeot had a long legacy of producing open-top variants of its cars. The company had developed the first car in the world with a retractable hard-top, the 1934 402 Decapotable. In 1969 they worked with Pininfarina to create the 504 convertible, but it was the Peugeot-Talbot union that brought a small convertible back into the company's range with the Samba Cabriolet, launched in 1982.

To develop the rag-top 205, Peugeot once again collaborated with Italian styling house Pininfarina, who undertook the design work required to create the convertible. Starting in 1983, the Italian company strengthened the 205's shell by adding two cross members, one at the front seats and one at the fuel tank. The shell also gained thicker, wider sills; a thicker, steel-tubed windscreen frame; and a brace bar across the middle of the cabin, which helped maintain the car's structural rigidity, carried the car's seat-belt mounts and offered protection in the event of an accident. Neat quarter-light windows were added to the frameless doors for extra strength, the rear passengers were offered wind-up windows, and the hood's rear window was made of plastic rather than glass. The car retained a large chunk of the

SPECIALS AND VARIANTS: FROM COMMERCIALS TO THE CTI

This cutaway shows how the 205 was strengthened in order to lose its roof.

hatch's practicality, too. Alhough the hood made the boot shallower, its depth and width remained the same as that of the closed car.

The extra metalwork needed to strengthen the car meant it tipped the scales at almost 90kg (200lb) more than the equivalent hatch. The company worked quickly and by late 1985 the first cars were ready, with the all-new convertibles proudly wearing the Pininfarina signature on their hindquarters. To produce the convertible, common components from the hatchback were shipped to Italy where the bodies were built up on a robotic assembly line capable of producing fifty CTI shells a day. Once painted and fully trimmed, the CTIs were returned to Peugeot's Sochaux and Mulhouse plants to be fitted with their mechanical and suspension components.

As a cabriolet the 205 remained a pretty little car, with its frameless doors and neatly stowed hood. Peugeot stated that the 205 CTI offered 'exhilarating performance in true sports car style'. It was no doubt helped by the fact that it looked so similar to the GTI, with the same 14in alloy wheels, chunky halogen driving lamps and distinctive red stripe running around the car. Mechanically, the CTI remained identical to the GTI, with the same 1580cc power unit developing 115bhp and 98lb ft of torque. The CTI's suspension, however, took a lead from the lower-powered versions. The GTI's lower wishbones were replaced with track control arms and a rear-facing anti-roll bar. The spring rates and damper settings were also focused more towards comfort, while softer suspension mountings were also employed. These changes helped to reduce any sensation of body flex without damping down the 205's drivability. The ventilated disc brake set-up remained identical to that of the GTI.

The convertible's UK launch took place in Wales in June 1986. Customers in France were offered two versions, the CTI or the less powerful CT, but in Britain the CTI was,

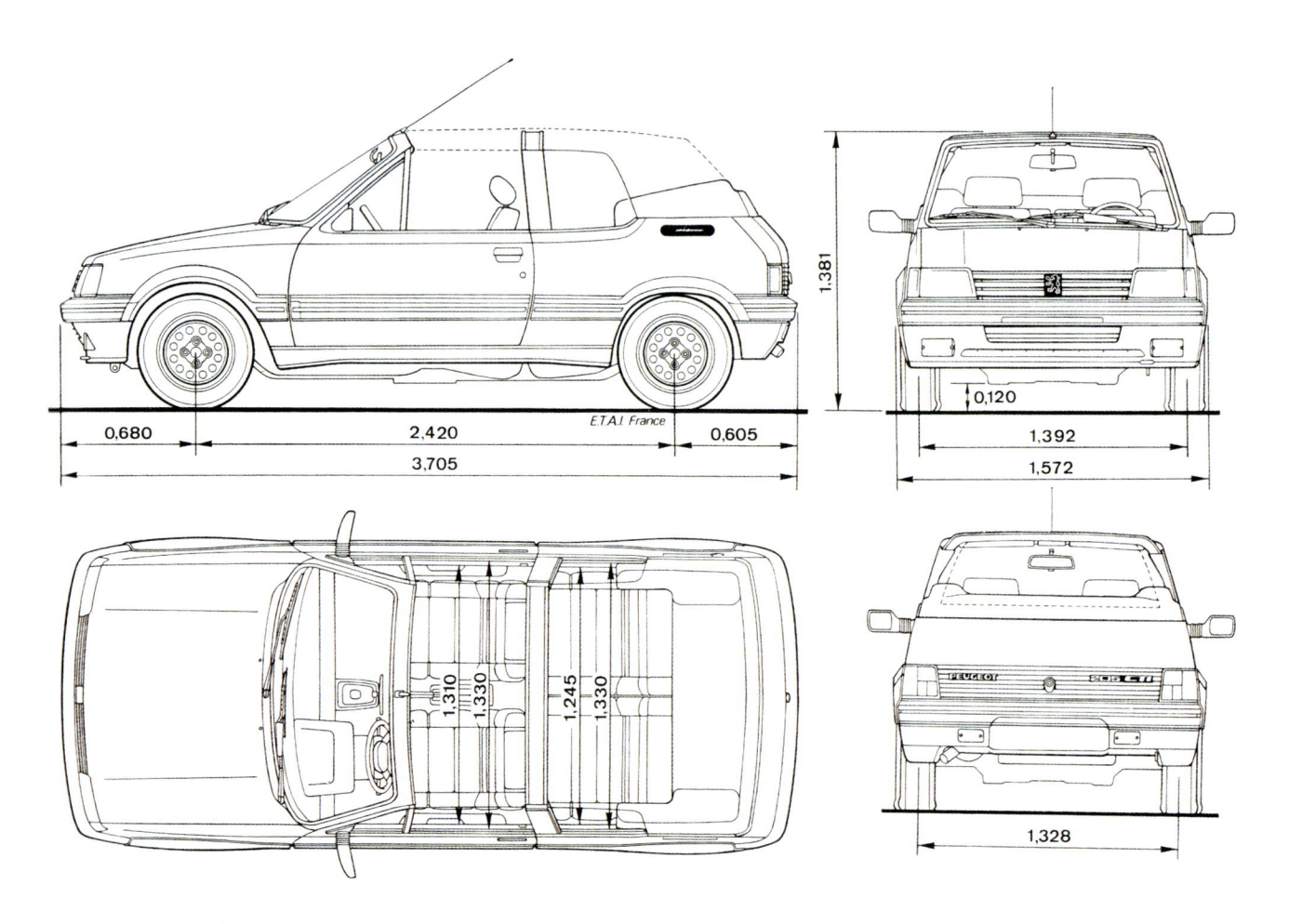

■ SPECIALS AND VARIANTS: FROM COMMERCIALS TO THE CTI

Conversion from fixed-head to drop-top was handled by Pininfarina, who completed the task with aplomb.

PEUGEOT 205 CTI, CJ AND ROLAND GARROS

Production: 1989–94
Body style: Convertible

Designed by Pininfarina and part produced at their Italian factory, the convertible 205s brought the car to a whole host of new customers.

SPECIALS AND VARIANTS: FROM COMMERCIALS TO THE CTI

RIGHT: **The 205 CTI arrived in Britain in 1986 and was met with a warm response, notably because of its similarity to the GTI.**

BELOW: **Peugeot made sure that the new convertible was available to as many customers as possible, so in 1988 they launched a budget version, the CJ, or Cabriolet Junior.**

131

■ SPECIALS AND VARIANTS: FROM COMMERCIALS TO THE CTI

CTI advertising played heavily on the aspirational aspect of the cabriolet.

initially at least, the only convertible 205 offered. It cost £9,495, which represented a significant £2,000 premium on the equivalent GTI, putting it squarely up against its rivals from Ford and Volkswagen. Road testers of the day were largely positive about the CTI, praising the car for its similarities to the fixed-roof version.

As with the standard hatchback, Peugeot was keen to offer the convertible in as broad a range as possible. As part of the company's revision of the entire 205 range, a lower-power model – the CJ, short for 'Cabriolet Junior' – was added in 1988. Power came from a carburettor-fed 1360cc TU engine, as found in Citroën's AX. To cope with the extra weight of the cabriolet body, Peugeot tuned the 1.4 unit to develop more torque, meaning it developed 65bhp and 83lb ft of torque. Despite the extra weight, the CJ was still capable of 100mph (160km/h), while remaining surprisingly economical, attaining almost 40mpg (7ltr/100km).

At £8,835 the CJ was Britain's lowest-priced convertible, coming in almost £2,000 below the cheapest Escort cabriolet. Aimed at younger buyers, the CJ was, thanks to its smaller engine, cheaper to insure than the CTI and came with unique, denim-styled seat trim. *Autocar* tested the CJ in October 1988 and declared: 'Modern four-seater, open-top fun comes no cheaper. We like it.'

A third version of the convertible arrived in 1989. The Roland Garros featured a distinctive white hood and dark

The 205 Electrique was the result of a programme that began back in 1978.

SPECIALS AND VARIANTS: FROM COMMERCIALS TO THE CTI

green paintwork and used an 85bhp version of the 1.4 engine. Only 150 right-hand-drive versions were made available to the UK market, making it highly sought after.

Coming later in the lifespan of the 205, the convertibles did not receive as many revisions as the hatchbacks, but in 1991 the 1.6 CTI was dropped as the engine was phased out, meaning that the CTI would now be offered only as a 1.9. That year also saw the CJ being revised, with a catalytic converter now becoming standard. The engine was therefore reworked with an increase in power to 75bhp.

PLUG IT IN

In 1984 Peugeot unveiled the 205 Electrique, a battery-powered concept vehicle used to showcase PSA's continuing research into battery-powered vehicles. The car was fully automatic, had a top speed of 62mph (100km/h) and could cover 87 miles (140km) between charges. The car took ten hours to achieve a full charge, with an operational life of almost 125,000 miles (200,000km).

The vehicle was developed by PSA's Department of Research and Scientific Affairs in conjunction with the French battery company SAFT, a division of the GEC group, with part-funding from French government agencies. The research programme began in 1978 with tests on batteries and by 1981 had advanced to electric propulsion systems.

The 205 was chosen as the most appropriate host vehicle for the programme, partly because it had been designed from the outset to accept a broad range of engine options. The engine bay could be adapted for use with battery packs and an electric motor without any modification to the standard production shell, meaning that the passenger compartment and luggage space remained unaffected by the new, electric layout.

The programme made significant strides in realizing the concept of a truly practical electric vehicle, none more so

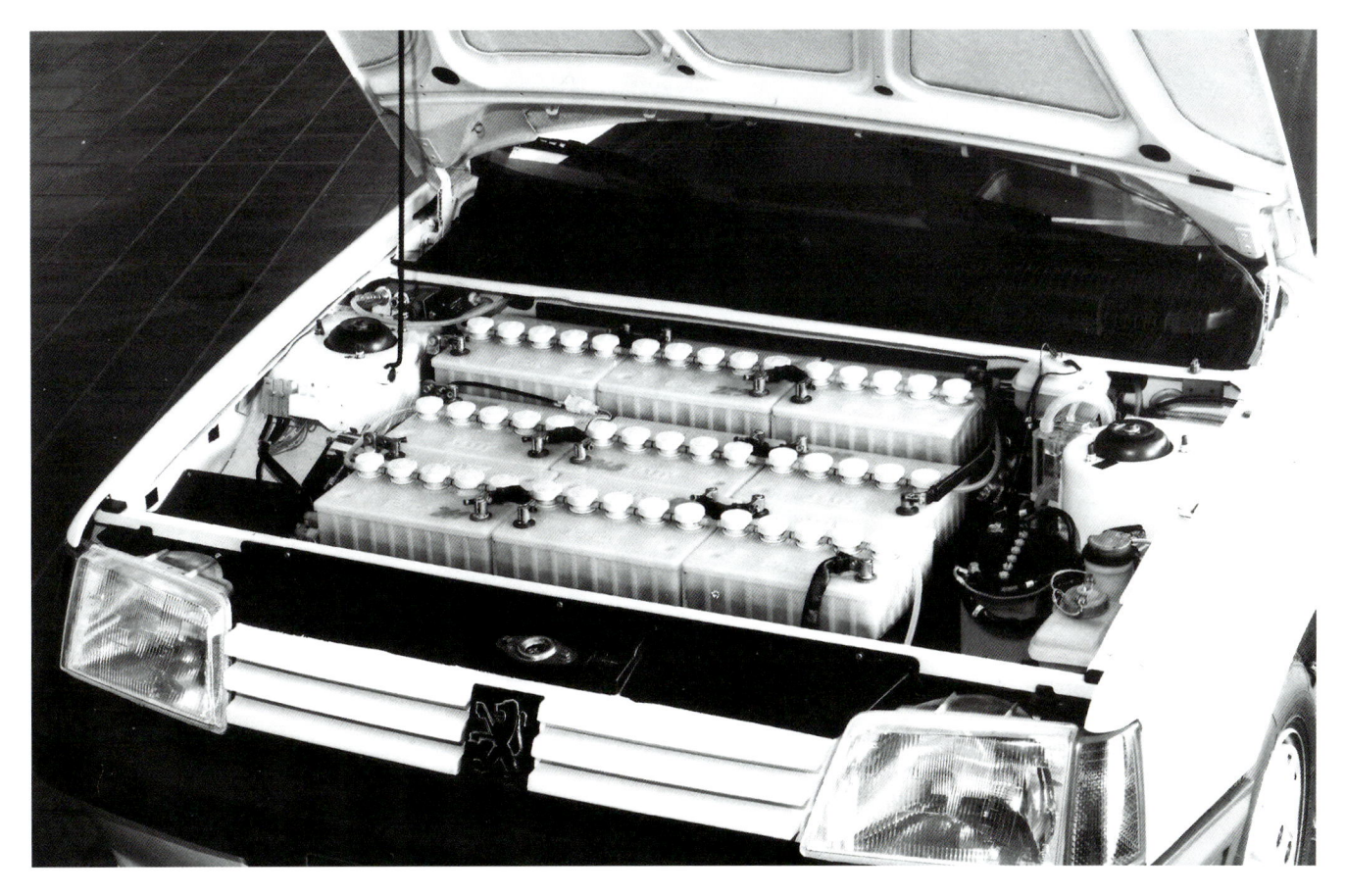

The internal-combustion engine made way for a bank of batteries to power the Electrique.

■ SPECIALS AND VARIANTS: FROM COMMERCIALS TO THE CTI

This design drawing shows how the Electrique's battery pack retained the standard 205's spacious interior.

than in the introduction of the nickel-iron battery. Developed by Peugeot and SAFT over a period of five years, the new battery was able to store twice as much power as a conventional lead battery of the same shape and size. Also, it boasted a life-span of at least 1,500 cycles, allowing Peugeot to accurately calculate the car's operational life.

In 1983 PSA and SAFT produced a five-cell unit, which they then set about testing in the 205 and the Talbot Express van. Peugeot's Electric Vehicle Research Unit was formed to evaluate the characteristics of the car and its batteries. The research team set about testing the battery pack's energy capacity, the power rating and how long the battery pack would be able to maintain these characteristics.

To this end, the team performed endurance testing, using robots to continually charge and discharge the battery packs over a twenty-four-hour period. The team also carried out simulated road testing during typical urban driving. They also discharged the battery at constant output, allowing them to determine the 205's electricity consumption. The tests were conducted at various temperatures, allowing the team to simulate a variety of environments the car might encounter.

Following successful laboratory testing, the Electric 205 began road testing. It retained identical dimensions to the traditional internal combustion version, with controls designed to be familiar to any normal driver.

The motor's electrical drain was controlled by two 'choppers'. One for the bottom third of the power range, the other kicking in when more power was needed. The system was also capable of recovering energy when braking and was equipped with a variety of fuses and trip switches to isolate and shut down the system in the event of an accident.

In total, the Electric 205 featured twelve, 6v battery modules, weighing 300kg (660lb), while the car charged via a standard power socket.

Driving the electric 205 was simplicity itself. A press of the accelerator got the car underway, lifting your foot from the pedal created engine braking, while pressing the brake pedal added further stopping power. While braking, the 205 gathered the kinetic energy and returned it to the battery. Putting it in reverse was achieved by simply flicking a switch on the dashboard as an electric vehicle did not have a conventional gearbox.

SPECIALS AND VARIANTS: FROM COMMERCIALS TO THE CTI

ABOVE: **The Electrique's interior showed little evidence of change, bar the unique steering wheel and bespoke instruments.**

RIGHT: **A close-up detail of the Electrique's instrument pack – note the original steering wheel has been replaced by a CTI item.**

135

■ SPECIALS AND VARIANTS: FROM COMMERCIALS TO THE CTI

Almost thirty years on, Peugeot's research continues with vehicles such as the 208 Hybrid FE.

Though it did not lead to a production version, the research proved that a genuine, modern, small passenger car could successfully be converted to a zero-emission vehicle. Peugeot's work and research foreshadowed the arrival of cars like the Nissan Leaf and the general direction of the car industry as a whole by almost thirty years.

Today, Peugeot is working hard in the area of alternative fuel and offers a range of hybrid vehicles. In August 2013 Peugeot unveiled the 208 Hybrid FE which combines a 1.2-litre, 68bhp petrol engine alongside a battery pack located under the back seat. It features a customized front bumper and grille, aiding a 25 per cent improvement in the FE's drag co-efficient, and is 20 per cent lighter than a standard 208.

The result is a car that emits 49g/km of CO_2 without any drawbacks on drivability.

Like the 205 Electrique, the Hybrid FE remains purely a concept, with no plans to put the car into production.

LIMITED EDITIONS

The 1980s saw many new ideas in motoring, one of the most popular, and broadly adopted, being the 'special edition'. The quality of these varied wildly. Some were simply normal cars with the addition of a few stickers, while others gained bespoke interiors, alloy wheels and other attractive

SPECIALS AND VARIANTS: FROM COMMERCIALS TO THE CTI

The first of a long line of special editions, the Lacoste, appeared in January 1985.

Changes to the XR were quite minimal, but included the colour coding of the bumpers, rear tailgate panel and wing mirrors to match the white body, alongside standard XR wheel trims, again in white. This was broken up by contrasting black piping trim on the body and bumper inserts, which was copied on the wing mirrors. The finishing detail was the inclusion of the brand's iconic crocodile logo applied to the front wings and boot lid. And, like the GTI, the Lacoste boasted a sunroof. The interior gained unique seat upholstery and door trims, as well as green carpets. It also boasted electric windows and central locking.

The Lacoste proved popular and in May 1986 was followed by the Lacoste All White. Like many other manufacturers in the 1980s, Peugeot discovered that for relatively little outlay they could provide customers with what was seen as a 'new' model. Buyers felt they were getting something different, bespoke almost, meaning their 205 stood out against their neighbour's. The Lacoste played well to the fashion-conscious 205 buyer, while delivering extra value thanks to the improved specification.

extras. Like many manufacturers, Peugeot offered a variety of 205 limited editions.

205 Lacoste

The first special 205 was the Lacoste, which arrived in January 1985. The 205 had been marketed as a chic, fashionable supermini so the use of the French fashion label made perfect sense. The car was based on a white 1124cc three-door XR, though for the UK market the Lacoste was fitted with the larger 1.4-litre petrol engine.

205 Junior

More specials followed in the Lacoste's wake, some more memorable than others. Some were simply intended to brighten an otherwise plain car, while others were aimed at a specific target market. The Junior, launched in 1986, was just such a car. Offered with little more than a set of stick-on 'Junior' logos and a 954cc petrol engine with a four-speed gearbox, the three-door Junior proved to be the ideal

Arriving in 1986, the Junior combined the basic 954cc engine and four-speed gearbox with the plusher interior from the 205 GR.

137

■ SPECIALS AND VARIANTS: FROM COMMERCIALS TO THE CTI

choice for those looking for a no-frills second car, or a car for younger drivers, where the XE was deemed too plain.

Customers responded well. In 1987 the Junior was joined by a five-door version and by February 1988 the limited edition had become a fully fledged member of the Peugeot range and would be offered for four years. Finished in either silver or white, it gained full-width wheel trims, exterior stripes and unique seat covers.

The Junior would be followed by the three- and five-door, 1.1-litre Junior Special, while in June 1992 the Junior itself would return as both a petrol and a diesel.

205 Roland Garros

Perhaps the next best-known 205 special was the Roland Garros. It arrived in June 1989 as a 1.4-litre, three-door hatchback. It took its name from the venue of the French Tennis Open and came in a model-unique Pinewood Green metallic finish, complete with body-coloured bumpers and alloy wheels. Unlike the Junior, the Roland Garros was intended to feel upmarket, almost luxurious.

The Garros featured GTI-style seats, uniquely trimmed with cream leather, electric windows and a sunroof. A year later it was joined by a convertible version. The cabriolet was finished in the same shade of green, with the rag-top finished in a contrasting white, neatly matching the interior theme. The Garros's convertible hood was also electrically operated. Both the hatchback and cabriolet proved to be good sellers and the Roland Garros name would later feature on other Peugeot models such as the 106 and 206.

205 1FM

In October 1992, almost ten years after its launch, Peugeot unveiled the 205 1FM. Twenty-five 1FMs were built to celebrate the twenty-fifth anniversary of the BBC radio station. The cars were used to raise money for the London-based Nordoff-Robbins Trust, a charity that uses music as therapy for children with disabilities. Peugeot hoped the sale of these exclusive cars would raise £100,000 for the charity. Priced at £17,000, many were sold to figures within the music industry and one was given away live on air.

Finished in black and uniquely numbered, the 1FM was marked out with '205 1FM' decals on its doors and badges on

The Roland Garros was a much more upmarket special with unique seats and carpets.

138

SPECIALS AND VARIANTS: FROM COMMERCIALS TO THE CTI

The IFM was based on the GTI, but with a plethora of additions.

its tailgate and 'tinted' alloy wheels. Mechanically, it remained identical to the more commonplace 205 GTI. It was, however, loaded with extras. Inside it boasted air conditioning, full leather trim, unique 'IFM' floor mats, electric windows and sunroof, immobilizer, and remote central locking.

Peugeot secured the services of then-Radio I DJ Simon Bates to promote the IFM, hosting a live broadcast from Peugeot's stand at the National Motor Show and the Ryton plant on the show's press day. With its links to Radio 1, it is perhaps unsurprising that the IFM also featured a much improved entertainment system. Peugeot claimed that the Clarion stereo fitted to the IFM had been 'specifically designed for this limited edition'. For the early 1990s, the specification was impressive, boasting a remote-control CD tuner, a six-disc changer in the boot and additional speakers fitted to an 'acoustic rear parcel shelf'.

Today, fifteen still exist, while six of these ultra-rare 205s have sadly been consigned to the history books.

Gentry and Griffe

The IFM was not the only 205 GTI to receive special-edition treatment. Following Peugeot's face-lift at the end of the 1980s, new colours were added to the 205 range in shades of Miami Blue and Sorrento Green. Just over 1,000 GTIs received the new paint – they also boasted power steering and full leather trim. A pair of limited editions were also released, the Griffe and the Gentry.

To some, the Gentry was not technically a GTI special since it lacked the GTI's front wishbone suspension, instead employing the track control arm set-up found on the regular 205. Power came from a 1.9 engine developing 105bhp (down on the 1.9 GTI's 122bhp) and was mated to an automatic gearbox. Inside, a full-leather interior with wood trim created a sense of opulence, while the specification also included power steering, anti-lock brakes and heated wing mirrors. The 300 Gentry that were built were offered in Aztec Gold and Sorrento Green. They featured unique

■ SPECIALS AND VARIANTS: FROM COMMERCIALS TO THE CTI

The Gentry's blend of GTI and automatic transmission added a sense of luxury to the 205 range, with power steering, leather interior and unique alloy wheels.

SPECIALS AND VARIANTS: FROM COMMERCIALS TO THE CTI

The Griffe wore similar alloy wheels to the GTI IFM and was finished in Laser Green.

In Britain the 205 Rallye was little more than a sticker special, but in Europe it was much more.

alloys and used the same wheel-arch mouldings as the GTI, leading to the belief by many that the Gentry was GTI-based.

Unlike the Gentry, the Griffe used the same suspension as the GTI and was first shown in 1990.

Around 3,000 Laser Green Griffes were built and it featured the same black and polished rim alloys that would later be seen on the UK-market IFM in 1992. This fully loaded model failed to see the light of day in Britain, but did prove popular in mainland Europe. Like the Gentry, the Griffe boasted every dealer option offered at the time, highlights including full-leather interior, power steering and a sunroof, while the GTI's red carpets were replaced by black ones – the only box not ticked on the options list was air conditioning.

141

■ SPECIALS AND VARIANTS: FROM COMMERCIALS TO THE CTI

The European Rallye's brakes and suspension were borrowed from the GTI, while the twin-carb, 1294cc engine developed 103bhp.

205 GTI Automatic

The GTI Automatic arrived in Britain in 1992. The car was never intended as a special edition, having originally been produced for the Japanese market. However, the Japanese order was cancelled, leaving Peugeot with several hundred right-hand-drive automatics. Since Britain was the 205's biggest right-hand-drive market it made sense for them to be sold in the UK.

The Automatic combined the 105bhp version of the 1.9 engine used on the Gentry with the braking set-up, smaller alloys and cloth seats of the 1.6. As befitting its intended Japanese market, it was fitted with air conditioning.

205 Rallye

Another special edition to arrive in Britain in 1992 was the 205 Rallye. As the name suggests, it played up to the 205's successes in the World Rally Championship but, for UK buyers, it boasted little sporting pedigree other than the wearing of the legendary Peugeot Talbot Sport colours. The Rallye marketed in Britain was, in truth, little more than a sticker-special. Its European namesake had considerably more appeal.

The European Rallye was a car created for motor-sport homologation and actually arrived four years before the British car. Buyers in Europe were offered a car that developed 103bhp from a 1294cc engine, fed by twin carburettors. Other components, such as the brakes and suspension, were based on the GTI. Peugeot kept the interior simple, with wind-up windows and basically trimmed seats. It found favour with privateer rally drivers, particularly those taking their first steps into competition.

By the time the Rallye arrived in Britain it was offered

Although the interior had hints of GTI it was kept simple with wind-up windows and plain seats.

in both yellow and white, neatly mimicking the WRC and Paris–Dakar winning cars, but it was a pale imitation of the continental car. By the end of 1992 the Rallye was no more, either in Europe or Britain. The next time the name 'Rallye' appeared on a Peugeot, the 106 in 1993, British customers would get the same deal as their European counterparts.

In its lifetime over thirty different limited-edition versions of the 205 would be sold, from the likes of the 'Trio' to the 'Zest' and the 'Look'. Naturally some would be more memorable than others, yet each – in its own way – would add to the car's legend.

LIMITED EDITIONS – THE PEUGEOT PERSPECTIVE

I recall one of the cheapest special editions we ever did was the 205 Junior. This was basically a base model three-door with the 1-litre engine, white paint, some nice pink and green body graphics, full-size wheel trims and denim upholstery. It sold very well. Later I think it was available in yellow but this was not a good colour combination. We also had the Roland Garros, a very fancy car in green metallic. I think it was based on the 205GT and it did very well in the French market, but was popular in the UK too. We also tried to sell the GTI with a 10bhp power hike, but this was a tough sell as it really did not feel any faster than the standard car. In any case, when the 1.9 engine came out, it was rendered irrelevant.

John Evans, Public Relations Manager, Peugeot UK, 1982–87

Plenty more limited-edition 205s would follow before the car's end of production, some of which would also be applied to the 309, such as the 'Look'. COVENTRY TRANSPORT MUSEUM

CHAPTER EIGHT

BUYING, MAINTAINING AND MODIFYING THE PEUGEOT 205

It might be over thirty years since the first Peugeot 205 hit the road but, rather than grow tired, time has allowed the baby Peugeot to mature – to become an icon and a true classic car.

The journey to classic status has been an interesting one for the Peugeot. It was arguably one of the most popular cars of the 1980s but that popularity was to be a double-edged sword. As discussed elsewhere, there were more than a few people willing to help themselves when they couldn't afford a car of their own. This did little to help the hot-hatch and performance market and, unsurprisingly, insurance costs rocketed. Thankfully manufacturers caught on and the proliferation of alarm systems and immobilizers, both as standard and in the accessory market, did much to curb the 1990s craze of joyriding.

The 205 would also have to contend with becoming the darling of the boy racer. It was perhaps inevitable that the 205 – particularly the GTI, but also the likes of the Rallye – would be snapped up when it moved into the second-hand market. After all, Peugeot had worked hard to promote the car's desirability, so it was hardly surprising that those who could not afford a 205 when new took the opportunity to experience one as a second-hand car.

205s are fast becoming a common sight at classic car shows.
AUTHOR

BUYING, MAINTAINING AND MODIFYING THE PEUGEOT 205

Despite its growing classic status, the 205 remains a popular choice for modifications. AUTHOR

VICKI'S VIEW – THE PEUGEOT 205 AND CAR CULTURE OF THE 1990s

Vicki Butler-Henderson is today well known as a former *Top Gear* presenter and one of the stars of the Discovery Channel's *Fifth Gear*. One of the founding steps in her journalism career was with the iconic modified-car magazine, *Max Power*.

I was Staff Writer on Max Power for its first year, as well as working on research and the dummy issue for six months before the first issue actually went on sale. I'd worked on the magazine for six months before the launch, in a room together with the Editor, Graham Steed. Max Power reflected what was on the street – the pages were packed with bright coloured cars, great body kits, dazzling alloys and filled with passion. The writers and the readers we featured lived and breathed their cars. Each car was unique whether you spent £50 on an air filter or £15,000 on a total modification. There were tips for all budgets and all levels of DIY enthusiasm. Car manufacturers started to make small cars, which lent themselves brilliantly to tweaking. And as these cars came onto the second-hand market, the Max Power brigade lapped them up. The 205 was an amazing, desirable car that remains one of my favourite hot hatches – especially the 1.9 GTI. There was a simple structure to the car world back then – small, medium and large cars. We didn't have people carriers, SUVs, 4x4s, super-saloons etc. The 205 was one of the best looking small cars you could buy. My father had a 1.6 GTI and the two GTIs were the halo versions of the model and they really did radiate greatness to the whole range. I just remember it being incredibly exciting every day, and the big discussions we had with the grown-ups (publishers) about putting MAX POWER in gold letters on the launch issue and which car was going to be on the cover. I am incredibly proud of being part of it. I have such fond memories and I hope everyone who appeared in it, and read it – especially in the first year when I was Staff Writer there (I subsequently left to become a Road Tester on another mag) – are doing well!

■ BUYING, MAINTAINING AND MODIFYING THE PEUGEOT 205

The 205's broad range means that there is plenty of choice when shopping for one. GERARD HUGHES

Big wheels, body kits and loud exhausts quickly became the order of the day. Magazines like *Max Power* were read by hundreds of thousands of car fans across the country and the magazine gained an almost cult following. The 205 was right at the heart of that scene.

The 205 successfully survived those awkward years and has now become an accepted retro classic, with all the specialist and club support one might expect of such a car. Its 2-series successors may have sold in greater numbers but the 205 enjoyed a particular affection that ensured that plenty of examples were cared for and treasured.

Owning a 205 today still makes lots of sense. The little Peugeot is relatively modern, surprisingly spacious and, in the case of the hatchback, remarkably practical. The lines of the 205 have only improved with age. While some of its contemporaries look dated, the Peugeot has managed to remain as good-looking as ever. It is a truly evergreen car.

The 205's popularity in its heyday means that they are plentiful today and finding a good one should not prove difficult. With a range that includes three- and five-door models and a cabriolet, there is an abundance of choice. The first step is to identify which particular car you want. Many will instantly reply 'GTI', which is understandable as it is arguably the most popular model. However, the other variants should not be discounted – even the most basic 205 can be great fun.

One of the 205's great strengths is its variety. With six petrol engines (including the T16) and one diesel there is something to suit a range of budgets. Another advantage to 205 ownership is its age. Given that even the youngest 205 is almost twenty years old, the vast majority now qualify for classic car insurance. Whether you opt for a 954cc base model, a 1.9 GTI or a Roland Garros, the 205 has an awful lot to offer.

Unlike many of its contemporaries the 205 has remained popular, especially models like the GTI and CTI, so even today 205s remain a common sight on the roads. The GTI's popularity has served as something of a double-edged sword. While some have been pampered and well cared for, many others have dents and dings caused by accidents. However, that popularity means that the 205 continues to be well served with regard to wheels, body kits and performance

BUYING, MAINTAINING AND MODIFYING THE PEUGEOT 205

modifications. While some 205s have arguably suffered at the hands of amateur modifiers, thankfully even the most ham-fisted attempt at improving the 205 can be reversed.

Whether you are looking for a completely original production model or one that has been modified there are plenty of 205s to choose from.

PICKING YOUR PERFECT PEUGEOT

Whatever your budget, chances are there is a 205 for you. While the very best GTIs are now reaching in excess of £7,000, a well cared for, lower spec model can be had for as little as £700. Whichever you go for, spares are plentiful and generally inexpensive.

There are also plenty of reasons to consider a 205 as a project car. A 205 in poor or unroadworthy condition can be had for very little money. Equally important, the 205 is DIY-friendly. Items such as front wings are bolted on, and the entire car can be stripped down with the minimum of tools. The 205 was intended to be cheap and simple to service, something that continues to pay dividends today. The 205 makes for an ideal learning car for those taking their first steps in repairs and modifications while those with more experience will find the 205 a rewarding car to maintain and modify.

Whether you opt for a GR or a GTI, the same basic checks apply.

Bodywork

A thorough check of the 205's bodywork is essential when considering any purchase and it is important to remain detached when viewing.

Check for rust in the sills, around the headlamps and the rear arches. It is also vitally important to look for signs of accident damage, especially on GTIs. Check the front end

Check wheel arches and sills for rust, and ensure the rear suspension sits as it should – it is susceptible to rear accident impact. AUTHOR

■ BUYING, MAINTAINING AND MODIFYING THE PEUGEOT 205

ABOVE: **Inspect metalwork around the headlamps and inner wings for rust. Take time to check the slam panel as well.** RICHARD GUNN

LEFT: **Look for damage to the rear including broken bumpers and poor panel fit. These could indicate the car has been spun off the road, or reversed into something.**
RICHARD GUNN

BUYING, MAINTAINING AND MODIFYING THE PEUGEOT 205

Badges can fade and suffer after years of polishing. Replacements are available. GERARD HUGHES

Rear bumpers can become brittle over time and can suffer badly from parking dings.

– items such as the bonnet slam panel and the front inner wings. While checking the inner wings, look for signs of rust. Spend some time checking the rear of the car – the 205's lightweight bodywork will betray any damage so check the car has not been hit from behind, reversed into anything or spun off into a ditch.

Peugeot's paintwork is generally of high quality. However, reds can suffer from sun bleaching and lacquer from metallic colours can become damaged. Make sure you view the car in good light and on a dry day. If the car is wet, take a chamois and dry the car thoroughly so that you get an accurate idea of the quality of the paintwork. Badges can fade over time –

149

■ BUYING, MAINTAINING AND MODIFYING THE PEUGEOT 205

The 205's interior is generally hard-wearing, though rattles and squeaks are to be expected. RICHARD GUNN

the 'chrome' effect applied to the Peugeot lion and the rear script badges can wear through.

Bumpers, too, can be fragile. It is not uncommon for the Peugeot's dark grey trim to become sun-bleached, turning lighter after years of exposure. Bumpers can also suffer from becoming brittle – as well as being at the mercy of years of car-park dings. Thankfully replacements are available.

Look at the panel gaps too, where the front of the door meets the back of the wing and where the wing meets the 'B' panel. The gaps should all be neat and even.

Interior

Like all cars of this vintage the interior plastics of a 205 can be somewhat fragile. The 205 was built to a budget and with even the youngest examples you should expect things to rattle and creak. Dashboard tops can split and crack after years of exposure to the sun. Seats, especially in the GTI, with their stronger, more supportive bolsters, can suffer badly from wear (replacement trim was available at the time but was prohibitively expensive).

Thankfully replacing these items is relatively simple and straightforward. The 205's lengthy production run means that the vast majority of interior parts are easily found and inexpensive to purchase. The GTI's red carpets can also suffer from sun damage and the pile can fray. It is a single-piece item and is simple to remove and renew.

If the 205 you are considering is fitted with a sunroof check that it opens and closes correctly. It is vacuum sealed – twisting the handle releases the air from a rubber tube allowing the roof to open.

Basic 205s are equipped with wind-up windows, headlights, a horn and little more. Over its lifetime the 205 gained options for electric windows, fog lamps, sunroofs

BUYING, MAINTAINING AND MODIFYING THE PEUGEOT 205

and even air conditioning. Check everything works as it should.

Under the Bonnet

The 205's simplicity makes it accessible to even the most inexperienced home mechanic. Smaller engines are fed by carburettor, and use a choke, while the GTI is fuel-injected.

However it is fuelled, the 205 should start easily. Be alert for masses of blue or white smoke, though some white smoke in lower temperatures is to be expected. If the car seems unhappy at idle investigate the condition of the distributor and other ignition components. Other causes of poor idling include air leaks, blockages, a worn throttle or possible a faulty airflow meter.

Most interior items are replaceable and inexpensive to purchase. RICHARD GUNN

Try each and every switch to ensure that all items work as they should. RICHARD GUNN

151

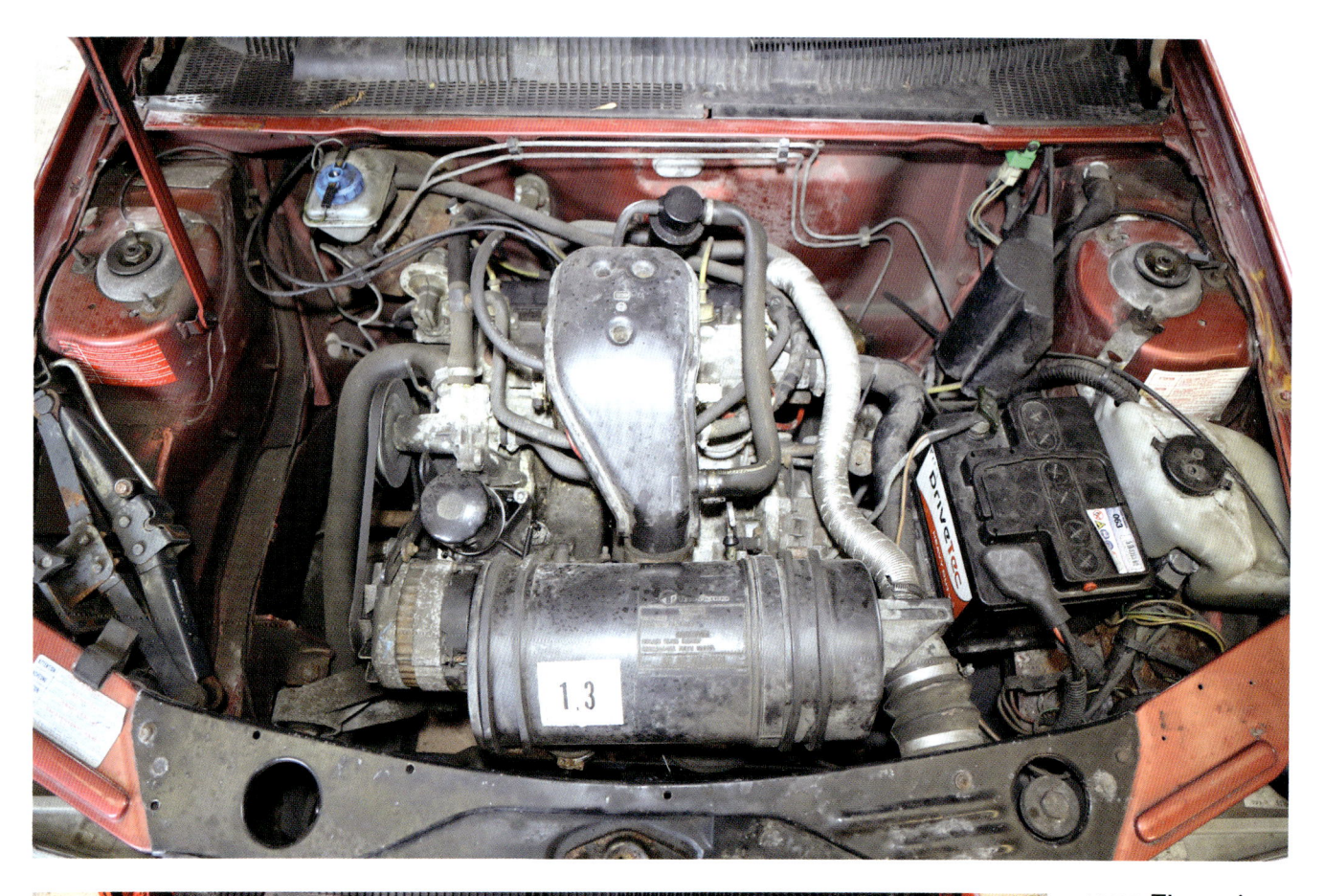

■ BUYING, MAINTAINING AND MODIFYING THE PEUGEOT 205

ABOVE: **The engine bay from this 1360cc GR shows how simple the engine compartment is.**
RICHARD GUNN

LEFT: **There are more components on a 1.6 GTI but basic maintainence remains straightforward.**
GERARD HUGHES

BUYING, MAINTAINING AND MODIFYING THE PEUGEOT 205

Diesel is also easy to understand, making it ideal for the home mechanic to maintain. GERARD HUGHES

For belt-driven models, like the GTI, the belt should be changed every 48,000 miles (77,000km) or 50,000 miles (80,000km) on the larger 1.9 GTI. Engine oil should be replaced every 5,000 miles (8,000km).

Gear linkages can wear out, resulting in a gear shift that feels sloppy. Again, replacements are inexpensive and widely available. If the clutch pedal feels stiff or awkward in action this suggests a worn clutch cable. Make sure that the gearbox and clutch operate smoothly and that the car can be put into each gear without issue.

On the Road

Simply put, driving any 205 should be great fun.

Even the most basic 954cc example is capable of being an enjoyable, engaging little car to drive. Through the bends the 205 should feel very direct and responsive. The GTI is fitted

The 205 GTI is all about raw driver appeal and it delivers it in spades.

153

■ BUYING, MAINTAINING AND MODIFYING THE PEUGEOT 205

A well-cared for 205 is capable of incredible mileages. This 205 has covered 338,000 miles – enough to travel to the moon and halfway back again.

with a quicker steering rack than other models so feels even sharper. The 205 is a wonderfully communicative car, with impressive levels of feedback offered by the chassis. Power steering was available on many models. Without power steering, the Peugeot – unsurprisingly – can feel heavy while manoeuvring, though non-assisted models should not be discounted.

The car should feel lively and keen to progress, particularly the sporting models – be wary of anything wearing a GTI badge that feels flat or lacking in urgency. Any noise from the front while turning would indicate wear in the constant velocity (CV) joints.

Brakes should be good and bring the car to a clean, controlled stop. Non-GTIs used 247mm, servo-assisted disc brakes with drums at the rear, while the 1.6 GTI used ventilated items. The 1.9 GTI improved things further still by adding rear discs.

The 205 is capable of achieving near astronomical mileage. In 2013 one 1990 Peugeot 205 notched up an incredible 338,000 miles (544,000km).

Finally, never forget the basics. Why is the car being sold? What service history does it have? Does the owner seem like someone who is enthusiastic about the car?

BUYING, MAINTAINING AND MODIFYING THE PEUGEOT 205

Peugeot Sport Club UK was born in the 1980s as the Peugeot GTI Club. Its formation was aided by Peugeot but today the club is independent of the manufacturer.

IN THE CLUB – THE PEUGEOT 205 AND CAR CULTURE

Like any popular car, the 205 quickly established its own community. The Peugeot Sport Club was formed in the 1980s as the Peugeot GTI Club. Originally it was run by Peugeot, before becoming independent in 1988.

The club's annual get-together, 'Pugfest', has been happening every summer since 1986, when a group of 205 fans met at Bruntingthorpe Proving Ground in Leicestershire. Peugeot clearly valued the club's members and provided indirect financial support to the club, allowing it to grow, and membership increased. Pugfest grew, too, and with support from Peugeot moved to Silverstone until 1995. The club began to fund the event themselves and since 2002 it has been held as a hill climb at Prescott Hill in Gloucestershire. Today the Peugeot Sport Club caters not just for the 205 GTI but for all sporting Peugeots launched since the 205.

Alternatively, there is Club Peugeot UK, which was founded in 1981 and caters for all Peugeots. The club attends a variety of events across the country each year as well as events in France and continental Europe. The highlight of their show season though is the Club Peugeot National Rally, which is held at a different venue each year.

MODIFYING YOUR 205

Since the very first GTI was launched owners have been seeking ways to improve the original Peugeot formula. Thanks to Peugeot's membership of the wider PSA Peugeot family, many parts from newer Peugeots and Citroëns will fit the 205.

Bolt-on Goodies

The most obvious place to begin when it comes to modifying the 205 is with simple, relatively inexpensive items such as air filters and exhausts. The 205 responds well to traditional tuning methods, such as porting and polishing the cylinder head. Alongside this, new inlet and exhaust valves can be fitted and uprated camshafts are also available. Enhancements such as these should see a power increase of around 20–30bhp.

For those looking to go further, and take a leaf from the T16's book, then the 205 can be turbocharged. This is a fairly involved process demanding significant work to the 205, especially given the age of the car and the additional stress placed on the engine's components by the process. As well as the turbocharger itself, the car will also require modifications to the exhaust system, an intercooler and a remapped engine control unit. The results of such work, however, can see a 1.9 GTI develop up to 170bhp.

Turbocharging can be expensive. While it may once have been a popular method of increasing the 205's power back in the 1980s and 1990s, since then other techniques have superseded turbocharging. This includes the development of stronger, more modern, more powerful engines by Peugeot themselves – engines that just happen to fit the Peugeot 205.

Swap Shop

One of the simplest ways to increase power is with an engine swap. Peugeot 205 enthusiasts seeking simple ways to make their car faster have followed this route using the likes of the 405 as a ready-made engine donor.

The 405 Mi16 used the 1905cc, alloy-block XU9 engine. As the '16' in its name suggests it was a 16-valve engine and developed either 145bhp (with catalytic convertor) or 158bhp (without). The XU9 was also used in the 309 GTI-16. The XU9 quickly became the popular choice for those undertaking an engine swap. The transplant was made easier by the fact that it used the same engine mounts as the 205's original item – the biggest hurdle being the mating of the 205's wiring loom to that of the new engine. This proved to be an insignificant hurdle to enthusiasts and Mi16-powered 205s soon became quite popular.

Peugeot's engine range continued to evolve and improve and when the 309 arrived it was offered with the XU10. With 160bhp, and a slightly larger displacement of 1998cc, the XU10 saw use in the 306 GTi-6 and Rallye. An engine with plenty of scope, it was quickly seized upon by tuning

■ BUYING, MAINTAINING AND MODIFYING THE PEUGEOT 205

The 205 has always lent itself to engine improvements – this car has undergone an engine transplant. GERARD HUGHES

firms and modifiers and naturally caught the attention of the 205 community.

One of the most recent evolutions of the 205 GTI to come into existence thanks to the XU10 is the near-200bhp Pug1Off conversion.

Produced by the Brackley-based company of the same name, the conversion involves replacing the 205's original engine with the 1998cc, dohc, 16-valve engine from the later 306 GTi-6. This has the immediate effect of increasing power to 167bhp, an increase of almost 40bhp, before any further modifications are made. Furthermore, because both of the engines are Peugeot units, the replacement 306 engine can be mated directly to the 205's existing five-speed transmission. Alternatively the 306's six-speed gearbox and limited-slip differential can be installed along-side the upgrades, including high-lift camshafts, revised inlet and exhaust manifolds and a reprogrammed engine management unit.

The cumulative effect of these modifications is a car that develops 195bhp @ 7,400rpm and 155lb ft torque. Larger 283mm discs can also be fitted alongside more modern, more efficient calipers as used on the 206 180 GTI to improve the car's stopping ability. By the time the suspension is uprated with improved dampers, springs, arms and anti-roll bars the car in question is drastically different to the one that Peugeot originally intended.

Somehow, though, the Pug1Off GTI retains the same irrepressible character as the standard car, albeit with a boost in power, bringing the 205 in line with many modern day contemporaries.

BUYING, MAINTAINING AND MODIFYING THE PEUGEOT 205

Specialist firm PuglOff has created the GTI-6.
GERARD HUGHES

157

■ BUYING, MAINTAINING AND MODIFYING THE PEUGEOT 205

Under the bonnet there's no hiding the changes – Pug1Off's installation is neat and could easily be mistaken for the work of Peugeot themselves.
GERARD HUGHES

THE 205 GTI-6

Specifications

Engine: 2-litre, 16v Peugeot XU10J4RS from 306 GTI-6/Rallye. 167bhp in 'standard' trim. Uprated '195' 195bhp spec with high-lift, long-duration camshaft. 221bhp per ton.
Transmission: Six-speed BE3/6 with Quaife ATB differential. Original 1.9 GTI driveshafts.
Suspension: Bilstein B6 dampers. Eibach springs. 309 GTI front arms. 306 rear arms. Fully rebuilt rear axle.
Brakes: Disc rear axle from 1.9 205 GTI. 283mm front brakes from 206 180. Optional Tarox discs with Ferodo pads, braided lines and uprated master cylinder.

Visually the car remains faithful to the 1.9 GTI, though changes are clear when the car is viewed in profile.
GERARD HUGHES

OWNER'S VIEW

Simon Rose
Car: 1991 1.6 GTI

I have owned this car since 2005. But I have owned 205 GTIs since 1999. I put in a 1.9 GTI engine, interior and rear disc beam from a crashed car I purchased for £50. Following this I put in a 1.9 Mi16 XU9J4 engine. This has a stage 1 inlet cam, Xsara VTS gearbox, sump baffle, and silicone oil and water hoses. It also has 309 GTi wishbones and driveshafts and 306 GTi-6 calipers, front discs and pads. I have a 309 GTi rear beam at home that I need to rebuild and fit and also some full leather front seats that I haven't got round to putting in the car.

I always remember that there was one near where I lived from the age of about thirteen onwards (circa 1994) and I loved it. It was a red 1.9 GTI and I was fascinated by it. I decided then that I wanted one. I also used to see it being driven 'enthusiastically' and I thought it was the best thing ever. At this time they were also appearing in car magazines quite a bit and there were lots of them around so I was hooked.

These days I think it is the rarity factor because you just don't see that many of them around. But the main thing is the way it makes you feel when you drive it. Mine is quite quick but compared to modern cars these days it isn't that quick. I think the combination of the speed, flimsiness and handling abilities makes you feel like you are driving so much faster than you are and you always feel in control because it is so grippy. I never drive it without a smile on my face, even when things go wrong! The other thing is whilst some parts can be expensive (OE parts that are no longer made), generally it is cheap to run and I do all the servicing/maintenance myself.

I think Peugeot marketed it very well because everyone wanted one back in the day. They linked it to the 205 T16 very well in some of the adverts and there was a lot of hype. It is a very good looking car and looked great back in the eighties and nineties but still looks great these days – I don't think it will ever look dated. Couple the looks with the handling and performance and you've got the icon that is the 205 GTI. I always get comments when I am out in it from people who either used to own one or their friend had owned one. I even got pulled over by the police once just so they could have a look at it and talk to me about it.

AUTHOR

■ BUYING, MAINTAINING AND MODIFYING THE PEUGEOT 205

OWNER'S VIEW

Craig Alexander
Car: 1991 1.9 GTI

I have, for better or worse, been surrounded by Peugeots most of my life. My parents had a string of 405s and 406s, I learnt to drive in a 307 and my first car was a little 106 1.1, so something must have rubbed off on me!

I mostly became aware of the 205 when I had my 106 (I'm a little too young to have really appreciated the 205 when it was new). I was just interested in how it was such a good looking Peugeot, which still looked fresh and modern today, and seemed to be from a time when Peugeot made fantastic cars! Once I drove one, with such sharp controls and responses I was hooked!

I have owned the car since the start of 2008. It has been on the road in one piece for a small proportion of the time since then. The car has been modified, but only in what I would consider an OE-plus manner. I have attempted to only fit modifications that are relatively subtle, or retain or improve the 205's innate character. Examples include the Speedline SL434 wheels, which are a modern alloy version of the magnesium Group A wheels, larger front brake calipers from a 306 GTi-6 and a quick power-steering rack from a Citroën Xsara VTS. The 205 is fortunate that many parts from later Peugeots and Citroëns simply bolt on. The options for upgrades are substantial.

Like a majority of owners these days I have opted to keep the exterior (bar the wheels, which are easy to swap back) completely standard, as I think the original design and styling suit the car perfectly. I am also undertaking slightly more ambitious modifications of A/C and ABS. Perhaps surprisingly, both systems were options that could be specified on the 205 GTI from new, and are being installed in a manner sympathetic to the OE installs, with modern components where necessary. For me it is a balance between the well-refined styling, which looks as fresh today as ever, and the steering response and feel. I think the thing people keep coming back to today are the controls. The hair-trigger throttle response and the fantastic steering. The fact that Peugeot took a well-tested hot-hatch typology and made it a little better in most ways. To me it's a little better looking than most similar cars, has aged better, and handles beautifully.

AUTHOR

OWNER'S VIEW

Craig Cheetham
Car: 1986 1.4 GR, 1989 1.4 CJ Convertible

I own two – a 1986 1.4 GR and a 1989 1.4 CJ Convertible. I've also owned both a 205 GTI and a 1.7 diesel in the past. I've had the CJ for four years, and the GR for two. My GR is completely standard and totally original – it was what made it appeal to me in the first place. The CJ has GTI alloys and also the interior from a later 1995 205 Mardi Gras, as the original denim-style seats had succumbed.

205s were everywhere when I was a kid, and I always thought they were such a pretty, harmonious design. The eighties was a great era for French car design in general, and I think the 205 has aged beautifully. The fact that they're such fun to drive and so incredibly well made is a bonus, frankly. I also loved Group B rallying, so the T16 probably had something to do with it as well. They seem immune to natural destruction. My father has a twenty-year-old 205 diesel that has covered over a quarter of a million miles. He leaves it parked in the street in all weathers, yet every time it gets a wash it looks brand new.

They cost peanuts to run, are incredibly simple to maintain even in performance trims, and even the puny-engined ones can be driven with gusto and put a smile on your face. They're also still quite cheap, though prices have started to rise of late, especially for good GTIs and diesel models. Put simply, I believe it's to be the best car ever from a French manufacturer. There were many more exotic, several that were more innovative and a few that were as well screwed together, but in terms of fulfilling its original design brief and being so right for its era the 205 is a phenomenal all-rounder. That, and Ari Vatanen, of course...

AUTHOR

■ BUYING, MAINTAINING AND MODIFYING THE PEUGEOT 205

OWNER'S VIEW

James Baggot
Car: 1991 GTI 1.9

I've always wanted a 205 GTI and when I was offered this one by a friend who collects them I had to have it. It needed some work to get it back to top condition, but I knew it was a worthwhile investment of my time and money. The car is already a classic. I've tried my hardest to restore the car to original condition. It spent a hundred hours in the paint shop after the restorers took it right back to the bare metal. They have done an incredible job of repainting it and it looks stunning now. I had to enlist the help of the Peugeot Owners Club chairman to help me find new headlights, fog lamps, red trim and some other bits. I spent £1,000 on these parts alone but it was worth it because they have really made the car look like new again. He searched France for me and eventually found a dealer with these original bits still on the shelf! The 205 GTI is an iconic hot hatch! I grew up wanting one as they were common on the roads when I was a teenager. I've looked at getting one many times, but finally took the plunge last year and am delighted with it. It's a cool car – a very special model in the history of hot hatches and one that quite rightly many petrol heads, like me, love.

The best thing about it is the looks it gets. As J39 JMR is so clean and new looking now the comments I get whenever I stop are amazing. I drove it back from London recently and stopped three times – each time a crowd gathered around the car. There's so much interest in GTIs still, especially ones in good condition!

The GTI was and still is a brilliant car to drive, simple and a beautiful design. The 1.9 was always classed as a giant-slayer and even now its performance figures are impressive. No 2-series Peugeot since has quite lived up to the greatness of the first and, in my opinion, that's because the 205 was perfect – and it's impossible to improve on that.

AUTHOR

OWNER'S VIEW

Simon Bennett
Car: 1988 CTI 1.6

I've owned my CTI for well over ten years, though it did spend two years in the ownership of a friend. It's standard apart from having the 1.9 wheels on instead of the 1.6 'pepperpots' and a Pipercross air filter.

I made up my mind that the 205 was the only car I wanted. A lot of my friends were into Golf GTis, however I have always had a soft spot for the 205 since the Group B rally days. For me a big part of the 205's appeal is the looks I get on a nice day with the hood down, its excellent performance and comfort. People will always approach you and mention when they or their friend's dad/family member had one. For a convertible it's also a practical car, having room for four adults. For me, several things made the 205 special. The look of the car for a start. It's very eighties in design and living in Coventry it meant that I was buying something local. I have owned three CTIs and three tin-top 1.9 GTis in total and cannot believe the smile I get every time I fire her up. The engine is one of my favourites of all time. Very revvy, and with performance that is still impressive even by today's standards. I work in the motor trade and drive numerous cars on a daily basis but nothing makes me feel at home more than sitting behind the wheel of my 205 CTI!

AUTHOR

CHAPTER NINE

PEUGEOT AFTER THE 205

It is perhaps understandable that, after the critically acclaimed 205, Peugeot struggled to recapture the magic of that car. The 106 and 306 launched in 1991 and 1993 respectively and it was Peugeot's intention that these two cars would eventually come to replace the ageing 205.

The 306 took much of what made the 205 popular and enlarged it. Its styling was very much an evolution of the 205, though this time it was solely the work of Pininfarina. Like the 205 it remained engaging to drive, particularly in the form of the 2-litre, 169bhp 306 GTi-6.

REPLACING THE IRREPLACEABLE

There was however still room in the Peugeot range for a 2 series. Five years after the 306's launch, the 206 arrived.

When it launched in 1998 it was built at multiple plants worldwide and remains in production and on sale in developing markets. It was sold as an estate and cabriolet, while in China it was restyled and sold as the Citroën C2. While the 206 went on to become Peugeot's best-selling car of all

The 206 arrived in 1998 with a range than was wider than the 205's.
It would become the best-selling Peugeot to date.

PEUGEOT AFTER THE 205

The 206 would be the final car to be produced in Coventry at the Ryton plant.

■ PEUGEOT AFTER THE 205

The Coventry-built 405, alongside the 309. COVENTRY TRANSPORT MUSEUM

time, it never received the plaudits of the 205 before it. It was also the final car to be built at the Ryton plant.

As more and more 206s found owners, its desirability ebbed away. As the 1990s turned into the 2000s, the competition for the hot-hatch crown was fierce, with everything from the MG ZR to the new Mini all aiming for the title the 205 had had all to itself a decade earlier. The 206 GTI failed to capture the public's imagination in any meaningful way. It is perhaps unsurprising that Peugeot found replacing the 205 as difficult as it did – the company had created something iconic, and icons are not easily copied.

The company found replacing the 405 somewhat easier. The 405 had ridden the crest of the 205 wave and after the Group B ban in 1987 would feature much of the 205 T16 technology, creating a mid-engined 405, christened the 405 T16 GR. It won the Pikes Peak Hill Climb and the Paris–Dakar Rally with Finns Ari Vatanen and Juha Kankkunen at the wheel, and Vatanen would star in the legendary cinéma-vérité short *Climb Dance*, which documented his 1988 Hill Climb win.

When the time came to replace the 405 in 1995, Peugeot had a wealth of experience to draw on. Saloons were

PEUGEOT AFTER THE 205

ABOVE: **With wins in the Paris–Dakar and Pikes Peak Hill Climb, the 405 would prove itself adept in motor sport.**

RIGHT: **That motor-sport success was brought to the road with the 405 Mi16.**

167

PEUGEOT AFTER THE 205

something the company knew very well and on its arrival the motoring media gave the 406 a warm response, commending it for the quality of its ride and the quality of its cabin. It would go on to be named the *What Car?* Car of the Year in 1996, narrowly missing out on the European Car of the Year that same year.

By the 1990s Peugeot had a strong reputation in motor sport so naturally the 406 undertook a racing career, though rather than rallying the 406 would see action as a touring car. It struggled for reliability in the British Touring Car Championship and endured a string of retirements, its best result being fourth at Norfolk's Snetterton in June 1996. It did much better in Europe where Frenchman Laurent Aïello would win the 1997 German Super Tourenwagen Cup, seeing off the likes of BMW, Opel and Audi in their homeland.

The 406 found plenty of customers, with the saloon and estate proving popular with both private and fleet buyers. Peugeot made the 406 even more desirable in 1996 when the simply stunning Peugeot Coupé (without the 406 branding) made its debut. Unveiled at the Paris Motor Show it boasted beautifully curved lines courtesy of Pininfarina, lines that would see it crowned 'Most Beautiful Coupé in the World'. It also won a 1997 Car Design Award at the Turin Motorshow before winning 'Most Beautiful Car of the Year' in 1998.

CONTINUED RALLY SUCCESS

While the 206 may not have been an icon of the times like

The 405 would be replaced by the stunning 406 – a car that would win plenty of plaudits.

PEUGEOT AFTER THE 205

RIGHT: **The 206 WRC** arrived right at the end of the century and would become the first championship winner of the new millennium. It would follow up that success with another title in 2002.

BELOW: **The 307 WRC** took to the stage in 2004 but it struggled to match the 206's successes.

169

■ PEUGEOT AFTER THE 205

The millionth 206 was produced at Ryton, but by 2006 the plant would be closed.

its predecessor, there was one area where it enjoyed similar success to the 205 – rallying. The 206 WRC arrived in 1999, winning the World Rally Championship in 2000 and 2002 with, fittingly, a Finn – Marcus Grönholm – at the wheel.

The 307 followed in 2001, succeeding the 306. It was larger than the car it replaced but made use of a reworked version of the 306's chassis. The 307 saw the continuation of Peugeot's new family look, a look that would extend across the range, with swept-back headlights and a more upright stance. It made its debut on the world rallying stage in 2004.

In Britain, Peugeot's UK arm built on the 206's rallying success, nurturing and developing future race and rally talent. The 307's rally career was beset with technical problems and it ultimately failed to repeat the success of the 206. It enjoyed a varied career, however, competing not only in the WRC but also in circuit racing, including the British Touring Car Championship and World Touring Car Championship.

Known as the 207 RC in mainland Europe, the 207 GTi was a UK-only model – it seemed the sun had set on the GTi name.

PEUGEOT AFTER THE 205

Peugeot left the WRC in 2005 as sister brand Citroën became the dominant power in the rally world.

The year 2006 saw the end of Peugeot production in Great Britain with the closure of the Ryton plant in Coventry. Despite being a leader for the company in terms of production levels, Ryton was deemed too expensive and Peugeot opted to produce the follow-up 207 in Slovakia rather than Britain. Some 2,300 people lost their jobs with the plant's closure, and the site was cleared for redevelopment, bringing to an end sixty years of car production in Coventry.

When Peugeot returned to rallying, the 207 would go on to win the Intercontinental Rally Challenge (IRC), an alternative to the WRC with a more TV-friendly format. The car was backed by Peugeot UK and wrapped in a patriotic Union flag-themed livery. In 2009 the car was driven to its third IRC title by British driver Kris Meeke. Meeke's championship win would see him star in a series of press and TV adverts for the 207.

Like the previous two cars in the 2 series the 207 duly received its own GTi, though only in the UK – in Europe the quick 207 was known as the 207 RC. The 207 GTi was considered a huge improvement over the 206 GTi but this didn't stop Peugeot's plans to drop the GTi in 2008 when Peugeot UK's then-marketing director Christian Stein told *Autocar* that Peugeot were now to focus on sports coupés, rather than hot hatches. The first step in this new direction would come a year later with the launch of the most desired and talked about Peugeot since the 205 – the RCZ.

A NEW GENERATION

The RCZ Concept caught many by surprise. Some felt it was too bold for a Peugeot. There was a sense that the company had lost its way in terms of design, but the RCZ would mark the beginning of a return to form for Peugeot.

Peugeot's stylistic return to form began in 2008 with the 308 RCZ Concept.

■ PEUGEOT AFTER THE 205

When it launched in 2010 the RCZ was met with strong demand and quickly began to win awards.

The RCZ arrived at the 2007 Frankfurt Motor Show as the 308 RCZ Concept, with no plans for the coupé to be put in to production. However, so positive was the reaction that the company looked to turn concept into reality. Though based on the 308 hatchback, the company chose to drop the '308' from the car's name, leaving it to become a stand-alone model, simply titled RCZ.

Production is handled by Austrian company Magna Steyr rather than Peugeot themselves. The car went on sale in spring 2010 and was immediately popular, with dealers reporting strong demand for the car that won 'Coupé of the Year' from the UK's *Top Gear* magazine as well as taking the title 'Most Beautiful Car of 2009' at the 25th International Automobile Festival.

As the RCZ wooed customers away from the Audi TT, the company also set about marking its 200th anniversary, celebrating at the Goodwood Festival of Speed with everything from a 205 T16 to its Le Mans 24 Hours machine, the 908. The RCZ also joined in the birthday celebrations, with two cars wearing numbers 200 and 201 competing in the 2010 Nürburgring 24 Hours race, finishing first in class and fiftieth overall.

The following year, Peugeot introduced the 508. Offered as a large saloon and estate, this was classic Peugeot territory and it was well received by press and public alike.

The stylistic return to form was further cemented by the launch of the 208 in 2012. The latest incarnation of Peugeot's 2 series certainly took inspiration from the 205 and, noting

172

PEUGEOT AFTER THE 205

the success of previous GTIs, reversed its decision to drop the legendary GTI badge, which –according to Peugeot – had never been its intention, rather that Stein had been misunderstood in his original interview. Either way, the announcement of a smaller, lighter 2-series Peugeot, complete with GTI badge, had the motoring press and Peugeot fans excited – an excitement shared by many within PSA itself.

The standard 208 arrived in June 2012 with a launch at MediaCity in Salford, Manchester. The 208 GTi was something of an open secret, Peugeot knew that the new 2 series would be expected to wear those three all-important letters. Peugeot teased with the announcement of the car, showcasing the '208 GTi Concept' at events such as the Goodwood Festival of Speed. In September 2012 Peugeot finally confirmed it – the GTi had been given the go-ahead for production.

The 208 GTi is powered by Peugeot's THP 200 1.6-litre turbocharged petrol engine, an engine shared with the Citroën DS3 and the 2007–2013 Mini Cooper S. In the 208 it develops 200bhp and 203lb ft of torque while meeting the demands of modern motoring legislation by emitting 145g/km.

It arrived in the UK in April 2013 with the roads of North Wales providing the perfect environment in which to showcase the GTi's capabilities. While perhaps not as sharp as the 205 GTi or contemporary rivals like the Ford Fiesta ST, the 208 GTi struck an impressive balance of sportiness and everyday usability – something Peugeot believes is a vital requirement for today's hot hatches.

The 205 GTI has cast a long shadow over each successive incarnation of the series and Peugeot acknowledged this by displaying a 205 GTI at the launch event. However, rather than draw a direct comparison with its 1980s forebear,

Like many many Peugeots before it, the RCZ would be campaigned on track, taking a class win in the 2010 Nürburgring 24 Hours race.

■ PEUGEOT AFTER THE 205

In 2011 Peugeot showed that they still knew how to make a big comfortable saloon in the form of the 508.

PEUGEOT AFTER THE 205

Peugeot has embraced the differences between the two cars. The 208 GTi marks a noted improvement over the 207 GTi and serves to highlight that, thirty years on, the French manufacturer still knows how to serve up a good looking and entertaining hot hatch.

The GTi was joined at the UK launch by the XY, a plush, upmarket 208 serving Peugeot's desire to move into more premium market segments. Featuring the same widened track as the GTi, the XY boasted Nappa leather and Alcantara upholstery, bound by purple stitching. The exterior was punctuated by chrome detailing alongside diamond-cut alloy wheels. The XY was offered with a choice of two petrol engines and three diesel, all of which fell into the sub-100g/km category, making them eligible for zero road fund duty in the UK.

As 2014 dawned almost 600,000 Peugeot 208s had been built in Europe and Brazil, with almost 9,500 buyers opting for the GTi or XY.

The 208 arrived in 2012 and many were hopeful that it would lead to a new GTI. AUTHOR

■ PEUGEOT AFTER THE 205

Something of an open secret, the **GTI** arrived in April 2013. It was quicker and lighter than the 207 GTI. AUTHOR

PEUGEOT AFTER THE 205

LIVING UP TO THE LEGEND – THE 208 IN MOTOR SPORT

At the Paris Motor Show in September 2012 Peugeot unveiled the 208 R5, announcing a return to rallying in 2013. Unlike the 205, the four-wheel-drive, 2-litre R5 – sporting the iconic Peugeot Talbot Sport colours once more – would not contest the World Rally Championship, with PSA's rallying focus remaining firmly centred on Citroën and the DS3. The 208 would instead be found in the European Rally Championship and in the less well-known World Rally Championship-2. Peugeot reinforced the message by producing a promotional video featuring all their previous 2-series rally cars in secure storage being joined mysteriously by a new rally-ready 208, much to the shock of the Peugeot 'security guard' – played by the one and only Ari Vatanen.

The GTI's interior was sporting, yet usable, which was an accurate description of the new car.

Rather than hiding from the 205 GTI, Peugeot played up to the legend with the launch of the 208 GTI.

177

■ PEUGEOT AFTER THE 205

Peugeot drew heavily on its history when promoting the motor-sport version of the 208 by draping the car in the legendary **Peugeot Talbot Sport** colours.

Like the 205 and 405 before it the 208 T16 set a new record at Pikes Peak...

...and will tackle the Dakar Rally in 2015.

PEUGEOT AFTER THE 205

Joining the 208 GTI at the UK launch was the 208 XY – a 205 Gentry for the new millennium.

As the 208's launch debut drew near, Peugeot opted to take even more inspiration from the 205, renaming the R5 the 208 T16. In late March 2013 Peugeot announced plans to enter the 208, like its namesake, in the legendary Pikes Peak Hill Climb.

Peugeot Sport were bullish from the outset, stating they would be returning to the hill with the intention of winning – a bold claim, but with legendary French rally driver Sébastien Loeb at the wheel it was easy to believe they could succeed.

On 30 June 2013, exactly twenty-five years after Ari Vatanen broke the record for Peugeot, they did just that. Loeb broke the 2012 record by over a minute, covering the 12 miles (19km) and 156 bends of the hill in 8 minutes 13 seconds at an average speed of 87mph (140km/h).

In 2014 the 208 will compete in the World Rallycross Championship with former Formula One world champion Jacques Villeneuve at the wheel. In an interesting repeat of history as this book goes to press, Peugeot have announced plans to return to the Dakar Rally as well.

■ PEUGEOT AFTER THE 205

MOTOR SPORT AND THE PEUGEOT 208

Though Peugeot continued to compete in high-level motor sport and win, particularly endurance racing, it could perhaps be argued that Peugeot's star had faded somewhat since the end of the 205 and 405's competition career. With the arrival of the 208, Peugeot chose to return to more mainstream motor sport. Citroën had dominated the World Rally Championship, but now it was Peugeot hoping to recapture the glory that propelled the company to the very top of the motoring world in the 1980s. Peugeot developed several variants of the 208 in the pursuit of their ambitions.

208 T16 Pikes Peak

The Pikes Peak-winning 208 T16 is a quite different beast to the 205 T16. Its power comes from a 875bhp, V6 bi-turbo engine developed for endurance racing, while it weighs in at just 875kg (1,929lb). Like the Group B 205, the new T16 features a mid-mounted engine and four-wheel drive. Much of Peugeot's expertise in developing the 208 came with its Le Mans-winning 908, with the smaller car inheriting running gear, brakes and air intake from the 908 HDi.

208 T16

180

PEUGEOT AFTER THE 205

208 R2

Designed to compete in rallying for cars between 1400cc and 1600cc, the R2 uses a tuned version of the 1.6 VTi petrol engine used in the 208 road car. The 1598cc engine develops 185bhp and is naturally aspirated. The gearbox is a manual, five-speed sequential unit. The car's steering has been revised too, with hydraulic assistance rather than the electric system used in the road car. Along with a faster steering rack it allows for greater precision and speed. It made its rally debut in the 2013 Tour de Corse.

(continued overleaf)

■ PEUGEOT AFTER THE 205

(continued from page 181)

208 Racing Cup

Unveiled in November 2012, the 208 Racing Cup is broadly similar in specification to the R2 but is tuned for circuit racing rather than rallying. It uses a slightly smaller 1587cc version of the VTi engine from the road car, with a 40ltr (8.8gal) fuel tank as opposed to the R2's 60ltr (13gal) tank. It develops 140bhp and has featured in races across Europe since its debut in 2013.

PEUGEOT AFTER THE 205

Peugeot Sport 208 GTi

Development of the Peugeot Sport GTi began in January 2013. It uses many of the same components as the 208 Racing Cup, although as with the road-going GTi it features a turbocharged 1.6-litre engine. Like the road-legal GTi it has a six-speed gearbox, though with a paddle shift. Power output was increased to 300bhp and, with a focus on endurance racing, it was fitted with a 100ltr (22gal) fuel tank. It made its debut at the Nürburgring 24 Hours race and took the top three positions in the SP2T Class.

■ PEUGEOT AFTER THE 205

AN UNCERTAIN FUTURE

Today, Peugeot finds itself in much the same position as it was in 1983. Though it remains Europe's second-largest car manufacturer, PSA continues to struggle financially. Unlike the Volkswagen Group, PSA do not sell their cars in the United States, concentrating instead on the European market. This meant that the global financial downturn of 2008 hit Peugeot particularly hard. Cars are becoming harder to sell in the European Union and manufacturers will and are turning to developing markets such as China in the battle to continue producing motor vehicles.

In February 2012, Peugeot and General Motors announced a global strategic alliance, with GM buying a 7 per cent share in Peugeot's parent, PSA Peugeot Citroën, together with an agreement to collaborate on small and medium-size vehicles.

In July, Peugeot reported a first-half loss of £638m in 2012 and announced a major restructuring plan, looking to cut some 8,000 jobs from its near 100,000-strong workforce. There were continuing rumours that the American giant would increase its stake in PSA in an effort to gain control of the French firm – rumours that caused considerable concern to workers in GM's European outfits Vauxhall and Opel as well as PSA Peugeot. GM had already announced intentions to close a factory as supply continued to outstrip demand. If the PSA plants joined the mix as well, redundancies and further factory closures were bound to follow – something the French government would do the utmost to prevent.

PSA Peugeot went on to record a record annual loss of €5 billion (£4.3 billion) in 2012. Simply put, the company owned too many factories producing too many cars for too few customers.

Peugeot's future is clouded as the company struggles to cope with a flat European market and increased competition from all corners of the globe.

PEUGEOT AFTER THE 205

PSA Peugeot continues to innovate with cars such as the Hybrid Air Tech.

In 2013 the company took strides to right itself. In January Peugeot showcased their Hybrid Air concept, a vehicle that uses compressed air as a method of propulsion in conjunction with a 1.2-litre, 3-cylinder petrol engine. The concept can operate in either pure air mode or work with the petrol engine. A tank of compressed air drives the vehicle. As the tank depressurizes, it displaces a volume of oil. This energy supplies a hydraulic motor, allowing the vehicle to move without using fuel or producing any emissions. When tested by Peugeot, a 2008 using this set-up was capable of 97.4mpg (2.9ltr/100km), while emitting as little as 69g/km of carbon dioxide.

Peugeot also succeeded in bringing a number of attractively styled, well-received cars to market, vehicles such as the crossover-cum-estate 2008 and the new 308, a car that would go on to be crowned European Car of the Year in March 2014.

PSA's financial troubles continued to make headlines in 2014, following General Motors' decision to sell its 7 per cent share in PSA in December 2013. Ultimately a deal was agreed with Chinese car maker Dongfeng Motors (PSA's joint-venture partner in China) that saw the Peugeot family finally lose control of the business. Dongfeng purchased 14 per cent of the group for £660 million, while the Peugeot family's shareholding decreased from 25 to 14 per cent. The Dongfeng stake was matched by the French government who, in an effort to protect the jobs of French workers, also took on a 14 per cent share.

Later in 2014 it will close its Citroën plant at Aulnay-sous-Bois but the future for Peugeot and PSA remains somewhat clouded and it is expected to continue to report losses until at least 2016. As the Volkswagen-Audi Group continue to increase market share right across Europe companies like PSA Peugeot will find it harder and harder to fight increas-

■ PEUGEOT AFTER THE 205

The 308, which launched in 2013, fought off fierce competition to win the 2014 European Car of the Year.

ing competition from the likes of VW-Audi and emerging manufacturing nations, such as South Korea and China. Following the investment Dongfeng said the deal would 'deepen their cooperation with PSA and strengthen overseas cooperation' while stating a goal of selling 1.5 million vehicles under the Peugeot, Citroën and Dongfeng brands from 2020.

While the company may never again reach the heady heights that 205 afforded it, it can at least pride itself on having created a true automotive icon, a car that, arguably, it will never better. Whether the 208 will have the same revitalizing effect on the company as the 205 remains to be seen, however if the relationship with Dongfeng proves successful and Peugeot is able to gain a foothold in lucrative emerging markets there always remains the chance that the Lion may yet go from strength to strength.

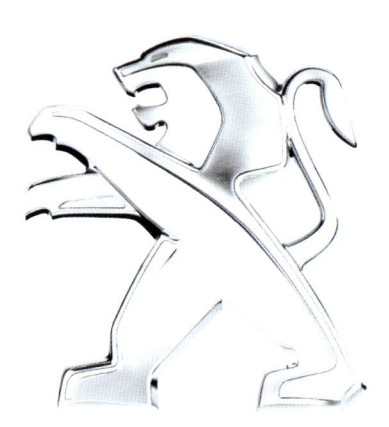

Peugeot's iconic lion logo was revised in 2010 and remains a symbol that has been at the heart of the Peugeot name for the last 200 years. What do the next 200 have in store for it?

APPENDIX

THE 205 IN NUMBERS

Production breakdown by factory:

Mulhouse:	2,229,242
Sochaux:	1,100,828
Villaverde:	1,191,237
Poissy:	604,694
Creil:	97,448
Aulnay:	21,140
Complete knock-down kits for export:	33,411
Total number of 205s built, 1982–99:	5,278,050

Production figures for the three and five-door hatchback:

1982 Three-door: 0 Five-door: 360
All 360 205 built in 1982 were fitted with five-speed manual gearboxes.

1983 Three-door: 154,915 Five-door: 96
In 1983 13,665 diesel 205s were built, all five-door. 62,005 featured four-speed transmission, 93,006 were manual.

1984 Three-door: 137,437 Five-door: 237,636
69,975 five-door diesels were produced in 1984. No three-doors as of yet. 146,441 were four-speed, 228,687 were fitted with the five-speed 'box.

1985 Three-door: 223,583 Five-door: 251,155
29,879 three-door diesels were built this year, alongside 72,607 five-doors. 176,096 were four-speed, 321,921 were five. Forty-five automatics were built.

1986 Three-door: 269,004 Five-door: 212,982
1986 saw 35,848 three-door diesels produced and 61,773 five-doors. Of the total built, 214,047 were four-speed, 297,576 were five-speed and 9,040 were automatic.

1987 Three-door: 287,889 Five-door: 222,557
35,844 three-door diesels were built in 1987, compared to 59,660 five-doors. 220,035 205s were fitted with the four-speed box, 320,222 with five. 9,183 were autos.

1988 Three-door: 233,001 Five-door: 293,404
In 1988 34,895 diesel three-doors were produced alongside 67,545 five-doors. Gearboxes were split with 171,197 four-speed, 389,293 five and 9,884 automatics.

■ THE 205 IN NUMBERS

1989　　　　　　　　　Three-door: 227,594　　　　　　　　　Five-door: 289,465

34,150 diesel three-doors and 66,907 five-doors were built in 1989. 179,568 205s featured a four-speed box and 375,712 boasted the extra cog. 10,550 were automatic.

1990　　　　　　　　　Three-door: 165,180　　　　　　　　　Five-door: 386,056

1990 was the third best year for diesel production. 33,210 three-doors were built that year, 66,907 five-doors. This was also the first year of the turbo diesel. 2,583 three-door and 2,336 five-doors were produced. 151,947 205s used the four-speed transmission, 44,196 went with a fifth gear. There were 12,941 automatic examples built.

1991　　　　　　　　　Three-door: 198,352　　　　　　　　　Five-door: 270,596

1991 was the biggest year for overall 205 production. 59,810 (15,708 turbos) diesel three-doors and 83,107 (10,507 turbos) were built. Automatics accounted for 10,395 of the cars built, with a further 98,128 being four-speed and 413,956 five-speed.

1992　　　　　　　　　Three-door: 92,595　　　　　　　　　Five-door: 220,827

48,603 (9,612 turbos) three-door diesels were built in 1992, as well as 72,885(7,095 turbos) five-doors. 51,115 used the four-speed gearbox, 295,965 the five. 10,721 were automatic.

1993　　　　　　　　　Three-door: 46,727　　　　　　　　　Five-door: 42,570

1993 saw 19,426 (6,153 turbos) four-door diesel built. 27,767(4,075 turbos) five-doors were built. 9,475 were four-speed with 97,461 using the five-speed. 4,908 automatics were built.

1994　　　　　　　　　Three-door: 72,294　　　　　　　　　Five-door: 46,713

26,295 (5,968 turbos) three-door diesels were built in 1994. 43,179 (5,499 turbos) five-doors were produced. 643 four-speed manuals were built as opposed to 142,383 five-speeds. 4,126 autos were also built this year.

1995　　　　　　　　　Three-door: 52,575　　　　　　　　　Five-door: 27,975

In 1995 17,625 (2,249 turbos) three-door diesels and 33,698 (2,544 turbos) five doors were built. The four-speed gearbox was discontinued by this point. 95,189 205s used the five-speed gearbox. The remaining 2,868 were automatic.

1996　　　　　　　　　Three-door: 46,383　　　　　　　　　Five-door: 19,954

1996 10,576 (1,747 autos) were three-door diesels produced in 1996 and 32,870 (1,400 turbos) five-doors were built alongside. 74,956 were five-speed manual, 1,118 were automatic. 1996 was the last year the 205 was offered with an automatic gearbox.

1997　　　　　　　　　Three-door: 24,799　　　　　　　　　Five-door: 42,363

1997 saw the Turbo diesel discontinued so from here on, all 205 diesels were naturally aspirated. 12,982 three-doors and 30,976 five-doors were produced.

1998　　　　　　　　　Three-door: 13,150　　　　　　　　　Five-door: 31,463

The 205's penultimate year saw 8,768 three-door and 21,126 five-door diesels built as production began to wind down, with the new 206 beginning to come on stream as its successor.

1999　　　　　　　　　Three-door: 8　　　　　　　　　Five-door: 2,370

The last year of 205 production. Of the eight three-door cars built, seven were diesel. 1,301 five-door diesels were produced alongside it.

In total 410,501 (44,020 turbos) diesel three-door 205s were built. 829,124 five-doors were produced, 33,456 of which were turbo-charged. 1,480,697 205s used the four-speed gearbox, compared to 3,711,574 five-doors. 85,779 were automatic.

T16s: 200 roads cars, plus approximately forty works cars

Van

Here are Peugeot's production figures for the 205 van. Initially it was offered with either a petrol or diesel engine. Diesel proved more popular and so by 1994 it was the only engine option for the van. The Fourgonette was only produced for three years and only available with diesel.

	Three-door	of which diesel	Fourgonette
1984	19		
1985	23,272	13,308	
1986	29,371	19,000	
1987	33,401	23,593	
1988	35,960	28,040	
1989	40,044	33,237	
1990	42,952	36,246	
1991	40,462	35,195	
1992	37,271	30,036	
1993	18,917	18,321	
1994	19,005	All	8,425
1995	11,841	All	5,466
1996	9,671	All	66
1997	7,196	All	
1998	3,360	All	
1999	9	All	

Peugeot 205 UK Sales figures

Year	Total	Market %
1983	2,883	0.2
1984	19,661	1.1
1985	30,842	1.7
1986	39,188	2.1
1987	49,129	2.4
1988	54,147	2.4
1989	52,740	2.3
1990	50,205	2.5
1991	46,615	2.9
1992	34,045	2.2
1993	23,065	1.3
1994	10,694	0.6
1995	8,944	0.5
1996	3,046	0.1
1997	4	
1998	3	

The 205 T16 – World Rally Championship Statistics

World Rally Championship Events: 22
Number of wins: 16
Driver's Championships: 2, Timo Salonen and Juha Kankkunen
Constructor's Championships: 2, 1985 and 1986

INDEX

Acropolis Rally 93, 100, 105, 117
Aïello, Laurent 168
Airikkala, Pentii 62, 115
Aitken-Walker, Louise 62, 114, 115
Alén, Markku 89, 92, 95, 104, 105, 106, 107, 109, 117, 120
Alexander, Craig 160
Allera, Hubert 86
Argentina 56
    Rally 94, 101, 106
Audi 82, 95, 100, 105, 115, 122
    quattro 81, 82, 87, 92, 102
Aulney-sous-Bois 29, 30, 185
Auriol, Didier 120
Australian market 55–6
Autobianchi Primula 25
Autocar 50, 63, 75, 91, 132
Axe, Roy 32

Baggot, James 162
Baker, Sue 52
Barras, Carlos 118
battery-powered cars 133–6
Bennett, Simon 163
Berglund, Bruno 121
Bettega, Attilio 99
Bézier, Pierre 36
bicycle manufacture 13–14
Biasion, Miki 105, 106, 120
Blomqvist, Stig 84, 86, 89, 100, 101, 104, 106, 107
body kits 71, 75–7
bodywork, wear & tear 147–150
Boillot, Jean 38, 83, 85, 87, 95, 117, 118–19
Bouvot, Paul 35
Bracq, Paul 36
British Leyland 26–7
British Touring Car Championship 168
Bruntingthorpe Proving Ground 155
Burns, Richard 114–16
Butler-Henderson, Vicki 145
buying used 205s 146–54

CAD/CAM systems 36
Caen 29
Charleville 29
Cheetham, Craig 161
Chrysler Europe, purchase of 23, 28, 30, 33
Citroën, purchase of 21
Citroën
    Ami 6 29
    C15 Berlingo 127
    Visa 58
Climb Dance (film) 166
Club Peugeot UK 155
Colombo 18
commercial vehicles 126–7
convertibles 128–33
Corse, Tour de 93, 97, 98–9, 105, 117, 181
Côte d'Ivoire, Rally 94, 103, 107
Coventry 23, 32, 166, 171
Coventry City F.C. 23
Cowan, Andrew 115, 123
Cresto, Sergio 105

Daihatsu Charade 57, 58
dashboard 51, 53, 55, 150
diesels 18, 56–9, 62–3
Dimma 77
Dongfeng Motors 185, 186
Douvrin, Française de Mécanique 29
Durisotti 127

engines 43–6, 50, 75–7
    modification 155–8
estates 18, 127–8
Evans, John 60

Falk, Peter 18
Fédération Internationale de l'Automobile (FIA) 82, 83, 105, 109, 114
Ferrari 17
Fiat 127 25
    Abarth 81
    Uno 27, 50, 62

Turbo 70, 72
financial troubles, 2008–14 184–6
Ford 104, 105, 117
    Escort 30, 57, 64, 81, 92
    Fiesta 25–6, 30, 47, 57, 58, 63, 73, 75, 173
        Fiesta van 126
        RS 200 102, 104
    Sierra 30
    Supersport 73
Formula One 81
Frankfurt Motor Show 172
French Grand Prix 14
Fréquelin, Guy 81, 84, 89, 95
Froumajou, Armand 84
fuel consumption records 57

gearbox 35, 45, 47, 153
GEC 133
General Motors, alliance with 184
Goodwood Festival of Speed 172
Grönholm, Maarcus 171
Group A cars 114
Group B rallying 82, 94, 105, 109
Group N cars 114
Gruau 127
Grundel Kalle 101, 103, 104, 115
GTI Rally Challenge 114, 116
Gumpert, Roland 82
Gutmann Automobitechnik 75–7

Harjanne, Seppo 109
Harryman, Terry 62, 101
hatchbacks, arrival of 25, 30–1
Heath, Nigel 116
heating & ventilation 38, 55
Hely, Tim 116
Heuliez 86
Hillman Avenger 32
    Imp 26
Hybrids 136
Air Tech 157, 185

Indianapolis 14

190

INDEX

Intercontinental Rally Challenge 171
interior design 36, 38, 50
   wear & tear 150–1
Ireland 49, 61–2

Jänner Rallye 81
joyriding 77–8, 144

Kankkunen, Juha 62, 98, 103, 104, 105, 106, 107, 109, 120, 166
Kollevold, Bernt 116

La Garenne factory 34, 85, 87
Laffite, Jacques 81
Lancia 95, 99, 105
   037 102, 107, 122
   Delta 62, 74, 102, 104, 105
   Stratos 81
Le Mans 35, 172
Levassor, Emile 14
Lie, Bjorn 116
limited editions 136–43
Linwood 28, 29
Lion logo 13, 22, 186
Lionne Sauvage kit 77
Llewellyn, Brian 61
Loeb, Sébastien 179
Lombard RAC Rally 94, 95, 103, 107, 114, 115, 116
Lotus
   Esprit 86
   Horizon 83
   Sunbeam 81, 84, 86, 95, 115

Maestro 32, 72
Magna Steyr 172
maintenance & repair 144–54
Mäkinen, Timo 83
Mangualde 29
Martin, Paolo 20
Max Power 145, 146
McCrae, Colin 114, 116, 121
Mehta, Shekhar 109, 112, 123, 125
Metro 26–7, 47, 50, 63, 64, 72, 102, 122, 126
Mikkola, Hannu 120
Mini 24–5, 27
Mini Cooper 69, 70, 81, 83
modifications, customer 155–8
Montecarlo, Rallye de 83, 87, 97, 104
Morgan, Ellen 62, 114
Morocco 49, 52, 60, 61
Mortefontaine track 87
Motor 50
Mouton, Michèle 95, 103

Mulhouse 29, 43, 44, 62

naming system 17
New Zealand Rally 93, 101, 106
Nicolas, Jean-Pierre 86–7, 89, 92, 93, 94, 95
Nürburgring 172, 183

O'Dell, Des 63, 84–5
Olympus Rally 109
Opel Ascona 92
   Corsa 27

paintwork & chrome 149–50
Paris Exposition 1889 14
Paris Motor Show 168
Paris–Dakar Rally 109–12, 113, 114, 117, 121, 122–3, 166, 179
Perron, Bernard 84, 85
Pescarolo, Henri 114
Peugeot, Armand 14
Peugeot, Jean-Frederic 13
Peugeot, Jean-Pierre 13, 16
Peugeot 104 20–1, 25, 30, 43, 47, 60
Peugeot 106 116, 164
Peugeot 201 16–17
Peugeot 202 17
Peugeot 203 17–18
Peugeot 204 18–20, 164–6
Peugeot 205
   aerodynamics 39, 43
   bodyshell 39
   brakes 47
   convertibles 128–33
   corrosion protection 43
   dashboard 51, 53, 55, 150
   design & development 34–46
   diesel 35, 45, 56–9, 62–3
   driving experience 153–4
   early history 13–14
   engine options 43–6, 50
   engine wear & tear 151–3
   estates 127–8
   fuel consumption 45
   gearbox 35, 45, 47, 153
   heating & ventilation 38, 55
   interior design 36, 38, 50
   launch 47–50, 52, 60–3
   layout 373
   Mk I 14
   prices 48
   production rates 43
   range of engines 35
   revisions, 1988 54, 55
   safety 37

   specifications 48, 54
   suspension 38, 41–2, 47
Peugeot 205 models
   IFM 138–9
   CJ 131, 132
   CTI 128–33
   Decapotable 128
   Electrique 133
   Fourgonette (F) 127
   GR 47, 50, 61
   GRDT 58, 63, 66
   GT 47, 50, 61, 65
   GTi 51, 55–6, 62, 63–80, 114–17, 144, 146
      Automatic 142
      buying 144, 146–7 150–3
      compared with 1.6 75
      creating 64–7
      Dimma version 77
      Gutmann version 75–8
      launch 69–70
      revisions 79–80
      rivals 72–3
      specifications 66, 67–9
      tuning 75–8
   GTi 1.9 74–5
   Gti-6 155, 158
   Gentry 139–41
   Griffe 56, 139–41
   Junior 137–8, 143
   M24 Prototype 34ff
   Nepala 128
   Rallye 142–3, 144, 155
   Roland Garros convertible 133, 138, 146
   T16 62, 65, 74, 84ff
      Evolution 1 84–90
      Evolution 2 94, 98–103
      M24 Rally (later T16) 84–6
      specifications 90
      world Rally debut 93
   T16 GR 109–30
   T16S 91
   van 127
   Verve 127
   VU 127
   X models 51, 53
   XA Multi 127
   XS 51, 55
Peugeot 206 WRC 169–70
Peugeot 207 Gti (RC) 170, 171
Peugeot 208 172–3, 175, 18
   R2 181
   Racing Cup 182
   T16 (R5) 177–9, 180

INDEX

Peugeot 305   30, 60, 83
   estate   126
Peugeot 306   164
Peugeot 307   170–1
Peugeot 308   172, 185, 186
Peugeot 309   114
Peugeot 403   18   404   18, 19
Peugeot 405   35, 56
   T16 GR   166–8
Peugeot 504   18–19, 30, 85
Peugeot 505   25, 30, 60
Peugeot 508   172, 174
Peugeot 604   30, 60
Peugeot 905 Spider   35
Peugeot 908   172
Peugeot 2008   185
Peugeot Citroën Group   21
Peugeot Coupé   168
Peugeot Electric Vehicle Research Unit   134
Peugeot M24 Project (later 205)   34ff
Peugeot M24 Rally (later T16)   84–6
Peugeot Partner   127
Peugeot RCZ   171–2, 173
Peugeot Sport Club   155
Peugeot Talbot Sport, creation of   84
Peugeot Talbot Sport rally team   65
Peugeot Type 5   15
Peugeot XY   175
Phelippeau, Jacques   116
Pikes Peak International Hill Climb   112, 114, 166, 179
Pininfarina   30, 34, 36, 127, 128–9, 166
Pirironen, Juho   109
Poissy   30, 32
Pond, Tony   81
Porsche   17
Portuguese Rally   97, 104, 121
Production figures   187–9
PRV Douvrin V6 engine   85
PSA Peugeot   23, 28
PuglOff   156–8

Quadrilette   15, 16

RAC Rally   62
rallying, development of   81–2

Renault   19, 36, 56
   16   25
   5   25, 47
   Alpine   81, 85
   Turbo   70, 73, 74
Rennes   29
restructuring 2012   184
Reutemann, Carlos   101
Richards, Dave   117
Röhri, Walter   89, 92, 93, 95, 97, 100, 112, 114, 117, 120, 122
Rose, Simon   159
Rover   56, 63, 105
Ryton plant, Coventry   23, 32, 166, 171

Sabine, Thierry   109
Saby, Bruno   95, 97–9, 103, 105–6
Safari Rally   18, 97–8, 105
SAFT   133–4
Salonen, Timo   95, 97–9, 100, 101, 103, 104, 106, 107, 109, 120
Sanremo, Rallye   81, 92, 94, 107, 109
Santos, Joaquim   105
Sarlat Rally   89
Scottish Sports Hall of Fame   115
Setright, L.J.K.   62, 69
Simca   28, 29–30
   Alpine   32
Smith, Trevor   116
Snetterton   168
Sochaux   14, 38
   FC Sochaux-Montbéliard   16
Solonen, Timo   62
South America   19, 56
Sport GTi   183
Stein, Christian   171
Sundström, Mikael   62, 103, 107, 115
Super Tourenwagen Cup   168
superminis   24–7
suspension   38, 41–2, 47
Swedish Rally   97, 104

Talbot   23, 28, 31–2, 47, 60, 81, 82
   Alpine   32
   Avenger   29

Cavalier   30
Horizon   23, 31–2, 47, 83
Minx   34
Rancho   31, 32–3
Samara   47
Samba   30, 31, 43, 47
   Cabriolet   128
Solara   30, 32
Tagora   31, 32
1000 Lakes Rally   94, 101, 107, 120
Todt, Jean   65, 77, 82–7, 89, 92, 94–7, 103, 109, 114, 117–19, 123
Toivenen, Henri   81–2, 89, 92, 95, 104, 105, 115, 117, 120, 122
Top Gear   172
Toyota Celica   98
Trémery   29
Turbo Technics   77
Turin Motor Show   168

Vatanen, Ari   6, 62, 70, 82, 89, 92–5, 98–9, 101, 107, 109, 110–14, 117–25, 166
Vatanen, Max   125
Vatanen, Rita   123, 24–5
Vaucard, Jean Claud   86, 114
Vauxhall Astra   30, 31, 64
   Chevette   26
   Nova   27, 50, 73
VERA research & development programme   35
Vigo   29,
Villaverde   30
Villeneuve, Jacques   179
Vokswagon-Audi   186
Volkswagon Golf   35, 56, 57, (as 'Rabbit')   56
   GTi   64, 72
Volvo   19   242   85
Welter, Gérard   34, 35
Welter, Rachel   35
What Car?   50, 57–8, 70, 168
World Rally   55, 62, 74, 94–103
World Rallycross Championship   179
World War I   14

Zanussi, Andrea   109, 112